The Illustrated Directory of

GUITARS

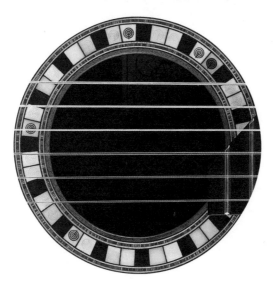

The Illustrated Directory of

GUITARS

Edited by Ray Bonds

PUBLISHED BY
SALAMANDER BOOKS LIMITED
LONDON

A Salamander Book

Published by Salamander Books Ltd.,
8 Blenheim Court,
Brewery Road,
London N7 9NT,
United Kingdom

© Salamander Books Ltd., 2001, 2002

A member of the Chrysalis Group plc

ISBN 1 84065 288 8

Credits

Project Manager: Ray Bonds
Designed by: Interprep Ltd.
Photography: Neil Sutherland, Don Eiler, John Alflatt
Color reproduction by: Studio Technology
Printed in: Hong Kong

The material that appears in this book is derived from *The Acoustic Guitar* and *The Electric Guitar,* both by Nick Freeth and Charles Alexander.

Contents

Part One

Acoustic Guitars

This book charts the evolution of the acoustic guitar from the sixteenth century to the present day. Our primary focus is on the instrument itself, although we also include some information about composers, players, and other figures who have had a significant influence on its development. We have been keen to place the guitar in its historical and social context, especially in Section One, which covers the pre-twentieth century period. It is easy to forget that early guitars, many of them museum pieces associated with archaic musical styles, often provided the popular repertoire of their day, and were once as actively used (though not as plentiful!) as Gibsons or Martins are today. We have done our best to bring these older instruments back to life for the reader, with contemporary accounts and quotations describing how and where they were played.

Sections Two and Three cover the years from 1900 onwards, which have seen the emergence of several entirely new categories of guitar, as well as significant advances in design and technology. Most of these are discussed in the main text, but one topic – the use of electronic amplification – is mentioned here because of the problems it poses for anyone trying to define exactly what is (or is not) an "acoustic guitar." Many *bona fide* acoustic instruments, fully capable of being heard without amplifiers, now feature built-in pickups designed for onstage use; while some leading musicians, Martin Taylor, favor guitars that can provide both acoustic and electric sounds. Where do these hybrids fit in? And if a synthesizer-guitar player selects a digital sample of an acoustic when he performs, should his solid-bodied, MIDI-equipped instrument also be featured here?

After considerable thought and discussion, we have decided that, for the purposes of this book, any guitar, nylon- or steel-strung, can be considered an "acoustic" if it has been designed to provide a full and satisfactory sound without amplification. As a general rule, any fitted pickups should not compromise the acoustic tone by being mounted directly onto the instrument's top, although we have made very occasional exceptions to this. Our definition permits the inclusion of archtop guitars with "floating" magnetic pick-ups, as well as classical or flat-top models with piezo-electric "bugs" built into their bodies or bridge saddles. It excludes any solid or semi-solid designs, such as the MIDI controller mentioned earlier.

These rules have allowed us to feature a wide diversity of instruments – from classical and flamenco models to new and ingenious designs by leading luthiers on both sides of the Atlantic. We have endeavored to provide a representative cross-section of the very finest acoustic guitars, past and present, and we hope that this book will be as enjoyable to read as it was to research and write.

*Above and right: **Chitarra battente by Giorgio Sellas, 1627.*** (Courtesy Ashmolean Museum, Oxford)

SECTION ONE

The Guitar's European Heritage

Despite their differences in size, pitch, and stringing, the earliest guitars, which appeared in Spain during the 1500s, shared some basic characteristics with their twentieth-century counterparts. Like today's instruments, they were versatile, portable, and suitable for simple playing styles as well as more elaborate music; and this widespread appeal was a key factor in establishing the primacy of the guitar over its rivals, the vihuela and lute.

The guitar's subsequent spread throughout Europe was aided by the activities of a number of widely-traveled composer/performers, one of the first of whom, Francesco Corbetta (1615–1681), helped to popularize it at the French and English courts. Later virtuosi, such as Fernando Sor (1778–1839) and Dionisio Aguado (1784–1849), made an even more direct impact on public tastes through their extensive concert tours. They also published music and instruction books, and were able to influence the development of the instrument itself through their recommendations and endorsements of individual makers. Gradually, the guitar, which had previously been subject to considerable local variations in construction and design, became more standardized; and by the late nineteenth century, larger, richer-sounding models of the type introduced by Antonio de Torres (1817–1892) and popularized by the player and composer Francisco Tárrega (1852–1909) had become the norm for concert use.

In this section, we trace the outline of the guitar's evolution throughout Europe, examining the work of the great Spanish, Italian, French, and German luthiers who laid the foundations for the instrument we know today. We also follow its progress in the New World, where émigré craftsmen such as C.F. Martin were soon to create a new, distinctively American version of the traditional design.

The Guitar's Origins

Fretted, plucked instruments small enough to be held in the player's arms have existed, in Europe and elsewhere, for many centuries. Some of their names (chitarra, ghiterra) seem to suggest direct links with the modern guitar. Names, though, can be misleading, and while the terms used to classify musical instruments have changed little since the fourteenth and fifteenth centuries, their meanings are now frequently quite different. One musical theorist, Johannes Tinctoris, writing in Naples in about 1487, refers to a "ghiterra" or "ghiterna," which he says was invented by the Catalans – but this instrument, described by Tinctoris as "tortoise-shaped," is probably a round-backed lute rather than a guitar. However, Tinctoris also mentions a "viola without the bow," favored in Spain and Italy as an alternative to the lute; and it is this, not the ghiterra, which is almost certainly the direct ancestor of the guitar as we know it today.

"Viola" is an Italian word; its Spanish equivalent is "vihuela." In

Right: The title page of Guillaume Morlaye's collection of music for the four-course guitar, which was published in Paris in 1552. The guitar in the illustration has a single top string, and double strings on its three remaining courses.

Renaissance Europe, the term covered a broad category of stringed instruments: some were played with a bow; others were held in the arms like a lute, and either struck with a pick, or plucked with the fingers of the hand. This third type (the "vihuela de mano") resembles the guitar most closely. Tinctoris says that, unlike the lute, it is "flat, and in most cases curved inwards on each side", suggesting the waisted, figure-of-eight shape now associated with the guitar. The vihuela de mano's strings were arranged in five or six pairs (or "courses") and the instrument may have been made in a number of different sizes; one surviving example in Paris is relatively large, and could have been designed to provide lower parts in ensembles and consorts.

By contrast, the earliest guitars, which probably emerged in Spain during the early 1500s, were smaller and higher-pitched, with four courses or groups of strings. None of them survive; but they are illustrated and described in a number of theoretical ▶

Acoustic Guitars

treatises, and in the collections of guitar music that began to appear in the second half of the sixteenth century. Guillaume Morlaye's book of songs and dances for the "guyterne" was published in Paris in 1552, and it was followed by other anthologies issued in Spain, England, and the Netherlands. Although one of these books refers to "the four-course vihuela, which is called guitar," and another contemporary source describes the guitar as "nothing but a vihuela shorn of its first and sixth strings," it seems clear that by this time, the guitar had developed its own independent identity and repertoire. Its restricted range made it well suited to simple dance-tunes and song accompaniment, while the vihuela excelled in more elaborate, contrapuntal music. The two instruments co-existed for a considerable period, but by the start of the seventeenth century, they were both being eclipsed by the growing appeal of the five-course guitar.

Right: The title-page of El Maestro, a collection of music for the vihuela by the Spanish composer Luis Milán (c.1500–c.1561), published in 1536. It depicts the mythological poet and musician Orpheus in an idealized sylvan setting, playing a six-course vihuela. Despite the number of strings, the illustration shows only ten tuning pegs; similar small inaccuracies are found in many other artists' impressions of early instruments. The vihuela's neck, headstock, and outline all resemble those of a guitar.

The Five-course Guitar

The musical limitations of the four-course guitar were clear to sixteenth-century players and theorists. As early as 1555, the Spanish composer Juan Bermudo, in his "Libro primo de la declaración de instrumentos musicales," pointed out that its range could be extended "by adding…a string a fourth above the present first course". The oldest surviving five-course guitar, dating from 1581 and shown below, was one of the first instruments to put Bermudo's prescriptions into practice. It was probably tuned in a way corresponding to the intervals between the top five strings on a modern guitar – a system outlined in the Spanish composer Miguel de Fuenllana's *Orphenica Lyra*, published in 1554.

Despite this superficial similarity, five-course guitars sounded very different from today's instruments. Their actual pitch was not standardized, but varied with individual guitars, string tolerances and musical needs. More significantly, the "bourdon" tunings used for the pairs of strings on some courses meant that notes assigned to these would be heard at both their fingered pitch, and an octave below. This created jangling doublings when chords were played, and allowed composers scope for a number of other effects that are difficult or impossible to reproduce on a guitar with six single strings.

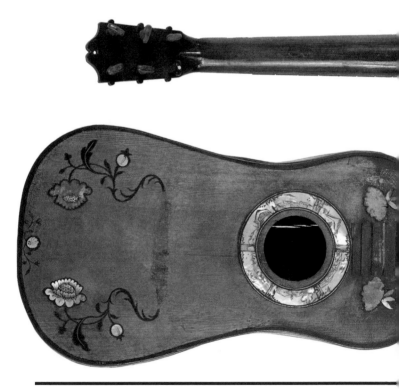

Below, middle and bottom: The top, side, and back of an elaborately decorated guitar, probably made in Italy around 1630, and later extensively altered. The top is made from a pine-type wood, and the illustrations of exotic animals, birds and plants are carved from ebony and ivory. The neck and six-string headstock are not original.

(Courtesy Edinburgh University)

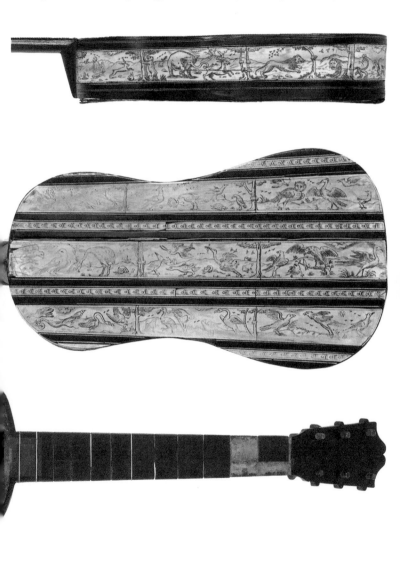

Acoustic Guitars

Music for the five-course guitar was of two main types. The easiest style of playing to master was the simple strumming popularized by Juan Carlos Amat's *Guitarra Española de cinco órdenes*, first published in 1596. The year before, Francisco Palumbi had introduced a new system of naming chords for the guitar using letters of the alphabet. His approach, which was even simpler to learn than the numbers and tables used by Amat, became widely known in the early 1600s; and the "alfabeto" system remained in vogue all over Europe for the next 100 years.

Alongside this basic, popular style of playing, more elaborate and sophisticated works for the five-course guitar started to appear throughout the seventeenth century, as the instrument's popularity spread across Europe. Most of these were created by professional court musicians, whose patrons could afford the finest performers, teachers, and instruments. In the next few pages, we examine the impact of one of the most important of these figures, Francesco Corbetta, and a few of his contemporaries, and also look at some of the finest guitars made outside Spain during this period.

Below and right: The earliest five-course guitar still in existence. It was made by Belchior Diaz in Lisbon, and is dated December 1581. It is relatively small – only 30in (76.5cm) long – and its open soundhole would originally have contained a "rose." Its bridge and belly are later additions, but its neck, headstock, sides, and back are all original.
(Courtesy Royal College of Music, London)

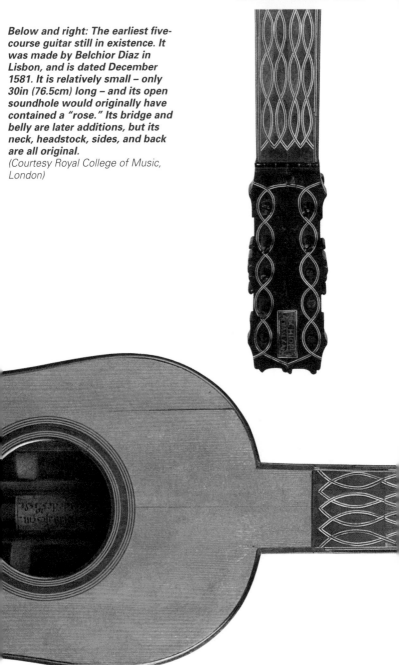

The Seventeenth Century Guitar in Europe

The "alfabeto" chordal system caught on quite quickly in early seventeenth-century Italy, creating a considerable demand there for instruments and music to play on them. Makers of lutes soon began to build guitars for this thriving new market, and among the leading craftsmen of the period were the Sellas family (notably Matteo and Giorgio), whose three Venice work-shops produced many fine five-course guitars. Some surviving examples of these (including, probably, the Sellas instrument shown below) have been converted to "chitarre battenti" – wire-strung guitars designed specifically for strumming dance rhythms and song accompaniments, and played with a pick.

Gradually, a demand developed in Italy for more complex guitar

Below and right: A five-course guitar built, in the Venetian style, by Jacobo Checchucci of Livorno in 1628.
(Courtesy Tony Bingham)

Acoustic Guitars

compositions, and "alfabeto"-type symbols were combined with other forms of printed tablature capable of showing melodies and inner parts as well as simple chords (standard staff notation was not used for the guitar until the eighteenth century). Among the early pioneers of this more substantial music was Giovanni Paolo Foscarini (d. 1649), a lutenist as well as a guitar player, whose compositions combined straight-forward strumming with lute-like "pizzicati."

Even more influential was Francesco Corbetta (1615–1681), whose first published music appeared in 1639, about ten years after Foscarini's. Corbetta traveled widely throughout Europe: after initial success as a virtuoso guitar player, composer, and teacher in Italy, he visited Spain, enjoying the patronage of King Philip IV, and went on to play a significant role in popularizing the guitar throughout Europe – and especially in France and England.

Below: The headstock for this instrument carries the maker's inscription "Matteo Sellas alla Corona in Venetia 1638." Beneath this, extending down the fingerboard, are a series of six ivory plaques engraved with a stag, a bear, a camel, a fox with a goose, a hare, and a hound. The guitar's table is made from pine, inlaid at the base and the neck joint with ebony.*
(Courtesy The Dick Institute, Kilmarnock)*

Right and above: A chitarra battente made by Magno Stregher in Venice in 1621. Its table is profusely inlaid with ivory, ebony, and mother-of-pearl. The headstock and fingerboard are also beautifully decorated, and Stregher's initials and the date are visible at the base of the fingerboard.
(Courtesy The Dick Institute, Kilmarnock)

Left: Chitarra battente by Matteo Sellas, 1638. The table is pine with a pin-style bridge, which is a nineteenth-century replacement for the original.
(Courtesy The Dick Institute, Kilmarnock)

The Influence of Francesco Corbetta

Francesco Corbetta first came to Paris in the mid-1650s, when Louis XIV (who had acceded to the French throne in 1643) was still a teenager. Over the following decades, French guitar music and its composers became a dominant influence throughout Northern Europe, and the popularity of Corbetta's performances, compositions, and teaching at the French court played a key role in bringing this about. However, the guitar had already been firmly established in France since the sixteenth century, and there was a long tradition of fretted instrument making in Paris and other centers.

The most distinguished heirs to this tradition were the Voboam family – René, Jean, and Alexandre. Their reputations as craftsmen must have been well known to the King, who was himself a keen guitarist; and at least two instruments by Jean Voboam were owned and played by Louis' daughters.

Voboam instruments also found their way to England, and Corbetta's first visit there, in 1662, soon created the same enthusiasm for the guitar at Charles II's court in London as already existed at Louis' court at Versailles. A contemporary observer commented that "the liking expressed by the King

Below and right: A five-course guitar made by René Voboam in Paris in 1641. The table is spruce, and the back and sides are tortoiseshell, with ebony and ivory inlays. The binding around the edge

of the body and the finger-board is also ebony and ivory, as are the bridge, soundhole, and fingerboard decorations.
(Courtesy Ashmolean Museum, Oxford)

for [Corbetta's] compositions had made this instrument so fashionable that everyone was playing it – well or badly. Even on the dressing tables of all the beauties one could rely on seeing a guitar as well as rouge and beauty spots."

Corbetta returned to France in about 1670, and continued to play, teach, and compose for the last 11 years of his life. Among his many pupils was the leading figure of the next generation of French guitar composers, Robert de Visée (c.1660–c.1720), some of whose music still remains in today's classical guitar repertoire. Corbetta died in

Paris in 1681: this touching tribute is said to have been written by another of his distinguished students, the guitarist and composer Remy Médard.

> *"Ci-git l'Amphion de nos jours*
> *Francisque, cet homme si rare,*
> *Qui fit parler a la guitare*
> *Le vrai language des amours."*

(Here lies the Amphion of our days,
Francis Corbet, this man of rare quality,
Who made his guitar speak
The very language of love's jollity.)
(Translation by Philip J. Bone)

Below and right: This guitar has a colorful legend attached to it: it is said to have been given by Mary, Queen of Scots (1542–1587), to her Italian-born private secretary, David Rizzio, who was murdered at Holyrood House, Edinburgh, in 1566.

However, the instrument's design and appearance make it much more likely to be a French guitar dating from around the 1680s. It was probably made in Paris by Jean Voboam.
(Courtesy Royal College of Music, London)

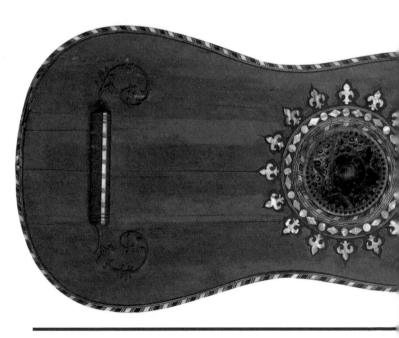

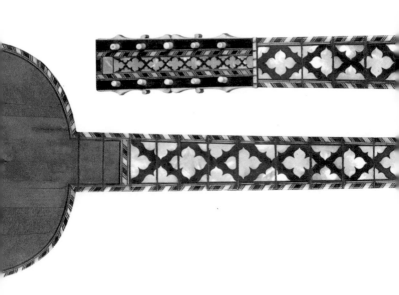

The Work of Stradivari, Tielke, and Vieyra

Corbetta's reputation helped to promote wide interest in the guitar throughout Europe. He, Foscarini, and others had begun to create a substantial repertoire for the instrument, giving it a musical respectability it had lacked in the days when it was associated only with simple strumming. This frivolous image was long established and took many years to dispel. In Spain, the guitar had developed strong links with

taverns, barbers' shops, and playhouses; and in 1619, the leading German musical historian and composer Michael Praetorius (1571–1621) described it as "used in Italy by...comedians and buffoons only for accompaniment to Villanelles and other foolish low songs." Despite these comments, there was enough serious demand for the instrument in seventeenth-century Germany to support an important center of guitar

Above right and right: A six-course guitar, made by Santos Vieyra in Portugal at the end of the seventeenth century.
(Courtesy Ashmolean Museum, Oxford)

Below: A five-course guitar built by Antonio Stradivari in 1688. Its table is spruce; the head, neck, sides, and back are maple, with ebony inlays.
(Courtesy Ashmolean Museum, Oxford)

Acoustic Guitars

making in Hamburg. Its founder was Hans Christoph Fleischer, whose son-in-law, Joachim Tielke (1641–1719), later became recognized as one of the finest luthiers in Europe.

Another sign of the instrument's growing acceptance in serious musical circles was the fact that the most celebrated of all stringed instrument makers, Antonio Stradivari (1644–1737) of Cremona in Italy, began to make guitars in the second part of the seventeenth century. Only four complete exam-ples of these survive; the one shown below is in the Ashmolean Museum in Oxford, and there is another five-course Stradivari in the Paris Conservatoire National.

Practically no Spanish guitars from this period are still in existence, and the final guitar shown here is one of the few surviving Portuguese instruments from the late seventeenth century. It is unusual in having six courses – anticipating one of the many important modifications to the guitar's construction that would start to take place in the following 100 years.

Right: Five-course guitar attributed to Jakob Stadler of Munich, c.1625
(Courtesy Royal College of Music, London)

Below: A late seventeenth-century five-course guitar by Joachim Tielke of Hamburg.
(Courtesy Royal College of Music, London)

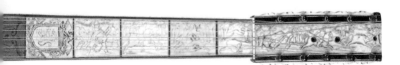

The Guitar: 1700–1900

During the eighteenth century, guitar bodies became larger, their internal bracing underwent radical improvements, and their stringing patterns began to change – from five to six courses (the six-course instrument was popular in Spain from the 1780s to the early 1800s, but failed to catch on elsewhere), and eventually to the modern system of six single strings.

These changes took place gradually, with different styles of guitar co-existing for many years. Some early eighteenth-century instruments were subsequently modified to take the new string configurations. The French guitar shown opposite originally had five courses; these have been replaced with six strings, and the fingerboard, metal frets, head-stock, and bridge are all subsequent additions. The elaborate parchment rose is part of the original design; it was soon to become less common, as more and more eighteenth century luthiers began to build guitars with open soundholes.

The design of the soundboard was also under scrutiny. Until the latter part of the century, guitar tops, whose vibrations play a crucial role in creating the sound of an instrument, were light and thin in construction, with little internal support to help them withstand the constant pressure from the strings. This often resulted in the kind of cracking and warping visible in the photograph of the "Zaniboni" guitar on page 34. The problem of providing adequate bracing for guitar soundboards, while

Below, right and far right: A French guitar made in the early 1700s, and attributed to a member of the Voboam family. It has been converted from five courses to six strings, and has also been fitted with machine heads, metal frets, and a pin bridge.
(Courtesy Edinburgh University)

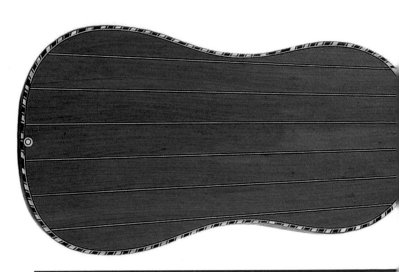

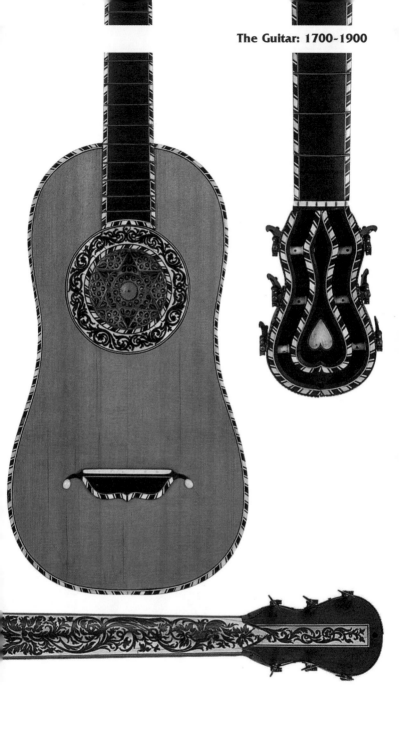

still allowing them to vibrate efficiently, was solved by the use of "fan-bracing," which involved gluing wooden struts onto the back of the soundboard in outwardly radiating patterns. The earliest maker known to have done this was Francisco Sanguino of Seville, whose first fan-braced guitar, made in 1759, is in the Gemeente-museum in the Hague. Other luthiers associated with the development of fan-bracing included Juan Pagés (d. 1821) and José Benedid (1760–1836) of Cádiz. The system was copied and adapted by later craftsmen, and eventually refined and perfected by the great nineteenth-century Spanish guitar maker Antonio de Torres (1817 –1892).

The eighteenth century also saw changes to the neck, headstock, and bridge. Gut frets gradually disappeared, to be replaced with metal ones permanently inlaid into the fingerboard. Geared machine heads began to be used instead of wooden tuning pegs; while bridges were fitted with ivory or bone saddles, and sometimes had pins to hold down the string ends. (Pin-style bridges continued to be used on gut-strung guitars throughout the nineteenth century, and later became standard on flat-top steel-strung guitars.)

In the following pages we will look at a cross-section of guitars from early 1700s to 1840, and trace the introduction of some of these developments. However, we begin by examining the range of playing styles that provided the basis for the instrument's ongoing popularity during this period.

Below, top right and right: This guitar probably had five courses. It was made in England or Ireland in the second half of the eighteenth century, and "Zaniboni" may have been either the maker or the owner. Its bridge is missing, and its body (made of maple) and table (made from pine or a similar wood) are both extremely thin. The purfling (inlaid bordering) around the edges of the body is a mixture of red dye and ink, and the inside of the instrument is lined with unbleached paper.
(Courtesy Edinburgh University)

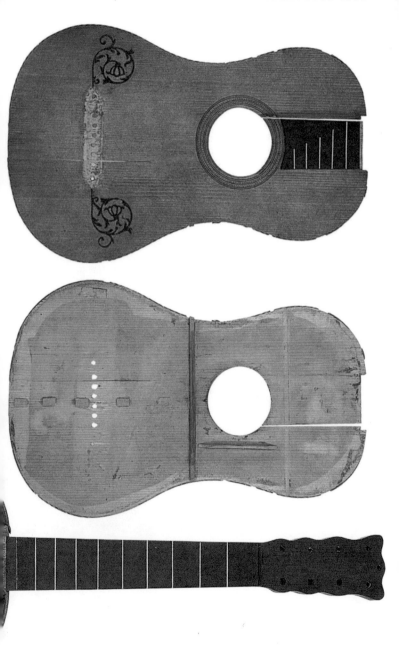

Playing Styles and Techniques

By the early 1700s, the guitar had largely replaced the lute as the favored instrument in royal courts and noble households. Francesco Corbetta and later player/composers such as Gaspar Sanz (1640–1710) provided their aristocratic patrons with melodious, refined music that made use of two contrasting ways of playing: the rasgueado or strumming style that had been associated with the guitar since the 1500s; and the punteado or plucked method that allowed the performance of more elaborate, contrapuntal works.

Punteado was a development of earlier vihuela and lute technique, in which the right-hand thumb and fingers are used independently to strike the strings. Its establishment led even the guitar's detractors to recognize the instrument's musical capabilities. One of these was William Turner (1651–1739?), an Englishman who had served Charles II as "musician in ordinary in his Majesty's private Musick for lute and Voyce." Turner commented scornfully in 1697 that "the fine easie Ghittar, whose performance is soon gained, at least after the brushing way *[rasgueado]*, hath at this present time over-topt the nobler lute" – but also

Right and below: Five-course French or Belgian guitar, mid-eighteenth century. This instrument, which has a pine top, is inlaid with ebony, ivory, mother-of-pearl, and tortoiseshell, and its soundhole contains a three-tier rose made from vellum.

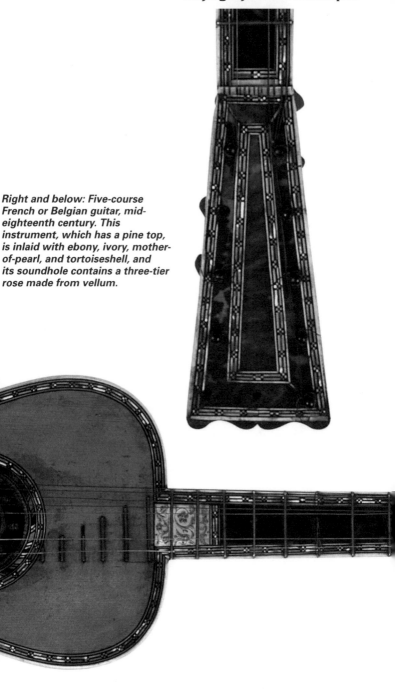

admitted that "after the pinching way [punteado], the Ghittar makes some good work."

The increasing acceptance of the guitar as a "serious" instrument was mirrored by its continuing success at street level, as the disdain once expressed by some educated listeners for the popular side of its musical character began to give way to appreciation and admiration. One French critic, François Raguenet, wrote in 1702 about the itinerant guitarists and violinists he heard performing in the streets of Rome, "accompanying their voices so justly that we seldom meet

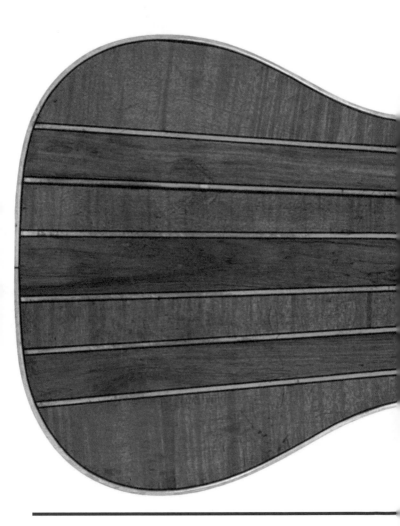

with much better music in our French consorts." His comments were echoed by later travelers; in the 1770s, the English musician, Dr. Charles Burney, enjoyed outdoor performances by peasant guitarists playing "a very singular species of music" in Naples and on the Piazza di San Marco in Venice, featuring "sometimes a single voice and guitar, and sometimes two or three guitars together." Traditional performing styles such as these had a perennial appeal, and played an important part in sustaining the guitar's vitality throughout the eighteenth and nineteenth centuries.

Below: The back is constructed from seven separate wooden strips – the four lighter sections are made of maple, the three other pieces of an unidentified darker timber. The guitar's appearance and design suggest an earlier period than the 1750s – it was probably made to special order for a player who required an instrument with older features. (Courtesy Edinburgh University)

The Evolving Guitar

The five-course guitar stayed in vogue for much of the eighteenth century. Large quantities of music and tutors continued to be published for it, and it remained a favorite at many European royal courts. However, even some of its finest players acknowledged its deficiencies – especially in the bass range. In the early 1700s, the great French guitarist and composer Robert de Visée (c.1660 –c.1720), who was Francesco Corbetta's pupil, and subsequently became Louis XIV's personal guitar teacher, observed that his own guitar music had unavoidable weaknesses in its part-writing, adding that "the instrument itself" was the reason for this. Despite such comments, no fundamental changes were made to the guitar's range and number of strings for several decades, and the two instruments shown here were tuned and played in exactly the same way as their seventeenth-century predecessors.

This guitar in the main picture was probably made in about 1730 by the Venetian luthier Santa Serafin. Compared to the richly decorated instruments from Venice shown in Chapter 1, it is more restrained and

Below and right: A guitar attributed to Santa Serafin, Venice, c.1730. Its table is made of pine or a similar wood, edged with ebony and ivory. The only *other body inlay is the soundhole decoration – a combination of purfling and circles of contrasting woods.*
(Courtesy Edinburgh University)

Above: The nut is ivory, and the fruitwood headstock is in a fan shape, with black inlays and tuning pegs of boxwood.

functional in appearance, and also has a narrower waist, a flat back (theirs were rounded), and a slightly smaller overall body size. It was restored by Andrew Dipper in 1985; guitars of this period, with their lightweight construction, are particularly prone to damage, and relatively few have survived intact.

Andrew Dipper was also responsible for the restoration of the five-course guitar shown opposite, which was made by José Massaguer

(1690–1764) in Barcelona in about 1750. In some ways, it seems more of a throwback to the previous century than the Italian instrument – although many other guitars of this period (especially Spanish ones) include "older" design features like the soundhole rose and elaborate body inlays seen here. Massaguer also made violins and other stringed instruments; only three other examples of his work are known to be still in existence.

Below and right: A guitar by José Massaguer, Barcelona, c.1750. The soundboard is made from fir, the back from flamed maple. The pattern of the rosewood inlay beneath the bridge is balanced by a similar design on the upper fingerboard (above the 8th fret), and the wavy inlay along the rest of the neck and headstock is bordered with strips of ebony.
(Courtesy Metropolitan Museum of Art, New York)

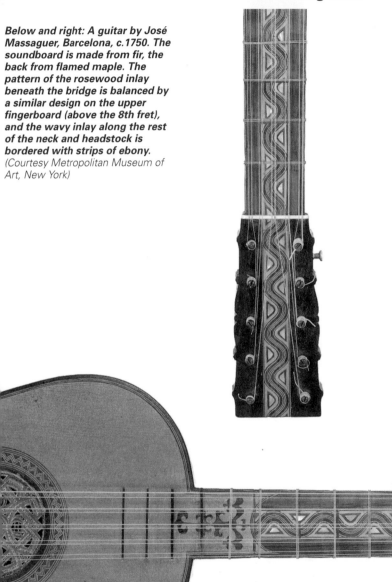

Bertet and Fabricatore

The guitar shown below, made by the Paris-based luthier Bertet in 1766, retains many features familiar from older instruments. Its soundboard is relatively unadorned, with Bertet's name stamped near the bottom edge. Gut frets and a sound-hole rose are still used, but the back, made from strips of maple and walnut, is flat, and the fingerboard completely plain.

Only about 15 years after this guitar was built, the first six-string instruments (the extra string extended their bass range by a fourth) began to appear in many European coun-tries. Except in Spain, where guitars with six double courses of strings were common until the early nineteenth century, these new designs were all single-strung. The most likely reason for

Below and right: A five-course guitar by Bertet, built in 1766. The luthier's name and the inscription "A PARIS" are branded onto the instrument's table; at this period, Bertet's workshop was near the Comédie Française.
(Courtesy Tony Bingham)

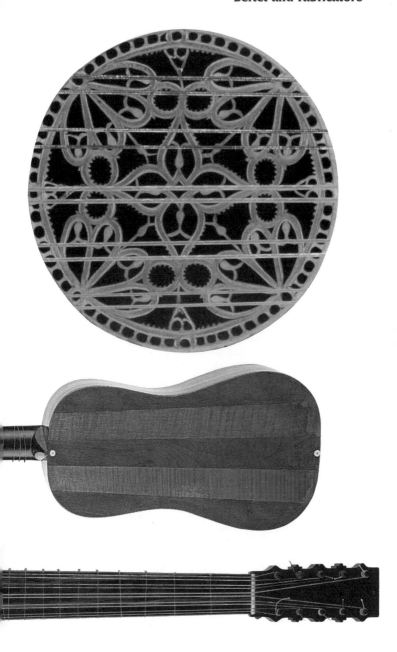

Acoustic Guitars

the change is that pairs of strings using bourdons or "re-entrant" tunings were becoming increasingly unsuitable for the music of the time. Julian Bream has described the five- and six-course guitar as "an admirable instrument particularly for songs and dances of a light, frothy character. Its ranks of paired strings, and characteristic split octave bass tuning, could produce a rash of wild harmonies and inverted counterpoint with a charm all its own." For classical and romantic music, these qualities were unwanted, and many composers and players would have welcomed the six-string's greater precision and depth of tone.

One of the leading early builders of six-string instruments was Giovanni Battista Fabricatore of Naples, whose first known guitar of this type was made in 1798. The guitar illustrated is a slightly later example of his work, from about 1805.

Below: A six-string guitar by Fabricatore, made in c.1805. Its soundboard is pine, and its fingerboard extends all the way down to the soundhole, as on most modern guitars. (Compare the Bertet guitar, the fingerboard of which ends well before the neck joins the body.) The soundhole and bridge are decorated with a combination of mother-of-pearl and red wax, and the same material is used for the purfling around the edge of the table and fingerboard.
(Courtesy Edinburgh University)

The Guitar Virtuosi

The early history of the six-string guitar is dominated by the careers and influence of a handful of Spanish and Italian virtuosi, who established international reputations with their playing and compositions, and inspired a wave of interest in the guitar throughout Europe. The first of these players to become well-known outside his own country was Mauro Giuliani (1781–1829), who was born in Bologna, but achieved his first major success in Vienna, and later had an English guitar magazine *(The Giulianiad*, published from 1833) named in his memory.

Paris was a city with an ever greater appeal to visiting guitarists, many of whom even-tually made their homes there. Ferdinando Carulli (1770–1841) was born in Naples, and settled in the French capital in 1808; he was joined there five years later by the celebrated Spanish player and composer, Fernando Sor (1778–1839), and, in the 1820s, by two other famous names: Matteo Carcassi (1792–1853) and Dionisio Aguado (1784–1849).

This musical activity led to an upsurge in guitar-making throughout France, and both instruments shown

Below and right: A guitar by Charles Lété, made in 1840. The inlays are mother-of-pearl, and the machine heads brass and ivory.
(Courtesy Tony Bingham)

Acoustic Guitars

here were built there during the height of the instrument's popularity. The guitar on the opposite page dates from the early years of the nineteenth century. It was made by Dubois of Paris, and was subsequently modified to take a seventh string – but has now been restored to its original condition.

The other guitar shown here is a beautiful instrument, made around 1840 by Charles Lété. Lété's workshop was in Mirecourt, a small town near Nancy in eastern France. The instrument's body is partly built of satinwood, an exotic timber from which Matteo Carcassi also had a guitar made at about this time. Despite their exquisite workmanship, such highly-decorated models were soon to fall out of favor with more serious players; one leading guitar historian, Graham Wade, has described them in his book *Traditions of the Classical Guitar* as "caught in the evolutionary process between ornamented *objets d'art* and genuine musical instruments."

Below: A guitar by Dubois, made in Paris during the early nineteenth century. It has ebony and mother-of-pearl purfling (in a chevron pattern) around its table, upper neck, and soundhole. There are also mother-of-pearl dots on the string pins and the edges of the "mustache" bridge. The body is made from pine and rosewood. (Courtesy Edinburgh University)

Sor's Choice

The popularity of the guitar led to a ready market for good-quality instruments throughout the musical centers of nineteenth century Europe. There was also a lively debate among professionals and the public about the relative merits of guitars from different countries. Instruments from Spain were often proclaimed to be the finest, although some virtuosi had vested interests in promoting guitars made in other places. The Italian player Luigi Legnani (1790–1877), for example, was one of the first musicians to endorse a specific make of instrument; in the 1820s guitars bearing his name were made and sold by two Viennese luthiers Johann Georg Stauffer and Georg Ries.

Perhaps the most useful and disinterested views on the subject of choosing a fine guitar were those of the great Spanish player and composer Fernando Sor, writing in the short-lived English guitar magazine *The Giulianiad*, in 1833:

"The manner of constructing the body of the instrument is almost everywhere understood extremely

Below: René François Lacôte (1785–1855), who had his premises at No. 10, Rue de Savoie, Paris, was acknowledged as the leading French luthier of his time. This guitar dates from 1825.
(Courtesy Horniman Museum)

Right and far right: A six-course guitar by José Pagés of Cadiz, made in 1813 – by which time paired stringing had largely fallen out of use. Its elaborate design, with ebony and mother-of-pearl inlays on the table and fingerboard, suggests that this was probably a "presentation" instrument, made to demonstrate the luthier's skill.
(Courtesy Edinburgh University)

well, and most Neapolitan, German and French guitars leave, in this respect, very little superiority to the Spanish. In the goodness of the body or box, the Neapolitans long surpassed, in my opinion, those of France and Germany; but that is not the case at present; and if I wanted an in-strument, I would procure it…from M. Lacôte, a French maker, the only person who, besides his talents, has proved to me that he possesses the quality of not being inflexible to reasoning."

Sor goes on to praise the work of (among others) Alonzo of Madrid, and Pagés and Benedid of Cádiz; but modesty or scruples prevent him from mentioning the London-based luthier Louis Pan-ormo (1784–1862), who consulted Sor on instrument design, used fan-bracing on his soundboards, and proudly proclaimed himself "London's only Maker of Guitars in the Spanish Style."

Hybrids and Curiosities

Above: Guitar "in the Spanish style" by Louis Panormo, 1838. The Panormo family were Italian émigrés who settled in London.
(Courtesy Tony Bingham)

Alongside musicians such as Sor, who encouraged guitar makers to refine and improve the quality of the regular six-string instrument, there were other players, luthiers, and inventors with more radical ideas. Some of them developed multi-stringed variants of the guitar, most of which had two (or more) necks, were difficult to tune and unwieldy to play, and did not survive for long. Other hybrid instruments were intended as a fusion of ancient designs and modern craftsmanship; the "lyre-guitar" is one example of this. Modeled on classical Greek lines, it ▶

Above: A "heptachord" made to Napoléon Coste's specifications by René Lacôte in Paris, c.1840.
(Courtesy Tony Bingham)

Left: Clementi and Company of London made this lyre-guitar in about 1800. The body is decorated in black lacquer with gilt arabesques, the upper arms feature a floral motif, and a female mask surmounts the head. (Courtesy the Dick Institute, Kilmarnock)

was introduced at the end of the eighteenth century, and, with its six single strings and extended bass range, was intended as an improvement upon what one commentator described as the "primitive" five-course guitar. Despite the appearance of a few other similar models in the early 1800s, the lyre-guitar was not a great success.

A number of eminent nineteenth-century guitarists had distinctive instruments made to their own special designs – and one leading French player with particularly unusual requirements was a former pupil of Sor, Napoléon Coste (1806–1883). Coste commissioned the guitar shown below from the Paris luthier René Lacôte; it was probably made in the early 1840s. It has seven strings, an extra-large body, and was tuned a fifth lower than normal. Also

remarkable are the massive bridge and tailpiece, and the elevated finger-rest at the side of the soundhole. Another of Coste's guitars can be seen at the museum of the Paris Conservatoire.

The final guitar shown here is an experimental model by Louis Panormo, built in 1831. In his London workshop at 46 High Street, Blooms-bury, Panormo offered "guitars of every description from 2 to 15 guineas," and this curiously shaped instrument is proof of the continuing lack of standardization in guitar design during the early decades of the nineteenth century. Although some guitars made in the first half of the nineteenth century bear an increasing resemblance to modern "classical" instruments, their shape and size was not finally settled until the advent of Torres in the 1860s.

Below: Experimental, oval-shaped guitar by Louis Panormo, London, 1831.

It has a rosewood body and is decorated with ivory and mother-of-pearl inlays.
(Courtesy Tony Bingham)

Mrs. Sidney Pratten's Guitars

Virtuosi such as Sor, Aguado, Carcassi, and Carulli made an immense impact on the concert-going public, and all four men wrote detailed guitar methods that sold in their thousands to amateur players eager to master the instrument for themselves. But a large number of budding guitarists set their sights at a more modest level, hoping to gain just enough knowledge of the instrument to use their skills as a social asset. It was at this sizeable public that England's foremost teacher and popularizer of the guitar in the Victorian era, Mrs. Sidney Pratten, aimed most of her work.

Mrs. Pratten (Catherina Josepha Pelzer), was born in Mulheim, on the Rhine, in 1821. She was the daughter of a leading German guitarist, Ferdinand Pelzer (1801–1860), who taught her to play the instrument from an early age. Catherina made her London concert debut at the age of about nine; soon afterwards, the Pelzers left Germany to settle in England, and she quickly built up an outstanding reputation as a soloist. As a young woman, she began to teach the guitar in fashionable and aristocratic circles, and in 1854 she

Below: This richly inlaid guitar was made in France in about 1850, and imported by a London company, Addison and Hodson. Mrs. Pratten used a photograph of herself playing this instrument on her visiting card.
(Courtesy Tony Bingham)

Above: A contemporary portrait of Mrs. Sidney Pratten (1821–1895). She had a distinguished career as a performer, and later became an influential teacher of the guitar in London.
(Courtesy Tony Bingham)

married an English flautist, Robert Sidney Pratten.

Some years later, Mrs. Pratten published a comprehensive method for guitar, drawing on the work of Giuliani and Sor; but, as one of her friends later wrote, "[she] found... that the amateur pupil was not inclined to devote sufficient study to the instrument to gain the necessary technique to grapple with the dif-ficulties of the music of the classic authors for the guitar."

Her solution to this was a book entitled *Learning the Guitar Simplified by Mme. Sidney Pratten,* a mixture of elementary exercises and "pleasing pieces and Songs." It was a huge success, and had been through 12 editions at the time of her death in 1895.

As a leading player and teacher, Mrs. Pratten owned some fine nineteenth-century guitars, and some of these (which may have been made to her specifications) are shown here.

Left and below: Another French guitar, with an ivory plaque bearing the name of Boosey and Sons, who were already well-established as musical instrument retailers in London. The original label inside the soundhole carries Mrs. Pratten's signature, and is dated July 2, 1859.
(Courtesy Tony Bingham)

Above: A "bambino" guitar, designed for children, and owned by Mrs. Pratten. It was made in 1870 and is shown here with its original case.
(Courtesy Tony Bingham)

The Carpenter From Almería

The importance of Antonio de Torres in the development of the guitar is hard to overstate. A gifted craftsman, who was also a fine player, his designs took the achievements of previous luthiers to new levels of refinement and sophistication, and many aspects of his approach have become de facto standards for his successors.

Torres was born in 1817 at La Cañada de San Urbino, just outside Almería in southern Spain. After a brief spell as a conscript soldier, he married in 1835, and began his working career as a carpenter in the nearby village of Vera. There, he was dogged by financial worries and family tragedy; two of his three daughters died in infancy, and following the death of his wife (aged 23), he left the area and settled in Seville.

It is not known exactly when Torres began making guitars, but he must have found the atmosphere of Seville a congenial place to develop his craft. The city had a thriving community of luthiers, and also attracted many leading players – among them Julián Arcas (1832–1882), who bought one of Torres' instruments, and encouraged him to become a full-time guitar builder. Torres followed this advice, and between 1856 and 1869 succeeded in establishing himself as the foremost luthier of his day – winning a medal at Seville's "Esposicion Agricola, Industrial y Artistica," and gaining commissions from a number of eminent clients – notably Francisco Tárrega (1852–1909).

Torres remarried in 1868; he had lived with his new wife, Josefa Martín Rosado, for a number of years

Right: By Torres' time, pin-style bridges were being gradually replaced by this design, in which the strings pass through slots behind the saddle, and are tied into position.

previously. In 1869 he left Seville, gave up guitar-making, and used some of his wife's capital to open a china-shop in his home town of Almería. Despite the endorsement of Tárrega and other virtuosi, it appears that the income from building guitars was insufficient (or too uncertain) for the needs of Torres' family. He eventually returned to his craft as a part-time activity, working at his home, 20 Calle Real, La Cañada, where he and his family also took in lodgers to help make ends meet. After the death of his second wife in 1883, he produced an increasing number of instruments, and by the time of his death in 1892, at the age of 75, he had made over 155 guitars.

Torres employed no assistants or apprentices, and his working methods were a carefully-guarded secret. His biographer, José Romanillos, has discovered and translated a fascinating account of his later life written by a local priest, Fr. Juan Martínez Sirvent, who was a close friend of the luthier. According to this, when performing critical tasks like gluing ribs, tops, and backs, "he always shut and locked the door of his workshop...so that no one could see him, not even his most intimate relatives." However, it seems unlikely that even the acutest observer could have discovered the key to Torres' genius simply by watching him. As he explained to Sirvent: "It is impossible to leave [my] secret behind for posterity; this will go to the tomb with me, for it is the result of the feel of the tips of the thumb and forefinger communicating to my intellect whether the soundboard is properly worked out to correspond with the guitar maker's concept and the sound required of the instrument."

Left: This guitar was built by Antonio de Torres in Almería in 1882. It has a spruce top, back and sides of cypress, and a French polish finish.
(Courtesy Guitar Salon International, Santa Monica)

The Construction of Torres' Guitars

Torres' guitars were not radical departures from tradition, but reflections and refinements of many previous developments, molded into a masterful overall design that has provided a model for nearly all subsequent luthiers. Compared with earlier nineteenth century French instruments (like those on pages 48-51), his bodies were larger and deeper, with a longer vibrating length for the strings (65cm/25.6in – now the standard for classical guitars) and a broader fingerboard. These changes, combined with Torres' improvements to the tops of his guitars, resulted in richer-sounding, more powerful in-struments capable of responding to the technical and

Right: "Tornavoz" fitted to a guitar made by Francisco Simplicio, 1929. This device, thought to have been invented by Torres, is a brass or steel cylinder attached to the guitar's soundhole, and is intended to improve its projection. It was used by Torres on several of his instruments, and taken up by his later disciples, including Simplicio (1874–1932). The tornavoz is one of the few Torres innovations that failed to catch on more widely, but it may have influenced the development of other internally fitted units designed to boost the volume of steel-strung guitars.
(Courtesy Gary Southwell)

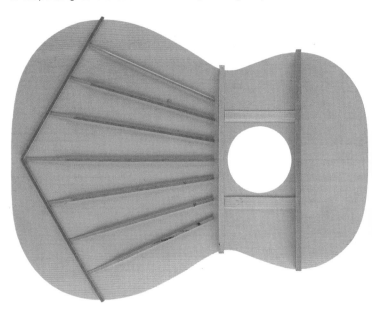

Above: Underside of top for a Torres replica guitar, made by Gary Southwell. The seven fan-struts reinforcing the lower part of the table are tapered, by careful planing, to the point where they meet the diagonal braces at its base. Two horizontal "harmonic bars" and two vertical supports strengthen the area around the soundhole.
(Courtesy Gary Southwell)

artistic needs of virtuoso performers. Torres was less concerned with decoration than his French and Spanish predecessors; his guitars are free from embellishments and elaborate inlays, and their elegant, understated appearance has set the tone for later instruments.

His advances in construction and bracing are based on the work of earlier Spanish luthiers, including Francisco Sanguino, Juan Pagés, and José Benedid. Their use of "fan-strutting" to reinforce the structure of the top (or plate) and modify the sound it produces contrasted with methods found elsewhere in Europe, where many makers preferred a system of transverse braces derived from lute design. This gave a bright, clear tone and a quick response when a note or chord was struck. Fan-strutting had a different effect, as British luthier Gary Southwell, who has built a number of Torres replicas, explains. "It's trying to control the plate a lot more, which tends to make the speaking time a bit slower, but gives you more harmonic richness of sound."

Torres' approach to fan-strutting, featuring seven braces (some previous makers had used as few as three), can be seen in the picture above, showing the underside of a Torres-style top built by Gary Southwell, and photographed before being glued into place. It provides a glimpse of Torres' solution to the perennial problem of making an instrument that is both tonally responsive and able to withstand the considerable pressure of its strings.

Tárrega and the Post-Torres Guitar

Francisco Tárrega (1852–1909) has been described as "the Chopin of the guitar" – a comparison that reflects his genius as one of its foremost players and composers. He was the first performer to demonstrate the increased tonal capabilities of the Torres-style instrument, and his extensive concert tours helped to spread its popularity throughout Europe. Tárrega was also an important teacher: his pupils included Emilio Pujol (1886–1980), Miguel Llobet (1878–1938), and a number of other players who later became highly influential in their own right.

As a young man, Tárrega met Torres during a visit to Seville in 1869, acquiring a guitar by the great luthier that he used almost exclusively for more than 20 years. During this period, he evolved a more expressive right-hand technique to make fuller use of the instrument's resources – although, like many of his predecessors, he continued to strike the strings with his fingertips, not his nails. He also introduced a new playing position, in which the guitar

Right: Francisco Tárrega was born in Villareal in 1852, and died in Barcelona in 1909. He was the most distinguished guitarist of his generation, and also an accomplished composer, arranger, and pianist.

Below: Guitar by Torres, 1889. The instrument's table is made from spruce, and has a finely decorated rosette; the rosewood bridge features bone edgings and mother-of-pearl dots.
(Courtesy Shel Urlik)

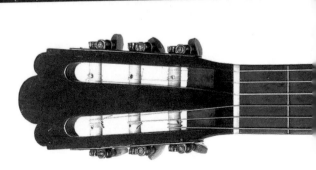

Acoustic Guitars

was supported on the left thigh. (This improves balance, allowing the left and right hand to move more freely; earlier, smaller instruments had been perched on the performer's right thigh, on the edge of a chair, or even on a tripod.)

Although Tárrega never published a guitar tutor (his pupil and biographer Pujol issued a detailed account of his master's playing methods in the 1930s), he produced a considerable amount of music for the instrument. Many of his own pieces (notably the famous tremolo study *Recuerdos de la Alhambra*) have become staples of the classical repertoire, while his transcriptions of other composers' material helped to broaden the guitar's hitherto limited expressive range. They include effective arrangements of piano music by his contemporaries Enrique Granados (1867–1916) and Isaac Albéniz (1860–1909) – richly-textured, colorful compositions that would have been impossible to perform adequately on a pre-Torres guitar. Tárrega's achievements also caught the attention of younger composers, such as Manuel de Falla (1876–1946) and Heitor Villa-Lobos (1887–1959), who were later to write major works for the instrument.

Right: The back and sides of the guitar are bird's-eye maple; the fingerboard is ebony.
(Courtesy Shel Urlik)

Below and below right: The label gives the instrument's date and number. Torres uses the words "segunda época" to differentiate his later (post-1875) guitars from those he made before his departure from Seville in 1869. The headstock is made from cypress; its face has a rosewood veneer.
(Courtesy Shel Urlik)

Towards the New World

By the mid-1800s, the guitar was growing in popularity not only in Europe, but also in the USA. It was first brought to the New World by the Spanish Conquistadores during the 1500s, and subsequently introduced to the native population in the schools set up by Franciscan monks throughout Spanish America. An English traveler, Thomas Gage, wrote of Indian children dancing "after the Spanish fashion to the sound of the guitarra" during his visit to a settlement near Mexico City in about 1625. Over the next hundred years, the instrument became increasingly popular with more privileged members of North American society. Guitars and printed tutors were readily available in many cities, and Benjamin Franklin (1706–1790) is said to have been a keen player.

Other plucked instruments came to America with its slaves. Among

Below: Christian Friedrich Martin made this guitar shortly before his departure from Germany to the United States. Its distinctive headstock follows the design created by Johann Georg Stauffer, the Viennese luthier for whom Martin worked in the 1820s.
(Courtesy Edinburgh University)

them were the banjo and the three-string "rabouquin," the close relative of an African instrument, the "raboukin," described by an eighteenth century French explorer, François Le Vaillant, as a "triangular piece of board with three strings made of intestines...which may be stretched at pleasure by means of pegs, like those of our instruments in Europe." Many African-Americans also experimented with other, home-made instruments, including rough-and-ready guitars. But black players were, for obvious reasons, almost totally cut off from the developments in commercial guitar making that began to take place in the early decades of the nineteenth century.

Quite a number of the creators of the modern American guitar industry were first- or second-generation émigrés from Europe, bringing their skills and business acumen to their ▶

Acoustic Guitars

new home. They included Orville Gibson (1856–1918), who was born near New York of English parents, and later moved to Kalamazoo, Michigan, working as a clerk before devoting himself to instrument building in the 1880s. Orville's use of carved, arched tops on his mandolins and steel-strung guitars (an idea inspired by his study of violin design) was a key breakthrough in construction. It led to the formation of the Gibson Mandolin-Guitar Manufacturing Company in 1902, and eventually to the creation of Gibson's innovative archtop guitars of the 1920s and 1930s.

Significantly, another classic twentieth-century American archtop guitar firm, Epiphone, also had its roots in violin-making. The company was founded in New York in 1873 by a Greek instrument builder, Anastasios Stathopoulo. Originally known as the House of Stathopoulo, its new name came from Anastasios' son Epaminondas (Epi), who took control of the business in the 1920s.

But the first, and arguably the most influential of all the Europeans who made acoustic guitars in America was C.F. Martin (1796–1873), a German luthier trained in Vienna, who settled in New York in 1833. The early history of his company is outlined on the following pages.

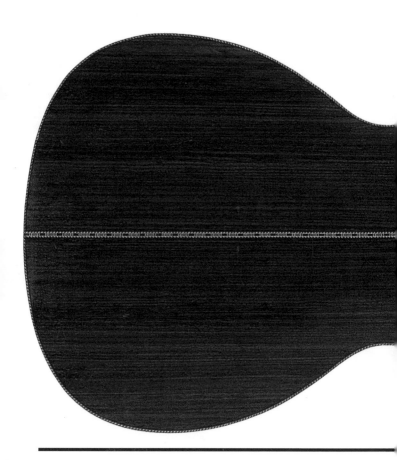

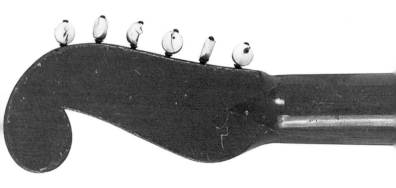

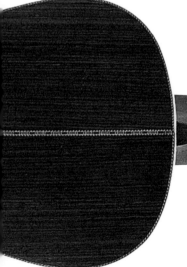

Above: Headstock details of C.F. Martin guitar.

Below: Back of the Martin guitar shown on previous pages.
(Courtesy Edinburgh University)

C.F. Martin –
Founding a Tradition

Christian Friedrich Martin was born in Mark Neu-kirchen, Saxony, on January 31, 1796. He took an early interest in woodworking, and learned the basics of the craft from his father, who was a cabinet maker. Soon, he was experimenting with building musical instruments, but after failing to gain an apprenticeship in his home town, he moved to Vienna in the 1820s, and was taken on by one of the leading guitar makers, Johann Georg Stauffer (1778–1853).

Martin eventually became the foreman at Stauffer's workshop, and was in day-to-day charge of the company's operations. However, he was keen to set up his own business, and left Vienna in 1825, returning to Saxony to try to fulfil his ambition. His

Below: Martin guitar in the style of Johann Georg Stauffer, 1834. It was made soon after C.F. Martin's arrival in America – its back is stamped "C.F. Martin, New York." The body is made from spruce, the bridge and fingerboard from ebony, and the

inlays around the soundhole and on the bridge and neck are mother-of-pearl. All "Stauffer-style" instruments feature a curved, violin-like headstock.
(Courtesy Martin Guitar Company)

Above: Stauffer developed a mechanism allowing the angle of the neck to be manually adjusted – the key at the base of the neck controls this.

plans were thwarted by the German violin-makers' guild, many of whom also built and sold guitars. They had a low opinion of guitar-makers, and did everything they could to prevent them from marketing their instruments. Martin fought and won a series of legal battles with the violin-makers' guild, but the lawsuits made life in Mark Neukirchen uncomfortable for him, and in 1833 he and his family emigrated to America.

Only a few months after arriving in New York, Martin opened a music shop at 196 Hudson Street, and for the next six years he built and sold his guitars from these premises. In 1839, he moved to eastern Pennsylvania, an area with a sizeable German-speaking community. The Martin Company has been there ever since, and its acoustic guitars, made in Nazareth, Pennsylvania, have achieved world-wide fame. It has remained a family business: C.F. Martin's son, Christian Friedrich Jr., became head of the company after his father's death in 1873; and the current Chairman, Chris Martin IV, is the original C.F. Martin's great-great-great-grandson.

Right and above right: Martin Stauffer-style commemorative reissue with special fingerboard inlay, 1996. A modern adaptation of the 1830s' Stauffer design, marking the 200th anniversary of C.F. Martin's birth. Unlike the original, which was gut-strung, this guitar has steel strings. It has a spruce top, Brazilian rosewood back and sides, and pearl/abalone inlays on its ebony fingerboard. These depict (left to right) Martin's North Street factory in Nazareth, Pennsylvania; the founder of the company C.F. Martin Sr.; and the top of a Martin flat-top guitar, with its distinctive X-bracing.
(Courtesy Martin Guitar Company)

Left: Martin 1-28 guitar built at the Martin factory in Nazareth, Pennsylvania, before 1867. Its headstock is an open, three-strings-a-side design similar to the type found on modern classical and flat-top guitars – by the 1860s, C.F. Martin had abandoned the Stauffer-style headstock. The rectangular bridge is almost certainly a later addition – the original would have had raised pyramid-shapes to the left and right of the string-pins.
(Courtesy Martin Guitar Company)

Above and right:
A Martin 00-42 flat-top,
steel-strung guitar from 1922.
Like nearly all Martin instruments of
this type, its top is made from
spruce; the back and sides are
rosewood, and the bridge is
"pyramid" shaped.
(Courtesy Real Guitars, San Francisco)

SECTION TWO

Twentieth Century Developments

By the early 1900s, the guitar had been slowly evolving for more than 300 years – but the pace of change was soon to change dramatically, with a range of radical innovations, driven by the demands of the American market, quickly bringing the instrument to the forefront of popular music. Accordingly, this section focuses on the USA and examines the work of the individuals and companies who helped to fashion the modern acoustic guitar.

At the beginning of the twentieth century, guitars were still outsold by banjos and mandolins, which dominated solo and group playing. By contrast, the guitar's place was mainly in the home – as an instrument to play in the parlor with family and friends, and as an accompaniment for singing. The main cause of this musical limitation was lack of volume, and as early as the 1880s, a number of makers were experimenting with the use of louder, more durable steel strings instead of the traditional gut sets. Their sound was not to everyone's liking. *Winner's Practical School for the Guitar*, an instruction book published in 1884, castigated the "cranks [who] choose steel strings, which are an abomination; any piece of pine board will answer just as well for an instrument to such depraved tastes". Nevertheless, the demand for them was strong, and by the mid-1930s, archtop, flat-top and resonator guitars, all steel-strung, were firmly established in American (and increasingly in European) popular music. The following pages look in detail at their design and development, and show how these instruments have con-tinued to evolve in the last half-century.

Towards the Modern Guitar

Orville Gibson (1856–1918) was the first major American luthier to apply the techniques of European violin-making to fretted instruments. During his childhood in Chateaugay, a small town in northern New York state, he had developed considerable skills as a wood-carver, as well as a strong interest in music. Later, he moved west to Kalamazoo, Michigan, where he began his professional instrument-building career in the early 1890s.

Orville's early efforts included a number of violins – one of them made out of wood salvaged from the old Town Hall in Boston – and he went on to introduce violin-like, arched sound-boards to his ground-breaking mandolin designs; previously, the instrument had always been fitted

with a flat or bent top. He later developed and patented another innovative design idea: the construction of a mandolin's neck and sides from the same piece of wood, with a partial hollowing-out of its neck to increase the instrument's internal volume.

Orville Gibson's guitars displayed many of the same characteristics as his mandolins, with carved, arched tops, and oval "Neapolitan"-style soundholes. During construction, their fronts and backs were "tuned" (to optimize their resonating properties) by a painstaking process of tapping and carving identical to the methods used by European violin-builders. The guitars, which were fitted with steel strings as standard, ▶

Below: Gibson Style U harp guitar, c.1915. Harp guitars were designed to provide players with an extended bass range, which was particularly useful for ensemble work. On this model, the ten "extra" strings would probably have been tuned chromatically.
(Courtesy Elderly Instruments; photograph by Dave Matchette)

were also considerably larger than any other contemporary luthier's; Gibson's biggest six-string model was 18 inches (45.7cm) wide. These features – combined with their elegant, often elaborately decorated appearance – made "Orville-style" instruments unique, and ensured their popularity among players looking for powerful, richer-sounding guitars.

The success of Orville's mandolin and guitar designs led to the formation of the Gibson Mandolin-Guitar Manufacturing Company in 1902. Surprisingly, he was only a consultant to the business, not its owner, and his direct involvement with it was relatively brief. He left Kalamazoo in 1909, and died in 1918, a year before the firm recruited Lloyd Loar – the brilliant young designer who was to take the archtop mandolin and guitar to new levels of sophistication and excellence.

Right: Gibson Style O, early 1900s. This model was introduced in 1902; the distinctive crescent and star inlay on the headstock was used on several of the first Gibsons. Unlike most other guitar makers of the period, Gibson fitted its instruments with steel strings as standard. The Gibson Style O later underwent considerable changes; a new version, launched in 1908, featured a scrolled body design, an elevated pickguard, and a floating bridge with a metal tailpiece. The model was eventually discontinued in 1923. (Courtesy Elderly instruments; Photograph by Dave Matchette)

Martin and the Birth of the American Flat-top

The Martin Company was already well-established by the time Orville Gibson began his career, and its guitar designs had evolved along very different lines. C. F. Martin Sr. (1796–1873) never used carved soundboards; he built his instruments with traditional flat tops, and, as we have seen, his earliest guitars were strongly influenced by the work of his former employer, the Viennese luthier Johann Georg Stauffer. However, soon after Martin's move from New York to Pennsylvania in 1839, one distinctive "Stauffer-style" feature, the scrolled headstock with its six-a-side tuning machines, began to be phased out in favor of a rectangular head like the one seen on the instruments here. The company's current Chairman, Chris Martin IV, suggests that the reason for this was, ▶

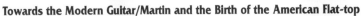

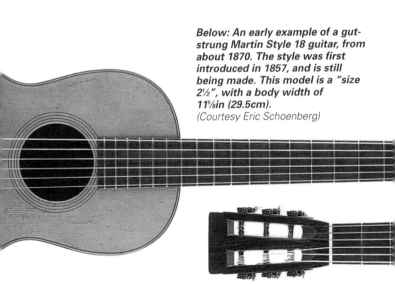

Below: An early example of a gut-strung Martin Style 18 guitar, from about 1870. The style was first introduced in 1857, and is still being made. This model is a "size 2½", with a body width of 11⅝in (29.5cm).
(Courtesy Eric Schoenberg)

in fact, purely practical: "The story I heard was that the tuning machine mechanism came from Europe, probably Germany...and the supply would occasionally be disrupted. So he would have guitars all ready to go, and no tuning machines. That's why he went to the rectangular headstock."

Another important innovation took place in the 1850s, when the Martin Company introduced a system of X-bracing on the insides of its guitar soundboards. (Previous Martin guitars had been fitted with a form of lateral strutting.) C.F. Martin may well have invented this revolutionary design, and was certainly responsible for developing and popularizing it, and X-bracing later became a major factor in the success and longevity of Martin's

classic twentieth-century steel-strung designs.

Steel strings were not fitted as standard on Martin guitars until 1922, although they were available as an option on some models from 1900 onwards. But many other now-familiar aspects of the Martin range were firmly in place well before the turn of the century. The system of identifying models by two hyphenated codes – the first denoting body size, the second "style" and materials – was adopted in the 1850s, and is still in use today. One of those designated "styles," Style 18, has been in regular production for over 140 years, and a number of other current models are also closely based on C.F. Martin Sr.'s original flat-top designs.

Below: A rare Martin 000-21 harp-guitar, built in 1902. Unlike the Gibson Style "U" shown earlier, this instrument has two necks; the upper one is an unfretted support for the extra 12 strings. These would have been used as "drones," or to provide extra bass notes.
(Courtesy Martin Guitar Company)

Right: Martin 000-42, 1918. The 000 size, which has a body width of 15 inches (38.1cm), was introduced in 1902 in response to players' demands for larger, louder guitars. This Style 42 is strung with steel, and has a distinctive ivory bridge.
(Courtesy Eric Schoenberg)

Gibson – the "L" Range

After the launch of the Gibson Mandolin-Guitar Manufacturing Company in 1902, the mainstay of the company's guitar range was the "L" series. There were initially four "L" models listed, but the original "Style L" was soon dropped from the catalog, the L-2 was discontinued in 1908, and the L-1 and L-3 were joined in 1911 by the larger L-4.

The instruments retained the steel strings and arched tops introduced by Orville Gibson, but differed substantially from his previous designs in other ways. They were plainer than their predecessors;

Orville's love of elaborately inlaid soundboards, fingerboards, and bridges was probably not commercially sustainable, and Gibson designs became increasingly standardized after his departure from Kalamazoo in 1909. The early "L" series guitars were smaller than the "Orville-style" instruments – the L-1 and L-3 had a body width of 13½ inches (34.3cm), and the biggest model in the series, the L-4, was a modest 16 inches (40.6cm) wide. And the "L" series also abandoned some of Orville's ingenious ideas about internal construction, including his

Below and right: The distinctive headstock logo was used on most Gibsons from 1903 until the mid-1920s – earlier "Orville-style" instruments featured a star and crescent inlay.

Left: A Gibson L-4, c.1924. The L-4 was introduced in 1912, and stayed in production until 1956.
(Courtesy Martin Taylor)

method of building an instrument's sides and neck from a single piece of wood.

However, by the end of World War I, other important new construction techniques were under development at Gibson. A member of the workforce, Ted McHugh, was responsible for the introduction of the truss-rod – a steel bar, fitted inside the neck, which greatly improved the guitar's strength and rigidity, and allowed the neck itself to be made slimmer and more comfortable for the player. Truss-rods were fitted as standard to most Gibson guitars from 1922 onwards (Gibson quickly patented the concept); the triangular cover for the one on the L-4 above can be seen clearly in the close-up picture. But the guitar that displayed the most dramatic design breakthroughs was the L-5, which set the standard for all subsequent archtop guitars, and was the brainchild of Gibson's chief instrument designer, Lloyd Loar.

American Archtops

Lloyd Allayre Loar (1886–1943) possessed an unusual combination of talents. He was a music graduate and a skilled performer on the mandolin and viola, as well as an engineer with a keen grasp of the technical aspects of instrument design. During his five-year stay at Gibson, he was responsible for product development, improving existing models and experimenting with new concepts, including electric guitars. But his great contribution to the evolution of the acoustic instrument was his work on the Gibson L-5, which first appeared in 1922, and is now recognized as one of the most important and influential archtops ever built.

Like Orville Gibson, Loar made his first breakthroughs in mandolin design, and then applied these innovations to the construction of the guitar. In 1922, he introduced the Gibson F-5, a mandolin that took ▶

*Above: A Gibson L-1,
c.1920. A late example of
an archtop design first
produced by Gibson in
1902.*
(Courtesy Real Guitars, San
Francisco)

*Left: The Gibson L-10's
headstock, tuners, and
neck are all similar to
those on L-5s of the
same period. Its
tailpiece (right), with
visible slots for the
strings, is a prototype
that was not used on
production models. The
fingerboard and bridge
are ebony; on later L-
10s, they were made of
rosewood.*

*Right: This Gibson L-
10 is dated 1928
(three years before
the model's official
launch). The glossy
black finish has
never been
retouched, and the
instrument is still in
near-mint condition.*
(Courtesy John
Monteleone)

Acoustic Guitars

Orville's innovative arched-top construction one stage further by using f-holes in place of the instrument's customary oval sound-hole. Later that year, the L-5 guitar appeared; it, too, had f-holes, as well as a number of other new features: a truss-rod, an adjustable bridge, and a system of top bracing that used two parallel wooden bars glued to the inside of the soundboard. The result was a guitar with a winning combination of playability, tone-quality, and power, which was quickly taken up by a number of extremely influential American players – notably Eddie Lang (1902–1933), whose recordings with fellow-guitarist Lonnie Johnson

(1889–1970), and collaborations with violinist Joe Venuti (1903–1978) helped to establish the guitar as a solo instrument in jazz.

Gibson responded to the resultant demand by bringing out three other "L" series archtops; the first of these, the L-10, was officially launched in 1931. It bore a strong resemblance to the L-5, but was not designed by Lloyd Loar, who left the firm in 1924 after it refused to back his plans to produce electric instruments. He continued to develop his radical ideas until the war years, setting up his own company, Vivi-Tone, with two other ex-Gibson employees in 1933.

*Below and right: Gibson L-5, 1937. It has a 17-inch (43.2cm) body, a two-piece spruce top, back and sides of maple, and an ebony-faced fingerboard with mother-of-pearl inlays. The "flowerpot" logo on the headstock is found on many early Gibsons, but the pickguard is probably a later replacement.
(Courtesy Dale Rabiner)*

Gibson – from L-5 to Super 400

Gibson continued to refine and develop its range of archtop guitars throughout the 1930s. The L-5 remained a key instrument in this range, but Lloyd Loar's original design underwent a number of changes in the years following his departure. In 1934, Gibson addressed the perennial need for extra power and volume by increasing the body width of the L-5 from 16 inches to 17 inches (40.6 to 43.2cm). At the same time, it enlarged three other "L" models (the L-10, L-7, and L-12) by the same

amount, and introduced a new, top-of the-line archtop with an 18-inch (45.7cm) body, the Super 400.

This guitar was designed to impress – a lavishly decorated flagship for the Gibson range, taking its name from its $400 price tag (a substantial sum, especially in the Depression years). It featured gold plated tuning machines, pearl inlays, an ebony fingerboard, and an elaborate tailpiece with the model's name engraved on it. The Super 400 was highly acclaimed – among the

Above: The Gibson L7 features delicate mother-of-pearl "picture-frame" inlays on its fingerboard. (Courtesy Mandolin Brothers, New York)

Below: Gibson L-7, 1937. The L-7 first appeared in 1932, and was enlarged from 16 inches to 17 inches (40.6 to 43.2cm) in 1934. (Courtesy Mandolin Brothers, New York)

players who could afford it – and it remains in use today, although some guitarists find it too large for comfort, and question whether its sound is significantly more powerful than a 17-inch Gibson's.

Gibson was the early pioneer of archtop guitar design, but by the mid-1930s it was no longer alone in the market. Epiphone had introduced a rival range of instruments in 1931, and several other important guitar-makers (including Stromberg and D'Angelico, whose work will be examined in later pages) were also launching new instruments. Gibson had to innovate to survive; and the

company's next major development the cutaway body, was introduced a an option on the L-5 and the Supe 400 in 1939 (see photograph at right Cutaways gave the player easie access to the higher reaches of th fingerboard; they were an immediat success, and not surprisingly, the were soon adopted by Gibson competitors.

Despite such rivalry, and th growing demand for electric guitars i the post-war years, the L-5 and Supe 400 acoustics retained their place in th main Gibson catalog until the 1980 and are still available as part of th company's "Historic Collection" serie

Right: This is a modern replica, from Gibson's "Historic Collection," of a 1939-style Super 400.
(Courtesy Dale Rabiner)

*Left: Gibson L-12P, 1948. The L-12
was introduced a year after the L-
7; the "P" (standing for Premier)
designates a cutaway model. The
"crown" inlay on the headstock
and the parallelogram fingerboard
decoration (right, inset) are still
seen on many Gibson guitars
today.*
*Courtesy Mandolin Brothers, New
York)*

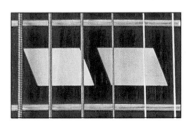

Epiphone – A Rival Range of Archtops

Epaminondas ("Epi") Stathopoulo (1893–1943) became President of his father Anastasios' New York-based instrument building company, the House of Stathopoulo, in the 1920s. For a number of years, the company had concentrated on banjo-making, and it was renamed the Epiphone Banjo Corporation in 1928. But in the early 1930s, Epiphone changed direction, focusing on the design and production of guitars, and providing the market-leaders, Gibson, with some serious competition.

Epiphone constantly sought to outdo Gibson's innovations. It challenged the dominant position o the L-5 with the launch of it "Masterbilt" range, comprising n fewer than nine new archtops, i 1931. When Gibson increased th body sizes on its guitars, Epiphon made its products a little larger sti And the company's two highly acclaimed flagship guitars, the D Luxe (1931) and the Emperor (1936 were conceived as direct rivals t their Gibson counterparts, the L-5 an the Super 400.

But Epiphone was certainly not mere imitator. Its guitars were th fruit of many years' experience i

Below and right:
Epiphone De Luxe,
1935. This model
features Epiphone's
famous "wandering
vine" design on its
headstock, which has
an off-center groove
on its right-hand side
- another "trademark"
for early Epiphone
instruments. The top
is spruce, the back and
sides maple.
(Courtesy Martin Taylor)

Acoustic Guitars

stringed-instrument construction, and were immediately recognizable on-stage, with their asymmetrical headstocks and elegant pearl inlays. The "wandering vine" design shown bottom right was seen on most Epiphones from the 1930s to the 1950s, and the company also used distinctive floral, diamond, and cloud-shaped markers for its fingerboards. Another Epiphone feature was the "Frequensator" tailpiece (seen on the Emperor and 1959 Deluxe models); it was intended to "equalize" treble and bass response by shortening the top three strings' path from bridge to tailpiece, and extending the length of

the lower strings. It is doubtful whether this made much difference to the sound, but the simple elegance of the "double trapeze" design ensured its lasting popularity.

Epiphone's post-war history has been a checkered one. Epi Stathopoulo died in 1943, and ten years later his family sold the business. Ironically, it eventually ended up in the hands of Chicago Musical Instruments (CMI) which also owned Gibson, and for a while Epiphones were made at the old competitor's Kalamazoo factory. Since the 1970s, guitars bearing the Epiphone label have been built in the Far East.

*Right:
Epiphone's
distinctive
"epsilon" logo
on the
pickguard of
the 1959
Deluxe.*

**Below: This Deluxe dates from
1959, and has a cutaway
and a "Frequensator" tailpiece.
The pickup (a De Armond model
popular with many archtop
players) is attached to the neck
and pickguard, and does not affect
the instrument's acoustic sound.**
*(Courtesy Mandolin Brothers, New
York)*

Stromberg and the "Orchestral" Archtop

Like Epiphone, Charles A. Stromberg & Son was a family firm. Its founder, Charles Stromberg, had emigrated from Sweden to Boston, Massachusetts; after working for a prominent local instrument manufacturer, Thompson and Odell, for a number of years, he formed his own company, which made drums and xylophones as well as banjos, mandolins, and guitars, in about 1905. Five years later, Charles' son, Elmer (1895–1955) joined the business as a 15-year-old trainee.

Elmer worked on a wide variety of instruments, and made his initial reputation in the 1920s as a banjo

designer. During this period, he had also begun to build archtop guitars, producing them in larger numbers as the banjo began to decline in popularity. The earliest Stromberg archtops were the "G" series: they had 16-inch (40.6cm) bodies, and were introduced in the late 1920s.

Like many other luthiers, Elmer Stromberg followed Gibson in increasing the size of his guitars. His G-1, G-2, and Deluxe models were widened to 17 inches (43.2cm) in the mid-1930s, and in 1937 he added two new instruments to the range: the Master 300 and 400. These were the largest and among the most powerful-

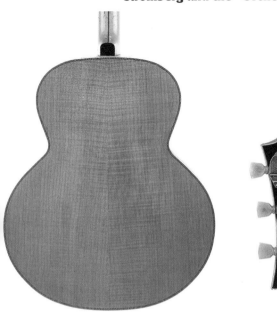

Above and below: Stromberg Master 400, 1948, made for Frank Bittles, guitarist with Fletcher Henderson. It has a spruce top, back and sides of maple, and an ebony strip inset into its maple neck. The body of the Stromberg Master 400 (top left) *is 19 inches (48.3cm) wide. Its headstock decoration (bottom of page) is not a pearl inlay, but has been carved out of the layers of plastic covering the wood.*
(Courtesy Derrick Weskin)

Acoustic Guitars

sounding archtops available, with a body width of 19 inches (48.3cm), and they proved popular with big-band players; Stromberg's customers included Count Basie's guitarist, Freddie Green, Frank Bittles of the Fletcher Henderson Orchestra, and Fred Guy from Duke Ellington's band.

Elmer Stromberg constantly dev-eloped and modified his designs. One of his most important in-novations was a new system of top bracing, replacing the parallel wooden struts he had used on his early guitars with a single diagonal bar running across the inside of his instruments' soundboards. This was in use on all his guitars by 1940, and was followed

by other refinements, including truss-rod systems and (after the war) body cutaways. The general trend towards electric archtops in the 1950s did not reduce the demand for Strombergs, and the production of instruments was only halted by Elmer's untimely death in 1955.

Above: This Stromberg Deluxe cutaway dates from the early 1950s. It is slightly smaller than the Master 400 (just over 17 inches, 48.3cm wide) but retains the distinctive headstock and tailpiece design.
(Courtesy Mandolin Brothers, New York)

D'Angelico –
A New York Classic

Archtop guitars by John D'Angelico (1905–1964) are among the finest instruments of their kind. Born into an Italian-American family in New York, D'Angelico was steeped in the traditions of European instrument building, and at the age of nine he began learning the basics of his craft from his great-uncle, who was a distinguished maker of Italian-style mandolins and violins. In 1932, D'Angelico set up his own workshop at 40 Kenmare Street, New York City, and started to develop his own guitar designs, which were strongly influenced by the Gibson L-5. Even at this early stage in his career, he was already attracting commissions from leading players. The "No. 2" instrument shown opposite was made for Benny Martell, the guitarist with the Buddy Rogers Orchestra – which had the dubious distinction of being a particular favorite of the American gangster Al Capone!

By 1937, D'Angelico was offering his customers four models of archtop guitar: Style A, Style B, the Excel, and the New Yorker. The first two designs were phased out during the early 1940s, and the Excel and New Yorker are the instruments on which his

Above: D'Angelico No. 2, 1932. This guitar, previously owned by Benny Martell of the Buddy Rogers Orchestra, has been restored by luthier John Monteleone. Like most D'Angelicos, it is made from American woods: the top is sitka spruce, the back and sides red maple. The pickguard is a later addition, probably made by John D'Angelico himself.
(Courtesy John Monteleone)

Above: D'Angelico Excel, 1939, with a 17-inch (43.2cm) body, pearl fingerboard inlays engraved with a distinctive diagonal pattern, and D'Angelico's "trademark" headstock, with its "keyhole" cut-out and finial.
(Courtesy Mandolin Brothers, New York)

reputation rests. The Excel has a 17-inch (43.2cm) body, and its distinctive cut-out headstock and urn-shaped "finial" were soon used on the larger-sized New Yorker as well. Both models underwent considerable changes over the years; D'Angelico would often add custom features tailored to his customers' requirements, as well as replacing or upgrading parts of his guitars when they were returned to his workshop for maintenance or adjustments.

Despite the substantial demand for his instruments, D'Angelico rarely made more than 30 guitars a year. They were built by hand with the help of two assistants – the first of whom Jimmy DiSerio, left the firm in 1959. For the last five years of his life D'Angelico's only regular employee was his apprentice Jimmy D'Aquisto who had started work with him in 1951, and came to play an increasingly important role as D'Angelico's health deteriorated and he suffered a series of heart attacks. Most of the instruments produced during this final period were built by D'Aquisto under his master's guidance. Following D'Angelico's death, D'Aquisto quickly established himself as a distinguished luthier in his own right.

Above and top: D'Angelico New Yorker cutaway, 1953. John D'Angelico first offered cutaways on his guitars in 1947, and the "natural" finish seen on this guitar began to be popular at about the same time. The engraving on the headstock (which has a finial but no cut-out) shows the outline of the Chrysler Building in New York. (Courtesy Mandolin Brothers, New York)

D'Aquisto – From Pupil to Master

Jimmy D'Aquisto (1935–1995) had been very close to John D'Angelico, and after the death of his former employer and mentor in 1964, he continued making D'Angelico's classic archtop guitar designs, the Excel and the New Yorker, under his own name. As D'Aquisto's friend and fellow-luthier John Monteleone explains, "Jimmy was bound by tradition. He had such a reverence for John [D'Angelico] that it took him a long time to build himself up to trusting himself. He had to prove himself to the people who loved John's work and solicited John's shop, and he did it by making his guitars just like John's – or as much as he could. Jimmy was always torn between living the legacy of John and being himself."

Gradually, D'Aquisto began to invest D'Angelico's designs with variations of his own. He altered the appearance of the f-holes on his Excels and New Yorkers, making them into elliptical s-shapes, and began using adjustable tailpieces with an ebony top and a brass hinge. On some models (see photograph below) he dispensed with D'Angelico's trademark finial, and streamlined the appearance of the pickguard. John Monteleone des-cribes the motivation behind these and other changes as the desire to break away from tradition, "to carry the instruments on from where they've left off," and this

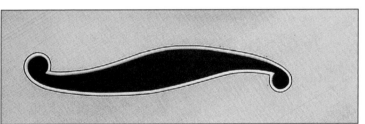

Above: D'Aquisto New Yorker, c.1980. While the body size and shape are similar to those on the D'Angelico New Yorker shown earlier, this guitar has many distinctive D'Aquisto features – notably the reshaped f-holes (above, inset) and pickguard, and the ebony-topped tailpiece replacing the metal "stairstep" type. The headstock (top, inset) still carries a stylized engraving of the Chrysler Building in New York, but the finial is gone from the cutout, and the truss-rod cover has been reshaped. (Courtesy Dale Rabiner)

process continued with D'Aquisto's later guitars, which are strikingly original and effective re-interpretations of the "traditional" arch-top.

Perhaps the most radical example of D'Aquisto's design philosophy is his "Solo" model – an instrument fittingly summarized by John Monteleone as "playable art." It has a carved-out headstock, dramatically reshaped soundholes intended to increase the guitar's projection, and a body made from spruce and Tyrolean maple (European "cello-wood" – D'Aquisto rarely used American woods for his acoustics). He made only nine Solos before his sudden death in April 1995, and among the advance orders he left unfulfilled was one from composer and guitarist Craig Snyder, who subsequently asked John Monteleone if he would be prepared to make a version of the Solo for him. The remarkable outcome of this request can be seen below.

Right: D'Aquisto Solo, 1993. Among its many striking features are the carved-out headstock and tailpiece, the massive ebony bridge, and the cutaway fingerboard. D'Aquisto made Solos in 17-inch (43.2cm) and 18-inch (45.7cm) sizes (this is a 17-inch), and there is some variation between individual models – particularly in the positioning of the soundholes, which are sometimes placed nearer the edges of the body.
(Courtesy Dale Rabiner)

John Monteleone's "Montequisto"

When he was commissioned by Craig Snyder to build a "Solo" guitar based closely on Jimmy D'Aquisto's original design, John Monteleone selected materials from D'Aquisto's own workshop, including wood, lacquer, and a partially completed neck and set of sides. Monteleone also had access to a number of earlier D'Aquisto Solos, taking tracings from them and examining their construction carefully. He explains that "out of respect for Jimmy, I felt it was a good idea to stay as close to the original design as possible. I knew that I could never duplicate the sound, and that wasn't my intention. Someone's sound and their tone is their thumbprint – and realizing that, when I got to building the inside of the guitar, I knew that I'd have to rely on my own instincts and ▶

Right and above: Monteleone Radio City archtop cutaway. An 18-inch archtop with a spruce top, curly maple back, sides and neck, and inlays made from tapered wedges of mother-of-pearl and abalone. The guitar's "Art Deco"

look was inspired by the appearance of New York's Radio City Music Hall. (Courtesy John Monteleone)

experience to get the best tone I could for this particular guitar. I stayed pretty close to the concept, but yet I went my own way a little bit, just to conduct it as I thought would be best." The outcome – a magnificent creation nicknamed the "Montequisto" by John's wife – is shown below.

Monteleone's own instruments (he builds flat-top guitars and mandolins as well as acoustic and electric archtops) are highly sought after by leading players. His close knowledge of the work of Jimmy D'Aquisto, John D'Angelico, and other leading luthiers, as well as his extensive experience as a guitar restorer, give him a special insight into the technical aspects of instrument construction. But he also draws inspiration from key figures in other areas of design – notably Raymond Loewy, who created the Lucky Strike cigarette packet, the Studebaker Avanti motorcar, and other classic American artifacts. Like Loewy and other commercial designers, Monteleone stresses the importance of simplicity and functionality in his work: "I never have an individual element of the guitar compete against another one. The first requirement is that [the instrument] has to play up to expectations. Once you've achieved that, then you can begin to look at how to make the parts harmonious in their appearance. It's another kind of vibration. The guitar has a sound – but it also has a look that moves."

Right: Monteleone Electric Flyer, 1997. An electric/acoustic instrument with a design derived from one of his earlier guitars, the Radio Flyer.
(Courtesy John Monteleone)

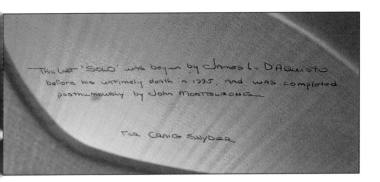

Above: The inscription inside the Solo: "This last 'Solo' was begun by James L. D'Aquisto before his untimely death in 1995, and was completed posthumously by John Monteleone. For Craig Snyder."

Left: D'Aquisto/Monteleone Solo, 1996. John Monteleone's version of Jimmy D'Aquisto's groundbreaking design. Although its overall appearance is similar to the D'Aquisto Solo shown on previous pages, there are a number of small differences. These include the bridge design, which is an easily adjustable "wedge" type, instead of the 1-piece unit favored by D'Aquisto. (Courtesy Craig Snyder/John Monteleone)

Robert Benedetto and "The Sound of Today"

Robert Benedetto was born in the Bronx, New York in 1946. His father and grandfather were master cabinet-makers (his grandfather worked for the Steinway Piano Company), and the skills he learned from them, combined with his passion for music, led to his first childhood experiments in creating instruments – miniature replicas that he carved out of discarded scraps of wood, using a knife he made from one of his grandfather's files. Bob soon graduated to building real guitars; and after a spell as a professional player, and service in the U.S. Air Force, he became a full-time archtop luthier in 1968. He now makes his world-famous instruments at his home in East Stroudsburg, Pennsylvania – with his grandfather's tools still close to hand.

Bob's designs have a strong affinity with European traditions of stringed instrument making; he produces violins, violas, and mandolins, as well as archtop guitars, and has recently completed his first cello. He acknowledges that "violin-makers have certainly been an inspiration to me – more so than guitar-makers really," and says he finds violins a greater challenge to build than guitars. "A violin is either 'right' or it's 'wrong' – there's very little room for subjectivity, and violin players are more in agreement than guitarists on what their instrument should play and feel and sound like."

Bob's approach to archtop guitar

Right: A partly completed body for a Benedetto La Venezia, showing the X-bracing on the top.
(Courtesy Robert Benedetto)

Left: Benedetto La Venezia (18-inch left-hand model) in a shaded natural finish. The top is made from European spruce, the back from highly flamed European maple. There are no bindings or inlays. The fingerboard and nut are ebony. The Benedetto S-6 pickup is a "floating" design, which does not make contact with the top.*
(Courtesy Dale Rabiner)*

design is based on years of practical experience as a player and luthier. He uses X-braced tops, which provide the combination of warmth and well-balanced tone he describes as "the sound of today" for the soloist. He has also moved away from the large, heavy body construction favored by some earlier makers; Benedetto archtops are lighter and more responsive, with distinctively shaped tailpieces made from ebony – not the more massive brass seen on other instruments in this section. Bob comments that "big isn't necessarily better or louder," and says the most popular body size for his archtops is 17 inches (43.2cm) – although he also builds 16-inch (40.6cm) and 18-inch (45.7cm) guitars.

In his 30-year career, Benedetto has completed more than 675 instruments (over 400 are archtops), and is generally regarded as the leading archtop builder of his generation.

Below and below right: Benedetto Manhattan (16-inch) in shaded green "jazz-burst" finish. This guitar was custom-made for Bob Benedetto's

Robert Benedetto – Innovation and Tradition

Robert Benedetto produces a varied range of models, and has been influential in developing the seven-string guitar, which features an extra bass string tuned a fifth below the existing low E. The seven-string adaptation to an archtop guitar was introduced by the great jazz guitarist George Van Eps (b. 1913) in the 1930s, and has since been used by a growing number of leading players, such as Howard Alden, Bucky and John Pizzarelli, Ron Esch'ete, and Jimmy Bruno – all of whom own Benedetto guitars.

The picture at right shows a customized seven-string made by Bob Benedetto for Jimmy Bruno, who was happy to let Bob make the essential decisions about its sound and feel. "The best thing to do with someone like Bob is to say, 'You make ▶

daughter, Gina. It has since been
played by many of the luthier's
endorsees, and was used by Andy
Summers (formerly of the UK rock
group The Police) when he appeared
at a concert featuring eight leading
"Benedetto Players" in May 1997.
(Courtesy Gina Benedetto)

*Below: The top of
this guitar is made
from sitka spruce,
and the body is
American maple
with ebony fittings.*

*Left: Benedetto seven-string guitar, custom-made for
Jimmy Bruno. Its 17-inch (43.2cm) body
is finished in honey blonde, and it has a floating Benedetto
S-7 pickup with volume and tone controls mounted
(almost invisibly) on the pickguard. The tailpiece inlay,
showing Jimmy Bruno's name, is mother-of-pearl.*
(Courtesy Jimmy Bruno)

it the way you want to make it.' Who knows better than the guy who's making it what's going to sound better?" Seven-strings now account for about 25 per cent of Benedetto's archtop guitar output, making him the most prolific builder of the instrument.

In his long career as a luthier, Bob Benedetto has been responsible for a number of significant developments in archtop design. In 1982, he constructed a guitar without inlays or bindings for the late Chuck Wayne, setting a trend for simplicity and purity that was followed by many other makers. Bob has also introduced "honey blonde" finishes, ebony pickguards and tailpieces, and the innovative "Renaissance Series" of instruments with standard f-holes replaced by unique clustered sound openings (see page 246). However, he remains cautious of change for change's sake In his book *Making an Archtop Guitar*, he reminds budding luthiers that "refinements, or so called improvements, are successful only when the player is involved. It is undeniably the player who will legitimize the maker's efforts." Significantly, Benedetto's highest accolades come from the musicians who use his instruments. These include Kenny Burrell, Cal Collins, Frank Vignola, Stéphane Grappelli (who played a Benedetto violin), and British guitarists Martin Taylor, Andy Summers, Andy MacKenzie, and Adrian Ingram.

Top right and right: Benedetto 25th Anniversary guitar. Made in 1993 to celebrate Bob Benedetto's then 25th year as a luthier. The shaded natural finish is a variation on Benedetto's signature "honey blonde" coloring, and the guitar is made from the finest European woods (spruce top, maple back). The burl veneer, also seen on the Cremona, is used here on the headstock, tuning buttons, pickguard, bridge base, and tailpiece.
(Courtesy Roy McDonald; photograph by Jonathan Levin)

Left: Benedetto Cremona (left-hand model). The 17-inch instrument takes its name from the town in Italy where the violin-maker Antonio Stradivari lived and worked. The top and back are **carved from European tonewoods, and the flared, burl-veneered headstock is inlaid with mother-of-pearl and abalone.**
(Courtesy Dale Rabiner)

John Buscarino and Dale Unger

Twenty-seven years ago, British guitarist Ivor Mairants wrote in the UK's *BMG* (*Banjo, Mandolin & Guitar*) magazine that the archtop guitar's days seemed to be numbered: "Most people hardly remember the instrument played by Eddie Lang… Development of it has almost stopped and until it again increases in popularity, very few makers will concentrate on its improvement." Thankfully, things have changed considerably since the early 1970s, and a wide range of first-class archtops is now being built and played. This healthy situation is at least partly due to the influence of luthiers like Bob Benedetto, John Monteleone, and the late Jimmy D'Aquisto, who have inspired younger guitar-builders to turn their attention to archtop construction.

Dale Unger, whose "American Dream" model is shown opposite, was born in 1954, and grew up in Nazareth, Pennsylvania, headquarters of the Martin Company. He has been strongly influenced by his contact

*Below and right:
"American Dream"
archtop guitar by Dale
Unger's "American
Archtop" company.
The instrument was
built using Bob
Benedetto's designs
and molds. Its top and
back are made from
laminated woods, and
it has a 17-inch
(43.2cm) body with a
3-inch (7.62cm) depth.
The logo on the
headstock was created
by Dale Unger with
Dick Boak from the
Martin Guitar
Company.
(Courtesy Dale
Unger/Robert
Benedetto)*

121

with Martin craftsmen and guitars, and by a three-year period working with Bob Benedetto, who lives in nearby East Stroudsburg. The American Dream is made from Benedetto's patterns and molds, but hand-crafted by Dale Unger with a laminated top and back, and maple sides and neck. Laminates are a less expensive alternative to the individual sections of premium tonewood traditionally used on archtop guitars; however, Dale Unger has braced and constructed his instrument "Bob's way," and the results are certainly outstanding.

John Buscarino is another former Benedetto apprentice, who also studied with the leading classical guitar-maker Augustine LoPrinzi. Buscarino is now based in Florida, where he builds archtops, flat-tops and nylon-strung guitars (see page 247 for a photograph of his innovative "Cabaret" cutaway classical design). His instruments are hand-made from American and European woods, and

are in strong demand from players and collectors – including the American guitar connoisseur Scott Chinery, for whom John made the "Blue Guitar" shown above. It is par

Modern American Archtops

The first guitar shown here has a fascinating history, and has traveled many thousands of miles from its "birthplace" in Toledo, Ohio (where it was built by W.G. Barker in 1964) to its current home with jazz guitarist Martin Taylor in Scotland. Originally destined for American jazz musician Howard Roberts, it was sold instead to a Hollywood studio guitarist, Johnny Gray, who used it on the soundtracks of many film and TV scores, including that of *Batman*. It can also be heard accompanying Elvis Presley's performance of "Love Me Tender." Subsequently, the instrument made its way to Australia, and was purchased and brought to London by Ike Issacs, guitarist with Stéphane Grappelli in the early 1970s. Issacs presented it to the young Martin Taylor as a 21st birthday present.

The other photographs feature two fine examples of 1990s archtops. ▶

of a group of 23 guitars (all blue 18-inch archtops) commissioned from leading luthiers which have been displayed at the Smithsonian Institution in Washington D.C.

Left and above: "Blue Guitar" by John Buscarino. Like the other 22 guitars in the series commissioned by Scott Chinery, this is an 18-inch (45.7cm) archtop. Buscarino has embellished the fingerboard and tailpiece with striking vine inlays which provide a pleasing contrast with the blue body.
(Courtesy John Buscarino)

Left and right, inset: Guitar by W.G. Barker, Toledo, Ohio, 1964. The distinctively shaped headstock has its present owner Martin Taylor's name inlaid on the truss-rod cover. The instrument's original metal tailpiece was replaced at Martin Taylor's request; the new one, which is ebony, was provided by Bob Benedetto.
(Courtesy Martin Taylor)

Acoustic Guitars

Mark Campellone (b. 1954) from Providence, Rhode Island, studied at the famous Berklee College of Music in Boston, Massachusetts. He began his career as a luthier in the mid-1970s after several years' experience as a professional musician, and built his first archtop in 1988. Campellone's instruments are strong-ly influenced by the work of Gibson and other classic archtop makers; he works largely alone, and is entirely self-taught. He currently makes about 30 guitars a year, offering three models, the Standard, Deluxe, and Special (shown here). Like a number of guitar-makers featured in this chapter, he has recently contributed a "blue guitar" to Scott Chinery's famous collection.

Bruce Sexauer (b. 1947) based in Sausalito, California, is an experienced maker of many different types of stringed instruments – in-cluding dulcimers, mandolins, psalt-eries, and harps, as well as electric and acoustic guitars. He began his career as a luthier in 1967, and started making archtops in the late 1980s.

The Ensemble JZ-17 is the second-largest of his three regular models; he has also recently developed a "Coo'stic Dominator" guitar, which combines elements of archtop and Selmer-Maccaferri (Django Reinhardt-style) designs.

Right: Campellone Special 17-inch (left-hand model). This guitar has a "thin-line" design, with a slimmer profile than most standard archtops. Its top is spruce, its back and sides maple, and its fingerboard ebony. The pickup, made by Ibanez in Japan, is a replica of the Gibson "Johnny Smith" model.
(Courtesy Dale Rabiner)

Above: Bruce Sexauer JZ-17. This "Ensemble" model (Sexauer also makes "Personal" and "Soloist" instruments with differing woods and finishes) has an Englemann spruce top, with a maple back and sides. The neck is also maple, and the headstock decorations are inlaid with ebony and mother-of-pearl. *(Courtesy Eric Schoenberg)*

American Flat-tops

In 1922, the same year that Gibson introduced the L-5 archtop, the Martin Company first fitted steel strings as standard to its model 2-17 flat-top guitar. This important move was probably hastened by the huge popularity of Hawaiian groups during the 1920s. Martin was already making a considerable number of the specially-adapted steel-strung guitars played by these musicians, and the transition to using steel on its regular models was relatively easy. The next year, steel strings were offered on Martin's Style 18 guitars, and Style 28 followed suit in 1925.

Like Gibson, Martin had been experimenting with bigger bodies in order to boost the sound and projection of its guitars – although it never built an instrument as large as the 18-inch Orville-styles. At the turn of the century, Martin's widest body was "size 00," which measured 141⁄8in (35.9cm). In 1902, the company launched the 15-inch (38.1cm) 000, and although guitars made in this size were initially slow sellers, they became increasingly popular in the early 1920s.

Soon afterwards, the 000 was the starting point for a significant design modification. It was inspired by Perry Bechtel, a leading banjoist planning to make the transition to the guitar, who approached Martin with a request for a flat-top that he would find more manageable to play. In particular, he wanted a narrower neck, and easier access to the higher reaches of the fingerboard. Martin responded by squaring off the top of the 000's body to

Right: Martin 000-45, 1929. This model features pearl inlays on its fingerboard, around its soundhole and sides, and adjoining the top and neck. It has 12 frets clear of its body. (Courtesy Martin Taylor)

Left: Martin OM-45, 1933. The OM version of Style 45 was introduced in 1930. The difference in body shape between this guitar and the 000-45 – the result of Perry Bechtel's request for an instrument with different dimensions – can be clearly seen. The neck now joins the body at the 14th fret.
(Courtesy Martin Guitar Company)

accommodate a re-shaped and re-positioned neck, which joined the body at the 14th fret. (Previous Martins followed classical guitar design, and had necks with only 12 frets easily accessible.) The new instrument, named the OM (Orchestra Model), was launched in 1930.

Fourteen-fret necks eventually became the norm not just on Martin flat-tops, but on their competitors' instruments too (they were already in regular use on archtop guitars). Martin's next major innovation, the large "Dreadnought"-size body, was also widely imitated. It was derived from a design the company had previously manufactured for the Boston-based Ditson retail chain, and its impressively bulky shape led to its being named after a famous class of battleship. Dreadnoughts quickly became the instruments of choice among players who needed the extra power they provided, and they are especially favored by folk and country music guitarists.

Martin – A Dynasty of Flat-top Designs

Martin is the longest-established and most consistently success-ful guitar-maker in the USA, and the company's flat-tops retain close links with the designs of its founder, C.F. Martin Sr. In the 1850s, he developed a system of X-bracing for the tops of his instruments, giving sweet-sounding results on the gut-strung guitars of the time. Later, when X-braces were combined with steel strings, they helped to create the "trademark" Martin sound – a rich, singing tone very different from the more cutting, less sustained quality of most archtop guitars. X-bracing is, of course, still in use today, as are several of the instrument "styles" from the turn of the century or earlier. Two of the guitars illustrated are Style 28s, with spruce top, rosewood back and sides, and Martin's famous ▶

Left: Martin D-28, 1945. The rosewood-bodied D-28 first appeared in 1931. This model is one of the last instruments of its period to feature Martin's distinctive "herringbone" decoration around its top.
The decoration was discontinued, due to shortage of supplies, in 1946, but has since been reintroduced thanks to customer demand.
(Courtesy Eric Schoenberg)

Below: Martin OM-28, 1931. An early "official" OM. This guitar is almost identical to the 000-28, but is fitted with a standard bridge, not a pyramid-shaped type. While OMs were successful for Martin, the constant

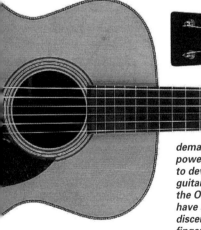

demand for larger-bodied, more powerful instruments led the company to develop the dreadnought-sized guitar, and eventually to discontinue the OM model in 1933. However, OMs have always been sought after by discerning players (particularly fingerstylists), and Martin has recently reintroduced them.
(Courtesy Eric Schoenberg)

"herringbone" trim around their edges; the first recorded example of this design appeared in 1870. The third instrument is an OM-45; the model dates from 1930, but the blueprint for Style 45 dates from 1904. Styles 28 and 45 both remain in Martin's current catalog with some minor changes.

Martin is a family business, and C.F. Martin's descendants have always retained control over it. For some 57 years between 1888 and about 1945, the founder's grandson, Frank Henry Martin (1866–1948), ran the company. He took over from his father, C.F. Martin Jr., and saw the firm through times of exciting opportunity, changing demand, economic depression, and world war.

Thanks to his guidance, Martin profited from the good times and survived the bad ones. It was active in other areas of instrument building, establishing successful mandolin and ukulele lines, and making short-lived attempts at archtop guitar and banjo manufacture, but continued to focus most of its energies on its core activity – the development of the flat-top. By the 1930s, the company had a flourishing range of small and larger-bodied guitars, and also undertook custom design work. This area was soon to grow in importance, as other star names followed Perry Bechtel in requesting specially modified and "personalized" instruments to suit their own needs.

Right and far right: Martin OM-45 Deluxe, 1933. This "Deluxe" version of the OM-45 features a pickguard with a pearl design, "snow-flake" inlays on either side of the bridge (matching the position marker at the first fret on the finger-board), and gold-plated tuners with pearl knobs.
(Courtesy Eric Schoenberg)

Below and bottom: Although it has almost all the features of the Martin OM design, including a neck with 14 frets clear of the body, it is labeled as a 000-28. One special feature of this guitar, *dropped from later "official" OMs, is its distinctive pyramid-shaped bridge; it also has "banjo-style" tuning pegs mounted vertically in the headstock.*
(Courtesy Eric Schoenberg)

Martin's "Special Projects"

Unlike some other guitar-makers, Martin has never made direct endorsement deals with its players. However, it does undertake "special projects" in conjunction with some performers, and one of the most famous of these is the collaboration with the "Singing Cowboy," Gene Autry (b. 1907). Autry had played Martin Style 42 guitars while he was still working as an Oklahoma telegraph operator in the mid-1920s. In 1933, after he found fame and fortune, he ordered one of the new Martin Dreadnoughts in Style 45,

asking for his name to be inlaid in pearl on the fingerboard. At the time, Dreadnoughts were only built in Style 18 (mahogany body) and Style 28 (rosewood body), but Martin created a D-45 especially for Autry, and subsequently produced the guitar (without the custom inlay) as a regular model.

Making the Autry D-45 was an exception to Martin's normal policy. As the company's current Chairman, Chris Martin IV, explains, "Our models are so well known, and it's not so much that we create a new model

Right: Martin 000-42EC, 1995. Eric Clapton played an active part in the development of this limited edition guitar – only 461 were made. The top is spruce, the body

East Indian rosewood; the instrument also features a beveled pickguard, and two pearl "snowflakes" on its bridge.
(Courtesy Martin Guitar Company)

Left: Martin D-45, specially made for Gene Autry, 1933. Unlike later models, this instrument – the first-ever Martin Dreadnought to be made in the rosewood-bodied Style 45 – has a 12-fret neck, and a slotted headstock.
(Courtesy Autry Museum of Western Heritage)

as adapt an existing one." This approach was followed in 1995, when Eric Clapton collaborated with Martin on a limited edition 000-42 with a number of other special features. Only 461 were made (the figure commemorates Clapton's 1974 "comeback" album, "461 Ocean Boulevard"), but the project was so successful that Martin went on to develop a "stock" Eric Clapton model, the 000-28EC, which is currently available in its "Vintage" series. Other leading musicians who have given their names to special Martin guitars include Paul Simon, country rock star Marty Stuart, Joan Baez and Sting.

A very small number of Martins are "one-of-a-kind"custom creations kept on permanent display at the firm's factory in Nazareth. These include the Stauffer-style reissue with inlaid illustrations, made to commemorate the 200th anniversary of the founder's birth (see page 77), as well as the 500,000th instrument to be produced by the company. This is an HD-28 Dreadnought, built in 1990, and signed by the entire workforce (see opposite).

Right: Martin HD-28, 1990. This guitar was the 500,000th instrument to be completed by Martin, and has been signed by the entire staff. It is now on display at the company's museum in its Nazareth,

Pennsylvania headquarters. The "H" prefix refers to the herringbone trim – a favorite Martin feature dropped after World War II, but reintroduced in 1976.
(Courtesy Martin Guitar Company)

Gibson's First Flat-tops

It took some time for Gibson to approach Martin's level of commitment to the flat-top. It did not enter the market until 1926, when it launched only two models: one of these, the L-1, "borrowed" its name from a previous Gibson archtop (seen earlier on pages 88-89), and was issued with a cheaper companion, the L-0. Gibson's third flat-top, which appeared in 1928, was endorsed by the American vaudeville and cabaret performer Nick Lucas. Six years earlier, Lucas (1897–1982) had recorded some of the first jazz-influenced guitar solos, including the classic "Teasin' The Frets," and in 1929 he went on to even greater success with his multi-million-selling hit, "Tiptoe Through the Tulips." The Lucas guitar was popular, despite its high price ($125); and over the next few years, Gibson's flat-top range started to make an impact as the company responded to Martin's OMs ▶

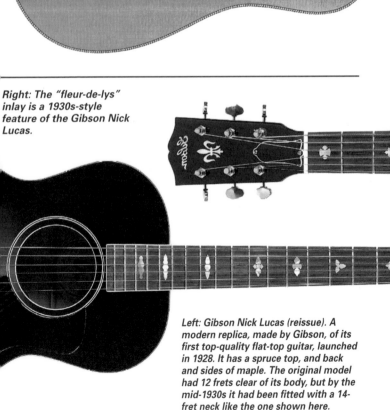

Right: The "fleur-de-lys" inlay is a 1930s-style feature of the Gibson Nick Lucas.

Left: Gibson Nick Lucas (reissue). A modern replica, made by Gibson, of its first top-quality flat-top guitar, launched in 1928. It has a spruce top, and back and sides of maple. The original model had 12 frets clear of its body, but by the mid-1930s it had been fitted with a 14-fret neck like the one shown here.
(Courtesy Mandolin Brothers, New York)

and Dreadnoughts with some innovations of their own.

In 1934, Gibson launched a large-bodied flat-top, the "Jumbo." The original model was superseded in 1936 by two new guitars, the "Advanced Jumbo" and the "Jumbo 35." All three instruments were 16in (40.6cm) wide, with 14 frets clear of their bodies. Like Martin's Dreadnoughts, they featured X-braced tops, but were slightly shallower-bodied and more "round-shouldered" than their rivals. They were competitively priced: the Advanced Jumbo sold for $80 and the J-35 for only $35. (Martin's D-28 Dreadnought cost $100 in 1935, while Gibson's own top-of-the-line archtop guitar was priced at $400.) The Gibson Jumbo range (the name would eventually be taken up by many other manufacturers of larger flat-tops) was later expanded, as the Advanced Jumbo gave way to the Super Jumbo (SJ), a model which is still available today.

Gibson also introduced a number of cheaper instruments during the early 1930s. The most basic model was the L-00, which appeared in the company's 1932 catalog and remained in production until the end of World War II. Early examples of this guitar, like the one shown here, had a black finish, and are thought to be the first Gibsons ever issued in a single color.

Right: Gibson L-00, 1934.
The L-00 was introduced
in about 1931 as the most basic
model in Gibson's "L" range of
small-bodied flat-tops. It sold for
$37.50, and later the price was
reduced to $30. Its back, sides,
and neck are mahogany, with a
spruce top and a rose-wood
fingerboard.
(Courtesy Real Guitars, San Francisco)

Left: Gibson Jumbo, 1934.
Gibson's first-ever Dreadnought-
sized guitar, in production for only
two years (1934–1936).
(Courtesy Mandolin Brothers,
New York)

The Gibson "Super Jumbo" Range

Gibson's "Super Jumbo" line evolved from a collaboration with "cowboy" singing star Ray Whitley, a major figure in pre-war radio and films. The instrument he helped to develop, which came to be known as the SJ-200, first appeared in the stores in 1938. It was named, like many Gibsons, after its price ($200), and its lavishly decorated body, originally 16⅞ inches (42.9cm) in width, was later enlarged to 17 inches (43.2cm). It had a more pronounced waist than Gibson's previous Jumbos, a distinctive, pearl-inlaid "mustache" bridge, and a large pickguard engraved with flowers and vines. The guitar stayed in limited production throughout the war years,

and in 1947 it was rechristened the J-200. It remains one of the most instantly recognizable and respected of all Gibson flat-tops. The many leading artists associated with it include Elvis Presley, Emmylou Harris, Rick Nelson, and bluesman Rev. Gary Davis – who used to refer to his J-200 as "Miss Gibson".

In 1942, another Gibson "SJ" instrument appeared. Confusingly, its initials stood not for "Super Jumbo" but "Southerner Jumbo" – a 16-inch (40.6cm) ,mahogany-bodied flat-top (although some wartime models had backs and sides made from maple) that remained in the catalog, with minor alterations, for over 30 years. Among its devotees were the Everly Brothers,

Above: Gibson SJ-200, 1950. Its top is spruce, its back and sides are maple. Among the SJ-200's many striking features are its elaborate bridge, with four rectangular pearl inlays above and below the string-pins, the "crest" fingerboard markers (similar to the "cloud" inlays first used in the 1930s by Gibson's competitors, Epiphone), and the beautiful hand-carved pickguard.
(Courtesy Hank's, London)

Left: Gibson B-25, early 1960s. The B-25 has a smaller body than the Country-Western (14¼in, 36.2cm wide) but is made from the same woods and has a similarly shaped pickguard with a point on its outer edge. The guitar remained in production until 1977.
(Courtesy Derrick Weskin)

Acoustic Guitars

who featured it on several of their hit records, including "Wake Up, Little Susie." In 1954, Gibson introduced a natural-color version; this was renamed the "Country-Western" two years later, and is shown opposite.

The third instrument illustrated here, a B-25, dates from the early 1960s, and was specially selected for its owner, Derrick Weskin, by the distinguished British jazz guitarist John McLaughlin, who was working behind the counter at a London guitar store at the time! The 1960s were a particularly successful decade for Gibson, thanks to the folk music boom and the impact of high-profile Gibson users such as the Beatles. Unfortunately, the next period in the company's history was a less happy one; the problems faced by Gibson in the 1970s and early 1980s, and the way these have now been solved, are discussed in later pages.

Below and right: Gibson Country-Western Jumbo, 1959. This natural-finish version of the Gibson Southerner Jumbo has a spruce top and mahogany back and sides. The guitar features a rosewood fingerboard displaying the company's distinctive "double parallelogram" inlays, which are also seen on many Gibson electrics.
(Courtesy Derrick Weskin)

Santa Cruz: Californian Craftsmanship

One of the most important developments in the recent history of flat-top guitar building has been the emergence of a number of small, dedicated companies committed to the highest standards of workmanship and design. They often draw inspiration from the work of earlier makers, but are also keen to introduce their own improvements and innovations, and able to tailor their instruments closely to the requirements of their customers.

Richard Hoover, of Santa Cruz, California, was one of the first American luthiers to set up such a firm. He began making guitars during the early 1970s, working alone in his garage, and explains that "in building on my own, I saw an impossible learning-curve ahead of me – years and years of experimenting to come up with the perfect guitar." Richard decided to take on two partners, and together they formed the Santa Cruz Guitar Company. "My intent was to

Below and right: Santa Cruz Tony Rice Model. This Dread-nought design has a 15½in (39.4cm) body, a top of sitka spruce, and Indian rosewood back, sides, and neck. The edges and soundhole are trimmed with the traditional "herringbone" inlays first made famous by Martin. The mother-of-pearl "Santa Cruz" logo can be seen at the 12th fret of the fingerboard. (Courtesy Santa Cruz Guitar Co.)

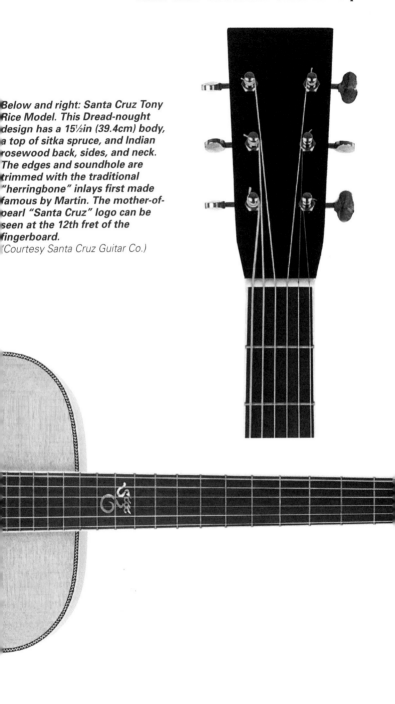

have each of us specialize in a certain aspect of guitar building, so that we could accelerate the learning process and make more guitars, while keeping to the principle of the individual luthier having control over each aspect of building."

This philosophy has created a thriving business. Richard Hoover now runs the Santa Cruz Guitar Company himself, employing 11 guitar-makers and six other staff. There is no assembly line; the builders work closely together on what Richard describes as "a logical series of processes that contribute to the whole; they can understand what they've done and how it affects the

guitar." Santa Cruz produces 15 basic models, and its instruments have been associated with leading players such as Eric Clapton and bluegrass guitarist Doc Watson.

The company's close relation-ship with a second major name in bluegrass, Tony Rice, led to the creation of the Santa Cruz Tony Rice Model (previous page). This is based on the classic Martin Dreadnought, but offers a more balanced response than the original 1930s D-28, which had a powerful bass but less treble and mid-range presence. Also shown here are two versions of another Santa Cruz guitar derived from a pre-War Martin design: their OM (Orchestra Model).

Right and left, inset: The headstock of the all-black Santa Cruz OM, showing the company's distinctive logo.

Above: A special version of the Santa Cruz Orchestra Model with an all-black finish, and tortoiseshell binding on its back and fingerboard.
(Courtesy Santa Cruz Guitar Co.)

Left: Santa Cruz OM. Santa Cruz's version of the "Orchestra Model," based on the design introduced by Martin in 1929. At 15⅕in (38.6cm), it is slightly wider than the Martin original. It has a spruce top and a rosewood body, and is particularly popular with players seeking to produce a powerful sound from a relatively small-bodied instrument
(Courtesy Santa Cruz Guitar Co.)

Santa Cruz: Anatomy of a Flat-top

Santa Cruz's first reworkings of vintage Martin styles were one-off custom orders for individual clients. But their guitars attracted so much interest that Richard Hoover eventually added them to the company's regular catalog. "Not only were these guitars in demand, but they were also really nice designs. At the time, Martin wasn't making them, so there was a lot of pent-up demand." Richard acknowledges the importance of Martin's influence on his own development as a player and luthier, and is proud that the appearance of Santa Cruz 000s and

OMs has encouraged Martin to restart production of these classic models themselves.

Like nearly all serious producers of flat-top guitars, Santa Cruz uses X bracing on its instruments. The tops themselves are made from sitka or German spruce, which is carefully selected and evaluated; more flexible wood tends to accentuate the guitar's bass response, while greater rigidity will boost the mid-range and treble. The positioning of the braces helps to "tailor" the sound of the instrument by stiffening some areas of the top, making them more responsive to

Right: This picture of the inside of the body of a Santa Cruz 000 under construction shows the central X-brace and the reinforcing struts.

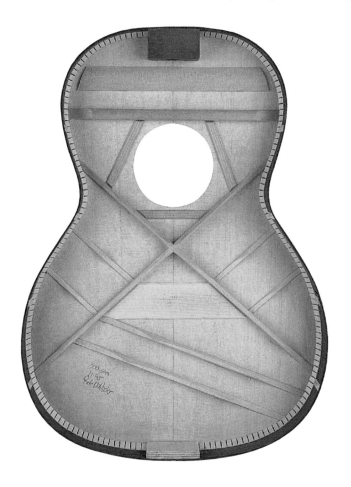

Left: Santa Cruz 000 (12-fret model). Another outstanding reworking of a classic Martin design, with a spruce top, and Indian rosewood back, sides, and neck. The top is fitted with a **central X-brace, as well as additional strutting to provide further stiffening and strength. The edges are lined with glued-in strips of basswood.**
(Courtesy Santa Cruz Guitar Co.)

Acoustic Guitars

higher frequencies, and the completed structure is sometimes lined with basswood to isolate it from the guitar's sides and back. Other factors influencing the overall tonal quality of the guitar include the size of the soundhole (a larger hole raises the fundamental frequency of the body, giving more mid-range and treble) and the selection of woods used for other parts of the guitar.

Santa Cruz instruments are a blend of tradition and innovation, and the company's pioneering approach to the business of guitar-making has since been followed by several other firms. Looking back over more than two decades as a luthier, Richard Hoover observes that "for the most part, there used to be nothing between the single builder and the factory. That's the niche we want to fill – to be a small company that is building superior instruments and really responsive to the players' needs."

Right: The headstock of the Santa Cruz Model F illustrated below bears the distinctive company logo.

Far right: Santa Cruz Model F twelve-string. This instrument is built from European woods: German spruce for the top, and maple for the back, neck, and sides.
(Courtesy Santa Cruz Guitar Co.)

Left: Santa Cruz Model F cutaway. Both the six- and twelve-string Model Fs have headstocks based on Epiphone's classic "asymmetrical" design (see pages 96-99 for the Epiphone originals). The six-string, made from spruce and rosewood, has a custom binding of Hawaiian koa wood. (Courtesy Santa Cruz Guitar Co.)

Bob Taylor – High Technology and Fine Design

In 1974, a young Californian luthier, Bob Taylor, started a guitar-making business with a colleague, Kurt Listug, in a small shop in Lemon Grove, near San Diego. The company they created, Taylor Guitars, has developed a unique, innovative approach to instrument building, combining traditional craftsmanship with high technology. Today, it is a major force in the industry, with almost 70,000sq ft (6,500m²) of factory space in El Cajon, California, a daily output of 100 guitars, and an enviable reputation among leading players throughout the world.

Among the many major performers associated with Taylor's instruments are Nanci Griffith, Kenny Loggins, Jewel, Kathy Mattea, Iris DeMent, Bonnie Raitt, Neil Young, and the late John Denver. Bill Clinton also has a Taylor; in 1997, the company presented him with a commemorative guitar (bearing his Inaugural Seal on the headstock) to mark his re-election to the US Presidency.

Bob Taylor's own innovative approach to lutherie lies at the heart of

Below: Taylor PS-14 "Presentation Series" Grand Auditorium model. Taylor's Grand Auditorium model is as deep and wide as their Dreadnought-size guitar, but has *a more pronounced waist and a slightly boosted treble response. The top is made from Engelmann spruce and the body from Brazilian rosewood.* (Courtesy Taylor Guitars)

Above: Taylor XX-MC 20th Anniversary Guitar. Bob Taylor celebrated his company's first 20 years in 1994 with a limited edition of 500 instruments. This guitar is one of the 250 made with mahogany bodies and cedar tops.

Its custom-tooled neck and soundhole inlays are mother-of-pearl.
(Courtesy Taylor Guitars)

Left: The "Byzantine"-style fingerboard inlays, made from abalone, are complemented by matching patterns on the headstock (which is overlaid with a rosewood veneer) and on the bridge.

Acoustic Guitars

the company's success. His skills have enabled him to create viable designs from unlikely materials such as "junk" timber from an abandoned pallet (see illustration), although for production models, he is committed to working with fine quality solid tonewoods. To manufacture his guitars, Bob makes use of Computer Numeric Control (CNC) systems, which drive machinery capable of cutting, carving, and planing at speeds and tolerances no human craftsman could match. CNC's precision removes the inevitable inconsistencies that occur when working by hand, allowing Bob and his staff to "get closer to actually producing what it is we had in mind." It also enables them to make even intricately carved or decorated parts quickly and in considerable numbers. However, as Bob emphasizes, this impressive technology is simply a means to an end: "We're guitar builders first. Choice of tools [comes] second, and we're very comfortable with high technology tools to make a low technology product. [CNC] makes us more consistent and more efficient, so that we can deliver more guitars to people at reasonable prices that really give them what they're hoping to have when they play that guitar."

Left (front and back): Taylor "Pallet Guitar". Its body was made out of a discarded oak pallet salvaged from a dumpster outside the Taylor factory. Bob Taylor and his team built a guitar from this waste material to demonstrate that top-grade tonewoods are not always essential for high-quality instruments. The result looks and sounds superb. Appropriately, the fingerboard shows a forklift truck (above), inlaid in yellow Formica, aluminum, and mother-of-pearl. On the back of the guitar, several nail-holes are still visible; these have been filled in with aluminum. (Courtesy Taylor Guitars)

Bob Taylor – The "Cujo" and Leo Kottke Models

Taylor's limited edition "Cujo" guitar is the product of two years' painstaking preparation and design. The instrument takes its name from Stephen King's 1981 novel, in which Cujo, a St. Bernard dog, is bitten by a rabid bat and becomes a crazed predator. The story was filmed in 1983 on a Californian ranch, and wood from a black walnut tree that grew there and was seen in the movie has been used to make 250 special guitars, each signed by Stephen King himself. The elaborate fingerboard decorations on these instruments, showing images related to the story, were all inlaid using computer numeric control. The fine detail achieved by the automated system would be difficult enough for a skilled engraver to match on a single custom guitar, let alone a production run of 250.

The CNC process turns out a series of perfect realizations of an original design; Bob Taylor points out that "every one's a master – none of them is a copy." In the development of that design, however, the emphasis is on traditional methods: experience, experimentation, and consultation with players. While working with bluegrass musician Dan Crary on the Taylor guitar that carries

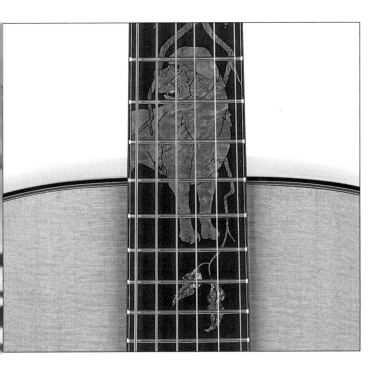

Below and above: Taylor "Cujo" guitar. One of a limited edition of 250 instruments made from the wood of the walnut tree featured in the film of Stephen King's novel. The fingerboard depicts a bat silhouetted against a full moon; the branches of the walnut tree; the barn from where Cujo the dog launches his crazed attacks; and Cujo himself. The inlays were created using mahogany, maple, walnut, green heart abalone, black oyster shell, and Formica.
(Courtesy Taylor Guitars)

Acoustic Guitars

his name, Bob and his team assembled a pair of rough prototypes, replacing tops, altering bracing patterns, and making constant comparisons and adjustments in order to achieve the sound Crary wanted. The creation of Leo Kottke's Signature Model twelve-string involved about four years of discussion with the artist. Such processes remain central to Taylor's approach to guitar building, and can never be replaced by technology.

The company's future plans focus on further refinements and improvements to the design and production of their instruments. Bob Taylor explains that "I still enjoy the traditional look and feel of what a guitar is. But what we'll be doing over the next five or ten years is redesigning the way a guitar goes together to really exploit the precision that we have at our disposal. I've been trying to do this for 20 years, and it's only now that I have the equipment to do it with."

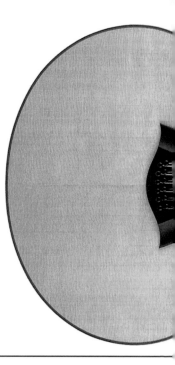

Eric Schoenberg – Growing Towards The Past

Eric Schoenberg brings a player's perspective to the art of guitar design. Since the 1960s, he has been searching for an instrument that would measure up to his own musical and technical needs, and the Schoenberg Soloist and its successors are the results of this quest.

As a distinguished performer of ragtime transcriptions and other elaborate fingerstyle arrangements, Eric Schoenberg's first requirement was for a guitar that would respond sympathetically to the subtleties of his technique. His initial choice, a Martin 000-45 with a 12-fret neck, could not provide the unrestricted access to the higher frets that he needed. He changed to a 14-fret 000-45, but found its scale length unsuitable. His next instrument ▶

Left: Taylor Leo Kottke Signature Model twelve-string cutaway. This guitar has a sitka spruce top, mahogany back, sides, and neck, and an ebony fingerboard. It is fitted with heavy-gauge strings, and is designed to be tuned a 3rd lower than normal.
(Courtesy Taylor Guitars)

Above: Schoenberg 000-28K. Modeled on Martin's 1923 000-28 guitar, and made from koa wood.
(Courtesy Eric Schoenberg)

Acoustic Guitars

solved the problem: "I ended up playing a Martin OM, and never found anything like it." The OM design, introduced in 1930 in response to a request from banjoist Perry Bechtel (see pages 126-127) offers a slightly modified 000-style shape and a long-scale neck with 14 frets clear of the body. Eric continued to use it for several years.

Eventually, though, he began to consider the possibility of creating a new guitar, combining the features of the original OM with a cutaway to make the top frets even easier to reach. The Schoenberg Soloist, designed with luthier Dana Bourgeois, was the embodiment of these ideas, and it first appeared in 1986. For the next seven years, Soloists were built at the Martin factory in Nazareth, Pennsylvania, with Eric and Dana

supplying the wood, the tops and bracing, the bridges, and the binding for the bodies.

Eric Schoenberg's subsequent design projects have been undertaken in partnership with Massachusetts guitar-maker Julius Borges. Their first production model was a replica of a 1923-style Martin 000-28, made in Hawaiian koa wood. More recently, they have realized what Eric describes as "one of my goals for years:" the creation of the Schoenberg Standard, a 12-fret 000 with a cutaway, offering an ideal combination of neck dimensions and fret access. Other instruments from Schoenberg Guitars include 12- and 14-fret 00 cutaways – further examples of Eric's policy of "backwards-looking innovation...learning from the past and growing towards it."

Right: Schoenberg Standard (prototype), 1996. An instrument based on Martin's 12-fret 000-design, but featuring a cutaway to improve access to the upper frets.

This is one of the recent batch of Schoenberg instruments made in Massachusetts in collaboration with luthier Julius Borges.
(Courtesy Eric Schoenberg)

Left: Schoenberg Soloist. Designed by Eric Schoenberg and Dana Bourgeois, and built at the Martin factory in Nazareth, Pennsylvania, to their specifications. Schoenbergs were made at Martin between 1986–1993.
(Courtesy Eric Schoenberg)

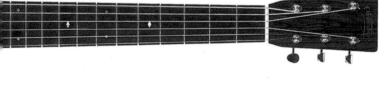

Steve Klein – A Fresh Approach to the Flat-top

Steve Klein, of Sonoma, California, is widely regarded as one of the most innovative luthiers on the current American scene. His instruments are strikingly radical in both appearance and construction; he has a highly individual approach to bracing, bridge design, and choice of materials, using traditional woods alongside "space-age" substances such as carbon fiber to create guitars with a distinctive sound and feel.

Klein guitars are built by Steve and his fellow-luthier Steve Kauffman, who constructs the instrument bodies. Klein himself produces fretwork and inlays, makes the bridges, and undertakes the final assembly. Unusually, no X-bracing is used: instead, each top features a "flying brace" (inspired by the flying buttresses used in European cathedral architecture) combined with a series of fan-braces that overlap the edge of the "impedance-matching" bridge. The bridge itself, which is in two pieces, is significantly broader on its bass side. Steve Klein explains the reason for this: "What the bass and treble strings are trying to drive the top to do are quite different. You've got a much larger wave-pattern happening in the bass frequencies – so the wider bass side causes a much slower and broader pumping motion to the top." The separation and balance provided by the bridge contribute to the tonal clarity of the instrument, and Steve describes it as "the heart of the Klein acoustic."

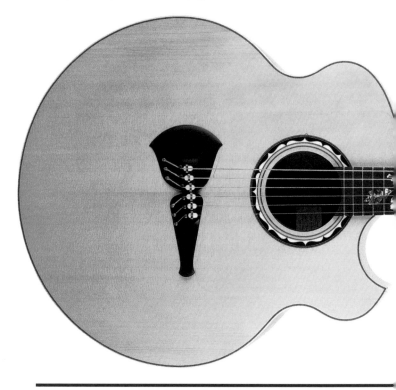

Above, below, and right: Steve Klein L-45.7C acoustic. A cutaway version of Steve Klein's larger acoustic model, with custom "mushroom" inlays on the fingerboard and headstock. Steve Klein's guitars are built for stability and longevity; their neck blocks are reinforced with carbon fiber, minimizing any fluctuation or movement that might otherwise be caused by changes in humidity or climatic shifts.
(Courtesy Klein Acoustic Guitars)

Acoustic Guitars

Steve Klein makes four basic models of flat-top guitar, the L-45.7, M-43, S-39.6 and N-35.6 (the numbers refer to the width, in centimeters, of the body's lower bout), and also provides custom inlay work for many of his clients' instruments. The guitar he built for Canadian singer-songwriter Joni Mitchell featured mother-of-pearl I Ching symbols and other person- alized images, while the cutaway model shown on the previous pages includes elaborate "mushroom" inlays. His L-45.7s are high-end instruments, "not the kind of guitars that people take out on the road," as Steve comments; but the many leading players who use them regularly for studio and high-profile concert and broadcast work include Steve Miller and Andy Summers, as well as Joni Mitchell. In contrast, Klein's new M-43 guitars are designed with the touring musician in mind, and are priced in the $5,000-$6,000 range, with pickups installed.

Right: Bridges for the Klein L-45.7C (top) and L-45.7 (bottom). The "impedance-matching" design is derived from the work of Dr. Michael Kasha, a physical chemist whose theories have also had an influence on some classical guitar-makers.

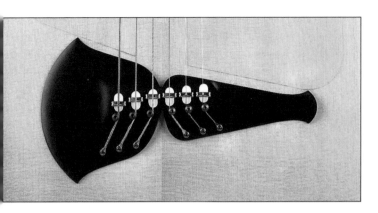

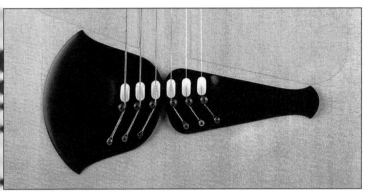

Left: Steve Klein L-45.7 acoustic. The top is spruce, the back and sides walnut. The neck – which, unusually for an acoustic guitar, is removable – is made from rosewood. The fingerboard and the "impedance-matching" bridge are ebony; all six string saddles are adjustable, and the strings' ball-ends are not pushed down into the body, but held on the surface of the bridge itself.
(Courtesy Klein Acoustic Guitars)

Modern American Flat-tops

The great archtop luthier Jimmy D'Aquisto (1935–1995) started making flat-tops as the result of a mistake by one of his suppliers. After receiving a consignment of German flat-top woods that had been delivered to his workshop in error, he began developing a number of unusual design ideas for the instrument, and went on to build flat-top guitars for Paul Simon, Janis Ian, and other well-known names. The model shown here, the "Forté," dates from 1981, and is made from spruce and maple. It has an exceptionally deep body and a bridge that shortens the length of the 5th and 6th strings. The resultant slight increase in tension improves the strings' "feel" and response.

John Buscarino, whose archtop guitars are featured on pages 122-123, offers a number of his models in a unique, "hybrid" form – with an archtop-style carved back and cutaway, but a round-hole, flat-top plate instead of an arched one with f-holes. The model illustrated is a 17-inch "Virtuoso;" Buscarino also makes the instrument in a 16in (40.6cm) body width, and in a range of different finishes.

Jean Larrivée, in contrast to D'Aquisto and Buscarino, is a specialist in more traditional flat-top design. A Canadian whose instruments have a worldwide reputation, he has recently celebrated 30 years as

Right: John Buscarino "Virtuoso" flat-top. The top is spruce; the back is carved from flamed maple. (Courtesy John Buscarino)

Above: D'Aquisto "Forté," 1981. The top is made from Tyrolean spruce, and the back and sides from German maple. The bindings and inlays are plastic, and the headstock features D'Aquisto's characteristic cut-out and finial.
(Courtesy John Monteleone)

a luthier. He started out as a maker of nylon-strung classical guitars, but began to build flat-tops in the early 1970s, in response to the folk music boom then sweeping Canada. Since then, his company has produced over 20,000 instruments; the Larrivée factory in Vancouver, British Columbia, uses some of the same computer technologies as Taylor Guitars, and Bob Taylor describes Jean as "one of my best guitar-building buddies." The beautiful headstock inlays found on many Larrivées are created by Jean's wife, Wendy. The model shown here features a mother of pearl, abalone and silver "Mucha Lady;" other instruments are decorated with dragons, jesters, angels, and djinns.

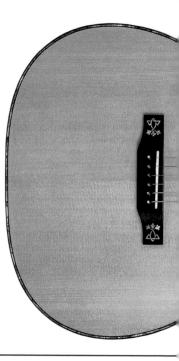

Right: Larrivée OM-10. It has a spruce top, a mahogany neck, and an ebony fingerboard.

American and Canadian Flat-tops

Bill Collings, whose D3 flat-top is illustrated, makes his guitars in Austin, Texas. He began his career in another Texan city, Houston, working as a instrument repairman while establishing himself as a luthier in the mid-1970s. During this period, he made contact with a number of leading musicians on the local scene, including singer-songwriter Lyle Lovett, and his reputation spread rapidly. Collings moved to Austin in 1980, and in 1988 he received a major commission from fretted-instrument dealer and expert George Gruhn – an order for 24 guitars to be sold in Gruhn's Nashville music store. Collings guitars are now available worldwide; they are sought after by a wide range of players, and the larger-bodied models are especially popular with bluegrass performers. The D3 is ▶

Right: Collings D3, c.1991. A Dreadnought design with a spruce top, rosewood back and sides, and abalone soundhole inlay. The bridge pins and nut are made from fossilized ivory.
(Courtesy Dale Rabiner)

**Bottom: The "Mucha Lady" on the
headstock is made from mother-
of-pearl, abalone, and ivoroid.**
*(Courtesy Mandolin Brothers,
New York)*

Acoustic Guitars

Collings' top-of-the-line Dreadnought: this instrument, made in 1991, has sides and back of Brazilian rosewood (the traditional material of choice for flat-tops and classical guitars, now in very short supply due to deforestation).

William "Grit" Laskin is a Canadian luthier who is also a successful performer and songwriter; his songs have been recorded by Pete Seeger, the Tannahill Weavers, and other leading folk artists. Laskin's superb flat-tops often feature elaborate inlays, like the ones on this "Grand Auditorium" custom cutaway guitar, made in 1991. The stylized scene on the headstock and fingerboard, showing a trapeze with two acrobats and a crescent moon includes a subtle visual joke: the seam of the female acrobat's leotard is positioned close to the tuning machine for the instrument's G string!

The third guitar shown is a Froggy Bottom model H, made in Newfane, Vermont by Michael Millard and his colleague Andrew Mueller. Millard has been building guitars for more than 27 years; the Froggy Bottom range includes everything from small-bodied instruments to Jumbos, Dreadnoughts, and twelve-strings. Among the leading names who play these guitars are singer-songwriter Dar Williams, and Will Ackerman, the co-founder of Windham Hill Records.

Right: Froggy Bottom Model H. A "Grand Concert"-size guitar similar in dimensions to a Martin-style OM, and especially suited to ragtime and other fingerstyle playing. Froggy Bottom also make larger Dreadnought and Jumbo designs.
(Courtesy McCabe's, Santa Monica)

Above: Laskin "Grand Auditorium" custom cutaway (1991). The term Grand Auditorium is used to describe medium-sized guitars, larger than **OMs (Orchestra Models) but slightly smaller than Dreadnoughts or Jumbos.** *(Courtesy Mandolin Brothers, New York)*

Three American Luthiers

James Goodall, whose twelve-string Rosewood Standard is shown below, is a self-taught luthier who grew up in California. A former seascape artist, he built his first guitar in 1972, bartering one of his paintings to acquire the wood he needed. (Coincidentally, his source for supplies was the shop in Lemon Grove, California later acquired by Bob Taylor and Kurt Listug of Taylor Guitars.) That instrument took him more than three months to complete, using tools borrowed from his father. Over the next few years, Goodall painstakingly acquired further knowledge and expertise, and in 1978, he became a full-time guitar-maker. Since 1992, he has been based in Kailua-Koni, Hawaii, where he currently produces about five instruments per week with the help of a small team of skilled employees.

James Goodall's mother was an art teacher in Southern California; one of her pupils, a teenager called Larry Breedlove, subsequently became production manager at Taylor Guitars. Larry Breedlove and another Taylor employee, Steve Henderson, soon became close friends; in 1990, they decided to set up their own guitar-

Below and right: James Goodall Rosewood Standard twelve-string. Goodall's Standard model is similar to a Dreadnought in size; he also offers a smaller Grand Concert instrument and a large-body Jumbo. The top on this twelve-string is spruce, the body rosewood, and the fingerboard ebony.
(Courtesy McCabe's, Santa Monica)

Acoustic Guitars

building business, and the Breedlove Guitar Company was born. The company's headquarters is just outside Bend, in the mountains of central Oregon, and since 1994 (when Breedlove left the firm), Steve Henderson has been in charge of instrument production there. Breedlove guitars are immediately recognizable, with their distinctively shaped headstocks and bridges, tight waists, and smaller-than-average soundholes. The company makes approximately 12 instruments per week, and in 1995 its CM "Asymmetrical Concert" model won the American Guitar Players Association's coveted

"Guitar of the Year" award.

Dana Bourgeois, who collaborated with Eric Schoenberg on the "Soloist" guitar (see pages 158-159 now runs his own guitar-making company, based in Lewiston, Maine He has over 20 years' experience as builder and restorer, and is also highly respected teacher and write on guitar design and construction Players of his instruments includ country and bluegrass star Rick Skaggs and leading British fo guitarist Martin Simpson. The Bou geois model shown here is a Jumb OM – a modern adaptation of Martin classic OM design.

Right: Breedlove C1. One of Breedlove's "Concert Series" guitars, with a sitka spruce top, rosewood back and sides, and 15⅜in (39cm) body width. The instrument is also made in walnut koa, and a variety of other woods (Courtesy Mandolin Brothers, New York)

Left: Bourgeois JOM. A Jumbo Orchestra Model combining the features of the Martin OM with a larger Jumbo body size.
(Courtesy Mandolin Brothers, New York)

The Gypsy Guitar

While leading American luthiers were developing their archtop and flat-top guitars during the pre-World War II years, a visionary European musician and designer was following a slightly different path. Mario Maccaferri (1900–1993) was born in Bologna, Italy, and made his early reputation as a virtuoso classical guitarist. He was also a skilled luthier, and in 1930 he accepted an invitation to collaborate with the Paris-based Selmer company on a range of new guitar models bearing his name.

Selmer insisted that one of these should be a steel-strung instrument aimed at jazz players, and Maccaferri, who was unfamiliar with jazz, decided to visit a night club to hear some. His impressions of the music were not very favorable, but he quickly concluded that the most important factor in jazz guitar design was the need for a powerful, cutting tone. He achieved this on the Selmer Maccaferri by using a slightly bent top to boost the sound (an idea borrowed from mandolin construction). The

The Gypsy Guitar

*Below: Selmer-Maccaferri, early
1930s. This is a superb example of an
original Selmer-Maccaferri, still used
regularly for concerts by its owner,
the leading gypsy jazz player Fapy
Lapertin. The slotted headstock and
horizontally mounted tuning
machines are characteristic features
of this design, as are the "mustache"
bridge and brass tailpiece. The
earliest Selmer-Maccaferris had a D-
shaped soundhole; the oval shape
was introduced a little later.*
(Courtesy Fapy Lapertin)

instrument also featured a distinctive D-shaped soundhole (changed on later models to an oval), and, on some early Maccaferris, a wooden resonator fitted inside the body.

The guitar, when it appeared, was highly successful throughout Europe, and became closely identified with the brilliant gypsy musician Django Reinhardt (1910–1953), whose recordings and performances as a soloist and with the Quintet of the Hot Club of France played a key influence in the development of the jazz guitar. Despite the success of his instrument, however, Mario Maccaferri's relationship with Selmer proved to be short-lived; he severed his relationship with the company in 193? after a disagreement, and eventuall left France to settle in the USA.

Selmer continued to manufacture Maccaferri's designs until the early 1950s; and since then several othe guitar-makers have created replicas and re-interpretations of his instruments. Among them are the leading French luthiers Maurice Dupont and Favino, and a British craftsman, D.J. Hodson of Lough borough, Leicestershire, who was recently commissioned to build a ⅞th size instrument for Django Rein hardt's grandson, David.

Right: D. J. Hodson Model 503 SRD. A replica of a D-hole Selmer-Maccaferri, made by a specialist UK luthier. The top of the instrument is spruce, its sides and back rosewood (the same woods were used on the original models). Hodson's logo, seen on the headstock, is modeled on Selmer's own trademark.
(Courtesy Charles Alexander)

Left: Dupont Selmer-Maccaferri replica, c.1990. Maurice Dupont is one of the most distinguished contemporary European makers of Maccaferri-style instruments. Apart from the lighter color of the top, *and the increased distance between the edge of the fingerboard and the soundhole, there is little to distinguish this guitar from the original on which it is modeled.* (Courtesy Dave Kelbie)

Maccaferri and Monteleone

After emigrating to America in 1939, Mario Maccaferri became involved in a wide range of design projects, working on the production of violins, saxophone reeds, guitars, and ukuleles, all made from plastic. He also remained active in more traditional methods of instrument building, and developed a close relationship with one of today's leading American luthiers, John Monteleone, who recalls him as "a beautiful, incredible man. When I went up to his place, we'd sit down with his wife, Maria, have lunch together and tell stories, and then Mario would pick up the guitar after coffee and play for half an hour –

beautiful classical arrangements. I was very fortunate to have had the opportunity to be a friend of his, and learn how to make a Maccaferri from Maccaferri himself."

During one visit to the Maccaferris, John Monteleone discovered a badly damaged Selmer-Maccaferri that had been given by Django Reinhardt's widow to the great American guitarist Les Paul. John successfully restored it, and went on to work with Mario on a number of instruments, including the "Django" model shown here. This experience led to the creation of his "Hot Club" model, which combines the Maccaferri-Selmer influence with

Left and top: Monteleone Hot Club, 1993. John Monteleone's modern reworking of the Selmer-Maccaferri . Unlike the original models, this guitar has a flat top, and a fixed bridge is fitted instead of the "mustache"-style one. Maccaferri's oval soundhole *has been replaced with an elliptical design that increases projection; it is edged with rosewood, which is also used for the back and sides. The top of the instrument is made from German spruce.*
(Courtesy John Monteleone)

Acoustic Guitars

John's own approach to body design. Unlike the original "bent-top" Selmers, the "Hot Club" has a flat top, and the oval soundhole is enlarged and reshaped to boost the bass and projection. On later versions of the guitar, the hole has been repositioned at a diagonal, and is higher on the left-hand bass side – a modification that further improves the instrument's treble and bass response.

Another departure from tradition on this and many other Monteleone guitars is the use of butcher bone instead of ivory for the nut and saddle. As John explains, he entrusts this material to an assistant: his dog, Sasha. "My dog is actually a participant – she is a luthier apprentice, and she has the benefit of preparation of the bone!"

Maccaferri and Monteleone

Below and right: Monteleone/ Maccaferri Django, 1987. A collaboration between the leading American luthier John Monteleone – whose signature (inlaid in mother-of-pearl) can be seen at the twelfth fret on the fingerboard – and the then octogenarian Mario Maccaferri, who remained active as a designer until his death at the age of 93.
(Courtesy Mandolin Brothers, New York)

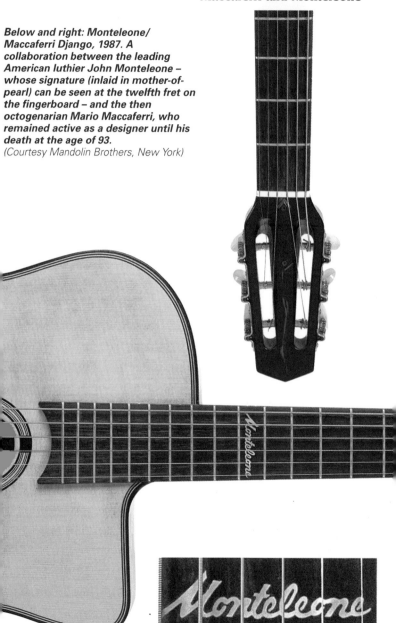

The Resonator Guitar

The need to boost the acoustic guitar's relatively quiet sound has been addressed in many different ways by modern luthiers; but perhaps the most radical solution was devised by John Dopyera (1893–1988), who filed a patent in 1927 for a guitar fitted with three aluminum resonators, and went on to manufacture his invention through the National String Instrument Corporation.

John and his four brothers, Rudy, Louis, Emil (Ed) and Robert, were émigrés from Austro-Hungary who had settled in California with their parents. By the mid-1920s John and Rudy were running a thriving banjo manufacturing business in Los Angeles, and John had already developed a number of ingenious devices for improving the sound and playability of various stringed instruments. At around this time, a vaudeville singer and guitarist, George Beauchamp, approached the Dopyeras. Like many other players of the period, he was having difficulty being heard on stage, and he asked John to build him a Hawaiian guitar with a phonograph-style horn to increase its volume. The outcome of this idea, which had been inspired by the violin-with-horn designs previously developed by several other companies, was unsuccessful, and John Dopyera began to experiment

Below: National Style 4 tri-cone, 1928. National's "top-of-the-line" Style 4 guitar was introduced in 1928 and remained in production until 1940. Its elaborate "chrysanthemum" engraving (inset panel, top right) was designed by George Beauchamp, the General Manager of the company. This is an early example of the model, which originally cost $195.
(Courtesy Mark Makin)

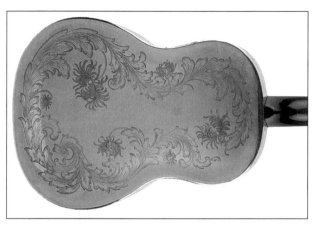

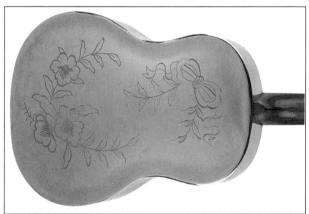

with other methods of making Beauchamp's guitar louder.

He eventually came up with the resonator concept set out in his patent application. His prototype "tri-cone" guitar had a body not of wood, but "German silver" (an alloy of nickel, copper, and zinc). It was fitted with an aluminum, T-shaped bridge, topped with wood where the strings made contact with it, and mounted over a set of three aluminum diaphragms. The bridge carried vibrations from the strings to the three diaphragms, and the extra resonance they provided gave the instrument a powerful and distinctive tone.

Soon after John Dopyera filed his patent for the tri-cone, the new guitars went into production – first in John and Rudy's Los Angeles shop, and subsequently, on a larger scale, under the auspices of a company set up in 1928 by George Beauchamp and the Dopyeras: the National String Instrument Corporation. National had a revolutionary new product and an eager market for it – but before very long the new firm would be torn apart by bitter disagreements between its founders.

Below and right: National Style 2 tri-cone, c.1929–1930. The Style 2 was one of National's most popular models; it was the cheapest of their resonator guitars to have a pattern engraved on it – a "wild rose" design (previous page, inset panel, bottom) created by Rudy Dopyera. This round-necked instrument is comparatively rare; most early National guitars were fitted with square necks for Hawaiian-style playing.
(Courtesy Mark Makin)

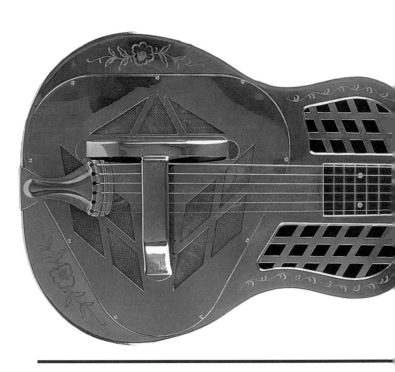

National – The Early Years

In 1928, National introduced another innovative guitar design, using just one aluminum resonator cone. This single diaphragm system was based on John Dopyera's ideas, but, in a move that infuriated Dopyera, George Beauchamp claimed the credit for it and eventually filed a patent for it under his own name. The ensuing row led to Dopyera's resignation from National in early 1929; later that year he formed the Dobro (Dopyera Brothers) Manufacturing Company, where he developed and marketed a rival single-cone resonator guitar.

This move led to deepening hostility with National. Beauchamp warned Dopyera's customers that the new Dobro guitar infringed National's patents, and Dobro reacted by bringing a $2,000,000 lawsuit against National. After a long and complex dispute, exacerbated by internal wrangles among National's directors, the case was settled out of court in 1933. The outcome was favorable to the Dopyeras; Beauchamp was ousted from the National board, and

Below and right: National Triolian wood-body single-resonator guitar, 1928. Not all Nationals were metal-bodied – the company made a variety of wooden instruments in the 1930s. This model, though, is a prototype; about 1,000-1,200 of them were produced between 1927–1928, mostly without serial numbers. Its design became the basis for the metal-bodied Triolian introduced in 1929. The plywood body and maple neck were constructed to be as dense and vibration-proof as possible. The colorful picture on the back is screen-printed, and was probably applied via a water-slide transfer. (Courtesy Mark Makin)

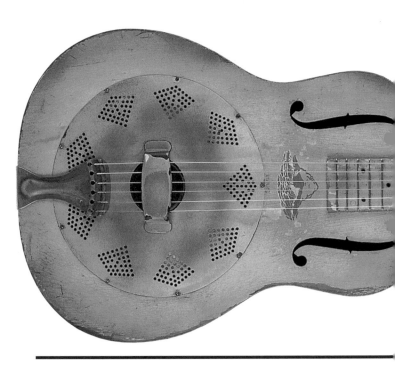

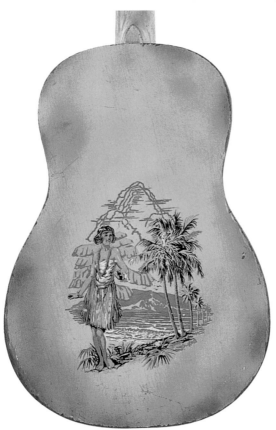

the two rival companies formally merged in 1935. The following year, the National-Dobro Corporation moved to Chicago. It continued building its resonator instruments (including ukuleles and mandolins as well as guitars) until 1941, when the company was forced to cease production in the wake of the United States' entry into World War II.

In its relatively brief period of operation, the pre-War National Corporation made a bewilderingly large number of different models. The guitar range featured four-string

tenor instruments, as well as Hawaiian and standard "Spanish" guitars, produced in a variety of decorative "styles." Some of these styles had names (e.g. "Duolian," "Triolian"), while others were simply known by numbers or letters (Style 1, Style 2, Style O, Style N, etc.) Many of these classifications were also used for National mandolins and ukuleles. The photographs here and on the previous pages show a cross-section of the designs produced by the company in the period between 1928 and the early 1940s.

Below: National Style N single-resonator guitar, 1931. This brass-bodied model has a mahogany neck, ebony fingerboard, and pearloid-inlaid headstock (bottom right), and is a more expensive version of the Style O, which featured a maple neck and fingerboard, and had no pearl finish. The instrument shown here has a 12-fret neck, but later Style Ns were built with a shortened body and 14-fret access.
(Courtesy Mark Makin)

Right and far right: National Style 3 tri-cone, 1929–1930. A square-neck model for Hawaiian-style playing. Style 3 instruments featured a "lily-of-the-valley" engraving designed by John Dopyera himself. They were made between 1928 and 1941.
(Courtesy Mark Makin)

National Reso-Phonic Today

National never resumed production of metal-body resonator guitars after the War, but the Dopyera brothers revived the Dobro line in the 1950s, and eventually set up the O.M.I. (Original Musical Instrument) Company to manufacture Dobros in wood and metal. Among its employees in the early 1970s was Don Young, a luthier who had been fascinated by resonator guitars since childhood. Don subsequently left the company, gaining other experience in instrument building and repair, but returned in 1984 as plant supervisor. During his absence, he met McGregor Gaines, a graphic designer and skilled woodworker; they became friends, and McGregor soon joined Don at O.M.I., where he became shop foreman. The two craftsmen were keen to make improvements to guitar production; but in 1988, after several suggestions were rejected by the management, they resigned and began building National-type designs by themselves.

For three years, Don and McGregor worked together to establish their new business, National Reso-Phonic Guitars, which is based in San Luis Obispo,

Right: National's headstocks carry the company's distinctive crest – a revival from the pre-war years.
(Courtesy National Reso-Phonic)

*Above and right:
National Reso-Phonic
Polychrome tri-cone
resonator guitar. This
instrument has an all-
steel body, a 1930s-style
headstock, and a baked-
on "wrinkle" finish. The
neck is maple and the
fingerboard is
rosewood.
(Courtesy National Reso-
Phonic)*

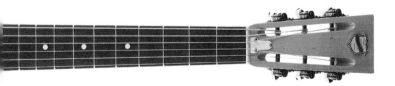

*Left: National Reso-Phonic Style O
single-resonator guitar. One of
National's biggest-selling guitars,
this is a recreation (with a striking
new finish) of a design introduced
in 1929. The body is made of
nickel-plated brass.
(Courtesy National Reso-Phonic)*

191

about 200 miles (320km) north of Los Angeles. They built their first instruments in a garage, and were initially restricted to wooden models; the tooling for metal guitars was too expensive, and, as McGregor observes, "We were definitely lacking in capital. Good ideas don't impress banks!" However, the instruments Don and McGregor created found a ready market among National devotees, and by 1992 they were able to begin production of the two classic metal-bodied designs that are currently their biggest sellers: the Style O and the Delphi. National Reso-Phonic now employs 17 people, and makes 80 guitars a month. Don describes their instruments as "pretty close, structurally, look-wise and tonally, to the 1920s- and 1930s-type Nationals. We have definitely made some improvements, but that's not to snub the old stuff – our hats are always off to the old makers, and we're directly linked to the Dopyera brothers."

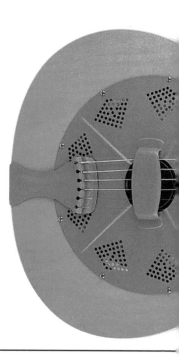

Recreation and Refinement

Don Young and McGregor Gaines had acquired a close knowledge of the Dopyera brothers' working techniques at O.M.I.; but they faced many difficulties in making National-style instruments for themselves. There were no written plans or blueprints for the original designs, and John Dopyera's patent applications, dating back to the 1920s, were not always a reliable guide to how the instruments had actually been produced. The only solution was to go back and examine the old guitars themselves: "We looked at them with a fine-tooth comb, studied the alloys, the resonators, the shapes, how they were put together." McGregor and Don quickly discovered that 1920s and 1930s Nationals had many design variations, even within production runs of the same model. When making their own versions of the instruments, McGregor explains that he and Don ▶

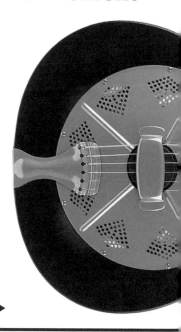

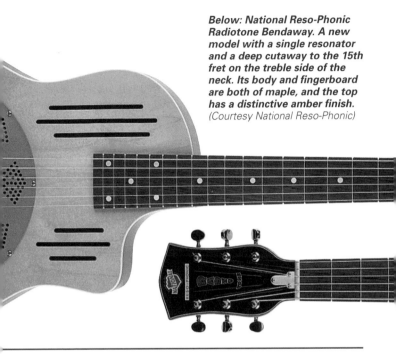

Below: National Reso-Phonic Radiotone Bendaway. A new model with a single resonator and a deep cutaway to the 15th fret on the treble side of the neck. Its body and fingerboard are both of maple, and the top has a distinctive amber finish. (Courtesy National Reso-Phonic)

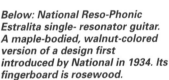

Below: National Reso-Phonic Estralita single- resonator guitar. A maple-bodied, walnut-colored version of a design first introduced by National in 1934. Its fingerboard is rosewood.

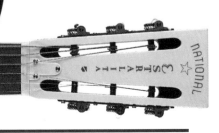

Bottom: The headstock is decorated with an ivoroid overlay and distinctive red lettering. The resonator cover-plate and tailpiece have a sleek, pewter-colored "baked-on" finish. (Courtesy National Reso-Phonic)

often had to "take a lot of different examples and try to work with the most graceful or most pleasing of the headstock styles or details."

The business of building Nationals for the 1990s involves both hand-crafting and high technology. Nearly all the company's necks – which used to take more than six hours to carve manually – are now made using high-precision Computer Numeric Control equipment. This completes the carving and fretting in only 12½ minutes, and can mill, slot and radius fretboards in seven minutes. Since acquiring CNC, National's production has increased by 80 percent. McGregor describes CNC as "a godsend – and it doesn't have mood swings or get cranky in the afternoon!"

Through their recreation of vintage National designs, and their development of exciting new acoustic and electric guitar designs, Don and McGregor have satisfied the demands of established resonator players, many of whom now play modern Nationals in preference to their fragile 1920s and 1930s instruments. And by raising the profile of the resonator guitar, the company is also helping to introduce it to younger performers, who, as Don Young observes, "are coming along, seeing this strange metal guitar with the hubcap on the front of it – and they go 'Wow!'"

Below: National Reso-Phonic Liberty single-resonator guitar. This is a custom model showing off some spectacular mother-of-pearl headstock and fingerboard inlays. The figure of Liberty (below right) on the tailpiece is gold-plated.
(Courtesy National Reso-Phonic)

Right and above far right: National Reso-Phonic Coy Koi tri-cone. Another custom guitar, with koi fish engravings on its body, and delicate fingerboard inlays. The brass bodies on the Coy Koi and other National instruments are nickel-plated using the same formulae and methods developed by the Dopyera brothers in the pre-war National factory.
(Courtesy National Reso-Phonic)

*Right: Headstock of the National
Reso-Phonic Liberty guitar.*
(Courtesy National Reso-Phonic)

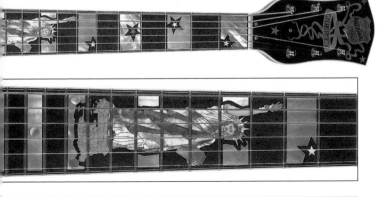

The Twentieth Century Classical Guitar

Antonio de Torres had a profound influence on later guitar builders in Spain and beyond. His reputation spread rapidly, and the innovations he introduced became established practice for most of his successors. However, the next generation of great Spanish luthiers came not from the south of the country, where Torres lived and worked, but from the capital city of Madrid. It was here that José Ramírez (1858–1923), the founder of a long and distinguished family line of guitar builders, opened his instrument-making workshop in the early 1880s. Ramírez and his

Below: Guitar by Salvador Ibanez, early twentieth century. The top is made from pine wood, and the back and sides are of maple edged in ebony. Mahogany is used for the headstock and bridge, and the fingerboard is teak.
(Courtesy Edinburgh University)

Right: Guitar by Domingo Esteso, 1923. This instrument has a spruce top, Indian rosewood back and sides, and a rosette inlaid with an elaborate ring of mother-of-pearl on a black background.
(Courtesy Guitar Salon International, Santa Monica)

brother Manuel (1864–1916) – who was his first apprentice – became major figures in the development of Spanish lutherie, and were responsible for training a great many other famous craftsmen.

After collaborating for a number of years, the two brothers quarrelled bitterly over Manuel's decision to set up his own Madrid-based business in direct competition with José. The disagreement led to a permanent split, but even before this, significant differences were becoming apparent in the Ramírezs' guitar designs. While José frequently built thinner-bodied, harder-toned instruments that were especially popular with flamenco players, Manuel preferred the richer-sounding Torres style. His tastes are reflected in the work of his former apprentices, especially Domingo Esteso (1882–1937), who stayed with him for over 20 years, only setting up his own workshop after Manuel's death in 1916.

Another important Manuel Ramírez apprentice, Enrique García (1868–1922), subsequently moved east to Barcelona, where he estab-lished himself as a highly respected maker of guitars in the Torres tradition, winning a number of international awards for his instruments. His pupil, Francisco Simplicio (1874–1932), followed the same stylistic approach; the labels on his guitars proudly proclaim him to be "the sole disciple of Enrique García."

The other instrument shown here (pages 196-197) is by a maker from outside the "Madrid School" of luthiers, Salvador Ibanez, who had a workshop in Valencia during the early part of the twentieth century. It was used by the young Julian Bream in 1946 to give his first public recital in the English town of Cheltenham at the age of 13, and can now be seen in the musical instrument collection at Edinburgh University.

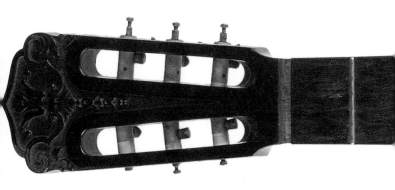

Left: Guitar by Francisco Simplicio, built in 1929. The absence of strings on the Simplicio guitar (it was undergoing repair when it was photographed) allows a clear view of the maker's label (top), which carries Simplicio's signature, and mentions the gold medal won by his teacher, Enrique García, at the *Chicago Exhibition in 1893. The Simplicio guitar is made from spruce and rosewood; its unusually tall and finely shaped headstock (above middle) is a characteristic of the luthier's work.*
(Courtesy Gary Southwell)

The Flamenco Tradition

The rich sonorities of the post-Torres classical guitar were not ideally suited to all musical styles and techniques. In particular, flamenco performers, playing the fiery, often fiercely percussive gypsy songs and dances of Andalucía, sought a brighter, more cutting sound from their instruments. For them, Spanish luthiers evolved an alternative gut-strung guitar design, offering the hard brilliance of tone they desired.

Flamenco guitars are usually thinner and more lightly-built than their classical counterparts. Their bodies are frequently made from cypress, rather than the rosewood traditionally used for classical guitar backs and sides, and their tops are protected by *golpeadores* (tap plates) mounted on one or both sides of the soundhole, which perform a similar function to the pickguards on steel-strung guitars. Flamenco-style head stocks are also highly distinctive; they have no cut-outs or geared tuning machines, and are fitted with simple vertically mounted wooden tuning pegs. Instruments of this kind were certainly available by the mid nineteenth century; Torres himself made some of his less expensive

Below and right: Flamenco guitar by Manuel Ramírez, probably 1914. Like most flamenco instruments, this guitar has a cypress body; its top is pine, and it is fitted with simple friction pegs for tuning.
(Courtesy Edinburgh University)

Left: The soundhole decoration on the Ramírez guitar is made from 12 narrow circles of black wood inset into the top, which is edged with ebony.

models from cypress, and later designers gradually introduced other modifications. José Ramírez I was one of several Madrid-based luthiers who stiffened the tops of their guitars by arching them (another technique previously used by Torres), and many of his flamenco-style models also had enlarged bodies which provided increased volume. His brother Manuel took a different approach; the guitar shown here, made by him in 1914, features a smaller body design and an unarched table.

Manuel Ramírez's flamenco designs were further developed by his former employee Santos Hernández (1874–1943), a distinguished luthier who also excelled at classical guitar construction. His designs have proved highly influential, and the important role he played in the early career of the great virtuoso Andrés Segovia, as well as the subsequent impact of his work on the leading German luthier Hermann Hauser, are examined below.

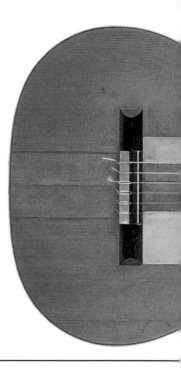

Andrés Segovia, Santos Hernández, and Hermann Hauser

Andrés Segovia (1893–1987) was soon to become internationally famous as the twentieth century's foremost classical guitarist; but in 1912, when he arrived in Madrid to make his concert début there, he was a relatively unknown 19-year-old without even an adequate instrument to use for the forthcoming recital. His search for a first-class guitar led him to Manuel Ramírez's workshop, where he made enquiries about hiring one. But having heard him play, Manuel is said to have been so impressed that he presented the young musician with a fine instrument that carried the Ramírez label, but was probably built by the luthier's foreman, Santos Hernández. Segovia used it not only for his Madrid performance, but also on many other worldwide concert engagements ▶

Below: Flamenco guitar by Santos Hernández, 1928. Its top is spruce, and its back and sides cypress. Note the "golpeadores" on either side of the strings.
(Courtesy Guitar Salon International, Santa Monica)

Below: Guitar by Hermann Hauser, 1936. This guitar is known to have been owned and played by Segovia himself. It was subsequently taken to Latin America by the Uruguayan guitarist Abel Carlevaro, and during the 1950s it was repolished – probably in Hauser's own workshop. Since then, the wood on the body has shrunk slightly, leaving some fine lines visible on the finish.
(Courtesy Guitar Salon International, Santa Monica)

over the course of the next two decades.

Despite his esteem for the Ramírez/Hernández guitar, Segovia never commissioned another instrument from Santos Hernández himself. Instead, after discussions with several other craftsmen, he chose to collaborate with a leading German luthier, Hermann Hauser (1882-1952), on the creation of what Segovia later described as "the greatest guitar of our epoch." While working on its construction, Hauser closely studied the Hernández as well as earlier Torres designs. After more than a decade of experimentation, he finally completed the instrument Segovia was seeking in 1936. It was used extensively by the great musician throughout the following 25 years,

and can be heard on many of his finest recordings.

Hausers are among the most sought-after of all classical guitars; but the precise reason for what one leading dealer, Tim Miklaucic, describes as their "intangible, clear, and lyrical quality" is harder to determine. Gary Southwell, a luthier who has recently built a series of Hauser replicas for the great English guitarist Julian Bream, suggests that the secret may lie in the "sympathetic tunings" of the instruments. The tops of Hauser guitars have a resonant frequency of F# or G#, while the backs are pitched a tone lower, at E or F#; and when Gary built a replica that incorporated these tunings, Bream confirmed that he had come close to attaining the sound of the Hauser original.

Andrés Segovia, Santos Hernández, and Hermann Hauser

Below and right: Guitar by Hermann Hauser, 1929. An instrument made during the period when Hauser was working with Andrés Segovia, perfecting the design for "the greatest guitar of our epoch." After Hauser's death in 1952, his son continued to make instruments to a similar design as the 1929 model, and the luthier's grandson, Hermann Hauser III, is now custodian of the family tradition.
(Courtesy Guitar Salon International, Santa Monica)

Segovia, José Ramírez III, and Ignacio Fleta

For much of the latter part of his career, Segovia played instruments by two Spanish luthiers, José Ramírez III (1922–1995, the grandson of José Ramírez I) and Ignacio Fleta (1897–1977). Ramírez's first assignment for Segovia was the repair of the maestro's treasured 1936 Hauser. He then began the lengthy process of developing his own designs to Segovia's satisfaction; his patience was rewarded in the early 1960s, when the guitarist started using Ramírez instruments regularly.

Ramírez made some significant departures from accepted tradition in his use of materials, preferring red cedar to spruce for the tops of his guitars, extending the string length of his instruments for extra projection and power, and creating special lacquer finishes to enrich their sound. Earlier, interest in exploring the

Below: Guitar by Ignacio Fleta, 1958. At this stage, Fleta was still using spruce for the tops of his guitars; he later changed to red cedar, as did José Ramírez III, the other luthier favored by Andrés Segovia during the last 30 years of his career. The instrument's headstock (bottom right) is based on the shape originated by Torres.
(Courtesy Ray Ursell)

Right: Guitar by José Ramírez III, 1979. This is Ramírez's "Centanario No. 2" model, with a spruce top and Brazilian rosewood back and sides. The neck is cedar; the headstock is overlaid with rosewood and inlaid with real ivory.
(Courtesy Mandolin Brothers, New York)

acoustical principles underlying the art of instrument-making had been a source of friction with his father, José Ramírez II (1885–1957), another fine but more conservative luthier, who felt that his son's researches were a waste of valuable time. However, José III's innovations – which also included the development of an efficient method of guitar production that enabled his craftsmen to turn out thousands of Ramírez instruments without sacrificing quality – have ensured him an important place in classical guitar history.

Ignacio Fleta was born at Huesa del Común, in the north-eastern Spanish region of Catalonia, in 1897. Trained as a violin and cello builder as well as a luthier, he made a variety of stringed instruments throughout the earlier part of his career, only focusing full-time on the guitar in 1955, after having heard a radio broadcast of Andrés Segovia playing a Bach transcription. Segovia was the first major player to use a Fleta (he acquired one in 1957, and sub-sequently bought two others), and since then, many other distinguished players, most notably John Williams, have been associated with his instruments. Fleta's two sons, Francisco and Gabriel, became partners in his Barcelona-based business during the 1960s, and they continued building guitars using the "Ignacio Fleta e hijos" ("and sons") label after their father's death in 1977.

Above: The label of the Ignacio Fleta, 1958, bears Fleta's name and shows the serial number of the instrument (No. 129).

Left and above: Guitar by Ignacio Fleta, 1960. Another Fleta from the same period, also with a spruce top and rosewood back and sides. The neck and the headstock (which is veneered with rosewood) are cedar, and the fingerboard is ebony. The instrument retains its original French polish finish.
(Courtesy Shel Urlik)

American Classical Guitar Makers

For many years, the main source for high-quality classical guitars was the instrument's birthplace – Spain. More recently, though, Spanish luthiers have faced growing competition from elsewhere in Europe, Japan, Australia, and, increasingly, the USA. American makers are now becoming as highly regarded for their classical designs as they have always been for archtops and flat-tops, and on these pages, we focus on three leading US luthiers whose guitars have achieved the acclaim of players and experts throughout the world.

Thomas Humphrey was born in Minnesota in 1948, but now lives and works in New York. He began his career there during the early 1970s in the workshop of Michael Gurian (a gifted luthier who was also associated with Michael Millard, the founder of Froggy Bottom Guitars – see pages 168-169), and started

Three views of a guitar by Thomas Humphrey, 1990. These show some of the revolutionary features that Humphrey has pioneered in his guitar designs – especially the sloping top and elevated fingerboard.
(Courtesy Shel Urlik)

Right: Thomas Humphrey uses an unconventional bracing system for his tops, preferring X-braces to the traditional Torres-style fan pattern.
(Courtesy Shel Urlik)

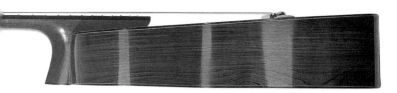

Acoustic Guitars

producing his own distinctive designs in the early 1980s. The most famous of these is the "Millennium," introduced in 1985, which features an unconventionally braced and steeply angled top. This is intended to increase the power of the instrument, while also improving access to the upper positions on the fingerboard. Humphrey's somewhat controversial designs are favored by leading guitarists such as Sharon Isbin, Carlos Barbosa-Lima, and Eliot Fisk; in 1997 he began a joint venture with the Martin Guitar Company to produce two classical models that will be built to his specifications.

Robert Ruck (b. 1945) is based in Hansville, Washington. A largely self-taught luthier, he produces approximately 30 instruments a year. He currently offers three basic sizes of guitar, which can be made as either "Standard" or "SP" (special, limited production) models. Robert Ruck guitars are used by a number of distinguished players, including the Cuban virtuoso Manuel Barrueco; he also builds a variety of other stringed instruments.

José Oribe (b. 1932) started making classical guitars in 1962 after earlier experience as an industrial machinist. Since 1973, his workshop has been in Vista, California. He offers his instruments in a variety of materials and finishes, laying great importance on the quality and seasoning of his tonewoods, all of which are aged for between 20 and 30 years before being used. Musicians playing Oribe guitars include fingerstyle jazz player Earl Klugh, and Angel and Pepe Romero.

Right: Guitar by José Oribe, 1982. This guitar features the same tonewoods as the Robert Ruck instrument. It is built in the style of José Ramírez III, whose work has been a major influence on Oribe.
(Courtesy Guitar Salon International, Santa Monica)

Above: Guitar by Robert Ruck, 1986. Its top is cedar, and the back and sides are Brazilian rosewood – a material the luthier has now stopped using, due to its acute shortage. Ruck's work is in great demand; he has made over 600 guitars, and there is an eight-year waiting list for his instruments.
(Courtesy Guitar Salon International, Santa Monica)

213

Three British Luthiers

Probably the most internationally famous of UK-based classical guitar makers is David Rubio (b. 1934), whose Spanish-sounding name can be misleading. He was born David Spink, and re-named himself (taking his new surname from a village in Spain) while studying and performing flamenco as a young man. Fascinated by this music and by all things Spanish, Rubio spent a number of years during the late 1950s at the workshops of leading luthiers in Seville and Madrid. After learning the principles of guitar building from them, he moved to New York in 1961, eventually setting up a lutherie business of his own in Greenwich Village. Rubio returned to Britain in 1967, and for the next two years he worked closely with the great English guitarist and lutenist Julian Bream,

Right: Guitar by Philip Woodfield. This instrument is built in the Torres style, with a spruce top, and back and sides of Indian rosewood. Unlike some modern luthiers, Woodfield prefers to finish his instruments with a coating of shellac (which was also used by Torres) rather than varnish or lacquer; he has found that it improves the tone noticeably. Although he sets great store by tradition, Philip Woodfield is also keen to experiment with new ideas – like the unusually carved and inlaid headstock (left) on this guitar.
(Courtesy Ray Ursell)

*eft: Guitar by David Rubio, 1969.
t was made soon after Rubio's
nove from his workshop close to
ulian Bream's home in Semley,
Dorset, to new premises in the
rillage of Duns Tew, Oxfordshire.
David Rubio is now based in
Cambridge.*
Courtesy Ray Ursell)

designing instruments for him and other leading players.

During the 1970s, David Rubio became involved with designing and constructing a variety of other stringed instruments, but is now focusing on the guitar once again. The example of his work shown below dates from 1969.

Philip Woodfield lives and works in rural Cornwall, an area of England that holds a particular attraction for luthiers; the biographer of Torres, José Romanillos, once described it jokingly as "the graveyard for guitar-makers." Woodfield, however, is prospering there, and has produced over 130 instruments to date,

including lutes, violins, and vihuelas as well as guitars. His designs are strongly influenced by Torres, and he prefers to work using traditional methods, avoiding the use of technology wherever possible. He has recently sold guitars to players throughout Europe, Japan, and the USA.

James Baker is a former student of Michael Gee at the London College of Furniture, which offers one of the UK's most highly regarded training courses for budding luthiers. He has now established a workshop in Suffolk, and Baker's instruments, like Philip Woodfield's, are in growing international demand.

Below and right: Guitar by James Baker. The top is spruce, the back and sides are Brazilian rosewood, and the headstock is faced with bird's-eye maple.
(Courtesy Ray Ursell)

SECTION THREE

Today and Tomorrow

In the early 1960s, a British recording company turned down the chance of signing the Beatles because it believed that "groups with guitars were on their way out." The instrument's death-knell has been sounded many times since then; but despite fluctuations of taste and fashion, the guitar – and especially the acoustic guitar, in all its forms – has never been healthier or more in demand than it is now.

One of the most important trends in current attitudes towards the instrument is the value placed on vintage designs. The most "collectible" of these are no longer simply tools of the performer's trade, but desirable possessions, commanding prices that would have astonished their original owners and makers.

This reverence for tradition is also reflected in the output of many contemporary guitar-makers. Gibson's success with its relaunched flat-top range is evidence of customers' appreciation for classic models and fine craftsmanship. Even the most radical departures from standard methods, such as Alan Timmins' use of carbon-fiber bodies for his resonator guitars, often go hand in hand with painstaking research and replication of earlier designs; while other present-day luthiers, including Gary Southwell draw more direct inspiration from the past as they build their new, innovative instruments.

In this section, we survey these and other recent developments in guitar-making, showing some of the ways in which today's luthiers are answering their customers' needs by creating instruments suitable for almost all playing environments – from stage and studio to the home and even the open road!

Left and below: Lowden LSE 1 cutaway acoustic guitar. This instrument, made by luthier George Lowden, whose company is based in Newtonards, Northern Ireland, features a sitka spruce top and mahogany back and sides. It is fitted with a built-in pickup, making it easy to amplify onstage; the volume control for this can be seen on the guitar's left shoulder.
(Courtesy Chandler Guitars, Kew)

Towards the Future

The town of Kalamazoo, Michigan, had been associated with Gibson guitars ever since Orville Gibson went into business there in the 1890s. But in 1974, the company moved its electric instrument making to a new factory in Nashville, Tennessee, and ten years later, when the production of Gibson acoustics was also transferred there, the Kalamazoo plant closed permanently.

Its shutdown was a sad footnote to a difficult chapter in the great guitar-maker's history. In the wake of its takeover by the Norlin company in 1969, some controversial changes had been made to production methods. These included the introduction of double X-bracing on Gibson flat-tops – which succeeded in making the instruments more resilient, but impaired their tone-quality. By the early 1980s, sales were suffering, and a radical shift in strategy was needed to put the company back on track. It came in 1985, when Gibson was sold to a new management team, who worked hard

Below and right: Gibson SJ-200. A newly-made instrument from the Gibson factory at Bozeman, Montana, closely based on the traditional J-200 design, which was originally launched in the late 1930s. The top is sitka spruce, the back and sides flamed maple. The acoustics currently being produced at Bozeman are among the finest Gibson have ever built.
(Courtesy Hank's, London)

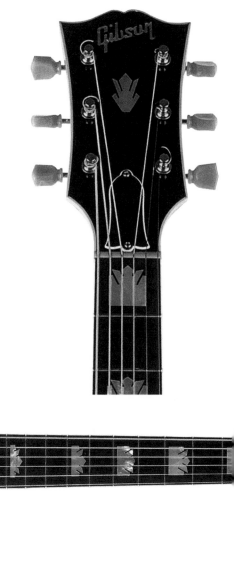

Acoustic Guitars

to restore the firm's fortunes. In 1987, Gibson acquired a former mandolin factory in Bozeman, Montana, and re-equipped it for acoustic guitar construction; since 1989, all Gibson flat-tops have been made there, while production of other instruments continues in Nashville.

The company's recent output, which includes new designs and "reissues" of classic models from the past, has been highly acclaimed by musicians and dealers. Staff at the new plant at Bozeman use a combination of craft skills and computer-controlled technology to produce their instruments, and there is also a busy Custom Shop, making special orders and limited editions. Perennial Gibson favorites, like the J-200 seen here, and the Nick Lucas model that was the company's first high-quality flat-top (see pages 134-135), are now being built with the care and attention to detail these fine designs deserve, and many players compare the Montana guitars favorably with their vintage originals.

Left and above: Gibson CL-40 Artist. One of a range of new acoustic designs produced by Gibson since their move to Montana. The CL-40 has a spruce top, rosewood back and sides, and an ebony bridge and fingerboard.
(Courtesy Hank's, London)

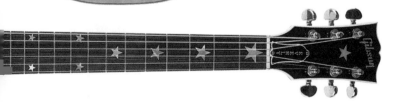

Left and above left: Gibson Everly. This guitar is based on the "Everly Brothers" Jumbo first introduced by Gibson in 1963, and later renamed the J-180. Don Everly was responsible

for designing the instrument's distinctive double pickguards, which were also fitted to the customized J-200s used by the brothers before the launch of their own model.
(Courtesy Hank's, London)

Modern British Flat-tops

For many years, top quality UK-made flat-tops were few and far between, and most serious British players would usually be seen with a Martin, a Gibson, or some other "high-end" American instrument. Thanks to the work of a handful of skilled and enterprising luthiers, this situation has changed. British designs are now competing with the finest US guitars, and a growing number of musicians, not just in the UK but throughout the world, are making them their first choice.

The English West Country is an important center for British guitar building, and the distinguished luthier Andy Manson has lived and worked in Devon for more than 20 years. His instruments are used by many discerning musicians, including Jimmy Page of Led Zeppelin and Ian Anderson of Jethro Tull, and the Manson range features Dreadnought models (the Sandpiper and the Dove), a Jumbo design (the Heron), and a guitar based on the classic Martin OM shape, the Magpie. Two of Andy Manson's associates, Andy Petherick and Simon Smidmore of Brook Guitars, are now building a number of his regular designs under license, allowing him to focus on the production of specialized and custom instruments.

George Lowden is another long-established name in British lutherie. His Ulster-based company produces

Right: Lowden O-12. Lowden's O (Original) series guitars are its largest instruments, with a lower bout width of 16⁹/16 in (41.8cm). The O-12 has a sitka spruce top, and mahogany sides, back, and binding. Like almost all Lowden models, it has a two-piece bridge saddle to improve intonation on the first and second strings.
(Courtesy Chandler Guitars, Kew)

Left: The Magpie includes a small pillar on the upper right side of its top, providing a safe place for the player to put his pick!

Left: Manson Magpie custom seven-string. Mansons all feature German spruce tops and Indian rosewood backs and sides. The Magpie is one of the company's *most popular models, and this customized version was made for British jazz guitarist Andy Robinson.*
(Courtesy Andy Robinson)

four basic models (with a wide variety of optional features), as well as a number of "Premiere Range" instruments made to special order from exotic tonewoods such as koa, black cedar, and Brazilian rosewood. Lowdens are played by singer-songwriter Richard Thompson, French fingerstylist Pierre Bensusan, and other leading guitarists on both sides of the Atlantic.

In 1973, Roger Bucknall, a British luthier with extensive experience of small-scale instrument production, set up the Fylde company, whose guitars gained a high reputation among leading UK folk performers such as Martin Carthy. Since then, Fylde's distinctive designs, often named after characters in Shakespeare plays, have attained a much broader popularity. As well as Dreadnoughts and smaller-body six-strings, the company has also pioneered two successful acoustic bass guitars, the King John and the Sir Toby. Fylde's customers include Sting, Pat Metheny, Martin Simpson, and English actor/singer Jimmy Nail.

Ovation Guitars

Twentieth-century luthiers have introduced many major changes in guitar construction; but – with the notable exception of the Dopyera brothers and their "German silver" instruments – they have nearly all continued to use wood as the basis for their designs. Companies experimenting with other materials, particularly man-made ones, have often had to face considerable resistance and criticism; and so far, only one large-scale American manufacturer, Kaman, has succeeded in overcoming this by achieving mass-market success for its "Lyrachord"-backed Ovation guitars.

Kaman was originally an aerospace engineering company, although its Chairman, Charlie Kaman, has always been a keen guitarist. In 1964, he and a team of technicians began analyzing the ways in which various guitars absorbed and reflected sound. Having found that ▶

Left: Fylde Oberon. This is Fylde's best-selling Dreadnought-style design, made in Penrith, Cumbria. The company's other models include smaller-bodied guitars like the Ariel and Goodfellow, and a Maccaferri-style instrument, the Egyptian.
(Courtesy Hank's, London)

Left: Ovation Custom Legend. A "high-end" Ovation with a sitka spruce top, mahogany and maple five-piece neck, and abalone purfling and fingerboard position markers. The tuning machines are gold-plated, with pearloid buttons.
(Courtesy Hank's, London)

Acoustic Guitars

instruments with rounded backs were more acoustically efficient than traditional flat-back shapes, they used their discoveries to create a radical new design – and the outcome was the Ovation Balladeer, which appeared in 1969. It had a spruce top, but its novel "bowl-back" was manufactured from Lyrachord, a specially-developed fiber-glass formulation that is strong, sonically reflective, and impervious to climate change.

The company's earliest models were entirely acoustic; but in the early 1970s, it pioneered the development of high-quality, feedback-resistant piezo-electric pickup systems for its guitars, and as a result, Ovations became especially popular for stage work. Although opinion remains divided about the instruments' sound and shape, a number of eminent players use them regularly. These include Glen Campbell (Ovation's first and most influential endorsee), as well as solo guitarists Adrian Legg and Al Di Meola, singer-songwriter

Joan Armatrading, and Latin jazzman Charlie Byrd (who plays a nylon-strung model).

Kaman has continued to experiment with other non-traditional materials, including graphite (which is used instead of wood for the top of its Adamas model); but only a handful of other companies and luthiers are currently working with synthetics. Among them is Alan Timmins, an English designer with a ground-breaking design for a carbon-fiber resonator guitar, whose highly distinctive work is featured on the following two pages.

Right: Ovation Celebrity Deluxe. It is a shallower-backed Ovation model, fitted with an under-bridge pickup system. The cutaway fingerboard edge, characteristic "leaf" design, and holes on the upper top are also found on other Ovations, including their top-of-the-range Adamas guitar.
(Courtesy Chandler Guitars, Kew)

Below: The Lyrachord fiber-glass material used for the Balladeer and its distinctive shaping were by-products of Ovation founder Charlie Kaman's earlier work on helicopter design. He explained recently that "In helicopters, the engineers spend all their time trying to figure out how to remove vibration. To build a guitar you spend your time trying to figure out how to put vibration in. But vibration is vibration."

Left: Ovation Standard Balladeer. The Balladeer was the first model introduced by Ovation; this is the current version, with a spruce top, two-piece neck, and mahogany fingerboard, and the company's distinctive Lyrachord back. The guitar also has a built-in pickup and preamplifier.
(Courtesy Chandler Guitars, Kew)

Alan Timmins and his Resonator Guitars

Alan Timmins, from Nottingham, was almost certainly the first luthier in Britain to build resonator guitars. Since developing a metal-bodied tricone in 1989, he has gone on to create carbon-fiber models now used by Mike Cooper, Dave Peabody, Michael Messer, and other leading players. Alan's wide-ranging technical expertise has been an important factor in the success of his designs, as has the support of his friend Mark Makin – the UK's foremost authority on the history of National guitars, who lives nearby, and commissioned Alan's

first instrument.

This was based on a National Style 97 (the design that replaced the company's Style 1 in the late 1930s), and was the first metal guitar Alan had ever made. He was soon working on other instruments: "I built half-a-dozen, maybe ten of them…but there were 16 bits of metal in each guitar, and it was a struggle, all the soldering, warping and lining up – a nightmare of a job." He decided to make molds, and use these to construct his guitar bodies from carbon fiber. This simplified the production process, which required

Below and bottom right: Alan Timmins F1 carbon-fiber tricone. The guitars' necks are made either from mahogany or, as on this model, from laminated maple with *an ebony strip. The headstock is carbon-fiber, and the "F1" inlay and fingerboard markers are abalone.*
(Courtesy Alan Timmins)

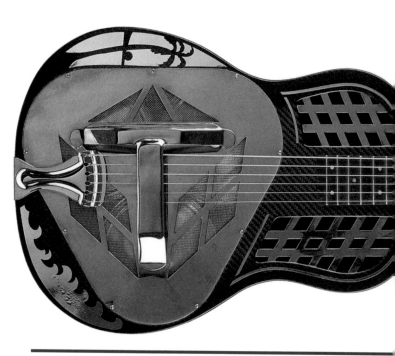

Above: The bodies for Alan's carbon-fiber instruments are molded in two pieces (sides/back and front), and then left to cure for up to a fortnight. The National metal-bodied instruments on which the F1 is based were made from shiny metal, with matt decorative patterns sand-blasted on. The F1 (left) reverses this: the bodywork is matt, the design (a version of Alan's "surfer girl") shiny.

only two moldings: one for the back and sides, and one for the front.

The outcome of Alan's experiments was his F1 model. The strength and durability of its body's carbon-fiber formulation provides remarkable stability. Alan guarantees his instruments "airport baggage-handler-proof," and unlike metal-bodied guitars, they do not expand and go out of tune when exposed to heat. Wood is still used for the neck, and the cover-plates are made from laser-cut brass.

The crucial question of how the carbon-fiber bodies sound is best answered by one of Alan Timmins' customers, blues guitarist Dave Peabody, who summarized his reactions – and those of his audience – in a recent edition of *Blueprint* magazine. "Apart from looking wonderful, being black and silver, it's got *the tone* to me. It's very loud and it projects brilliantly into a microphone...I picked [my instrument] up on my way to the Edinburgh Blues Festival, where it had its inauguration. And it got a round of applause on its own."

Below: Alan Timmins Style 97-type tricone, 1989. This guitar, custom-built for Mark Makin, was one of the first to be made since National stopped producing the designs in the 1940s. The back (right) features Alan's "surfer girl" and "palm-tree" decorations.
(Courtesy Mark Makin)

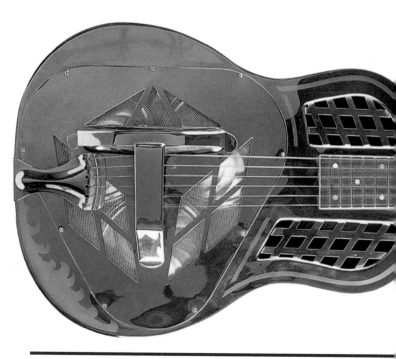

Travel Guitars

Acoustic guitars can be demanding traveling companions. Their dimensions make them unsuitable as in-flight hand luggage, and many musicians are unhappy about exposing their delicate instruments to the rigors of aircraft holds and baggage carousels. Other means of transport can be equally hazardous; yet keen players hate to be parted from their guitars on holidays or business trips. Recently, several American companies have offered a solution to this dilemma by developing smaller instruments that retain the feel – and some of the sound – of full-size models. Three examples are shown here.

The Baby Taylor is a remarkable piece of design, offering a deep, Dreadnought-style body and a standard-width neck on an instrument that measures only 34in (86.4cm) from headstock to endpin. It has many of the features found on full-size Taylors, including an X-braced sitka spruce top and ebony fingerboard, and unlike some travel guitars, it is designed to be played at standard pitch. The Baby Taylor was introduced

Below and right: Baby Taylor. A highly acclaimed instrument designed by Bob Taylor and his team for travelers and younger players – although it has also proved very attractive to more experienced guitarists. It has a spruce top, a mahogany neck, and mahogany veneer back and sides. The soundhole decoration is created using a computer-controlled laser etching process, and the fingerboard and bridge are ebony.
(Courtesy Taylor Guitars)

in 1996, and has proved popular not only with travelers and children, but with a number of leading professionals who have used it onstage and in the studio.

Martin's Backpacker has an unconventional look and feel. Its small, exceptionally light body is combined with a heavier, full-size neck, and a strap is needed to keep the instrument in the correct playing position. The guitar shown here is a steel-strung model; Martin also produces a nylon-strung Backpacker with a slightly wider and longer body. Both instruments can be amplified using built-in pickup systems. The provide excellent access to the uppe positions on the fingerboard, an have a pleasing, slightly banjo-lik sound.

Tacoma Guitars' P1 Papoose model is intended to be tuned a 4t higher than normal (i.e. the firs string, normally E, becomes an A). is fitted with a cedar top, featurin Tacoma's unusual low-mass tr angular bracing system, and mahogany back and sides. The Papoose has recently been en dorsed by country music stars Vinc Gill and Ricky Skaggs.

Below: Martin Backpacker (steel-strung). It features a 24in (61cm) scale length, solid wood top, and mahogany back and sides.
Martin's travel guitars are made under licence in Mexico.
Martin Backpackers have survived a number of grueling journeys – one owner was recently photographed playing his Backpacker on a Himalayan peak!
(Courtesy Martin Taylor)

Right: Tacoma Papoose. Tacoma describes the Papoose as "a professional instrument that happens to be small enough to be a travel guitar." Its wide neck (1¾in, 4.4cm at the nut) makes it easy to play in a variety of styles, and the asymmetrical soundhole i positioned in a low-vibration area of the top to maximize volume. The Papoose is also available with a built-in pickup system.
(Courtesy Eric Schoenberg)

237

Gary Southwell – Inspiration from the Past

British luthier Gary Southwell draws inspiration from a range of different classical guitar-making traditions. He has built Hauser replicas, as well as Torres-style instruments, and guitars based on earlier French and German models. Gary also creates his own strikingly original designs, which reflect his detailed knowledge of the past while offering ingenious new approaches and ideas.

Illustrated here is a Southwell replica of an instrument by the French luthier René Lacôte (1785–1855).

Guitars from this period were smalle than the Torres designs that late became the accepted standard fo makers and players; but their well focused sound provides sufficien volume for many modern concer halls, as Gary explains. "Althoug they don't have the warmth and dept of a post-Torres guitar, they do have a very clear, ringing tone which tends t penetrate and cut through very well. The Lacôte replicas are used by a number of distinguished players including early music expert Nige

Below: Gary Southwell replica Lacôte guitar. Its top is spruce, and the back and sides birdseye maple – a wood commonly used in nineteenth-century French guitars like the one on which this instrument is based. The neck is made from an ebony veneer, with an ebony fingerboard, and the edgings are a combination of ebony and sycamore.
(Courtesy Gary Southwell)

Acoustic Guitars

North, and David Starobin, who has also worked closely with Gary on the development of his "Series A" range.

Gary describes the Series A designs as "my modern interpretation of the Viennese tradition of classical guitar making." The "A" stands for "adjustable," and the instruments feature a refined version of the moveable neck system invented by Johann Georg Stauffer (1778–1853) and used on early guitars by his pupil C.F. Martin. A key in the heel of the neck allows the string action to be raised or lowered swiftly, even in mid-concert; and the "floating" fingerboard is free from contact with the top, increasing the overall vibrating area. The instrument's shape follows French and Viennese tradition, with a more pronounced waist than later Spanish guitars; while the intricately inlaid rosette is based on a Neolithic rock carving seen by Gary in Northumberland.

Gary aims to provide musicians with instruments that are inspiring, practical, and versatile. As he says, "To me the most important thing about a guitar is that it responds to what the player wants to do to it. A lot of guitars dictate to the player, I want to make an instrument that's full of character, but has the ability to be directed and enjoyed by the player."

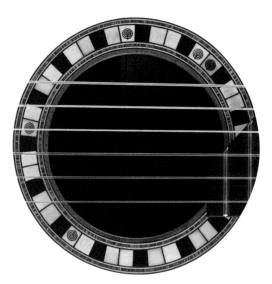

Gary Southwell Series A guitar. Again, a spruce top is used, with Honduras rosewood back and sides, a birdseye maple neck, and ebony fingerboard. The elaborate rosette is made from inlaid bone and ebony tiles, with a "Neolithic" design carved in. The removable key in the heel of the neck controls a mechanism allowing the height of the strings to be adjusted by the player.
(Courtesy Gary Southwell)

Martin Taylor and the Yamaha Electro-Acoustic

The defining line between "acoustic" and "electric" instruments is not easy to draw. Almost all steel-strung acoustic guitarists (and even a few of their classical colleagues) now use some form of amplification onstage, while a number of electric archtop players like to combine the signal from their magnetic pickups with natural, acoustic tones. When performing in a live, feedback-prone environment, this is often difficult to achieve – but one musician who can easily combine or alternate between the two sounds, thanks to the Yamaha guitar he helped to design, is distinguished British jazzman Martin Taylor.

In 1989, Yamaha approached Martin with an idea for a guitar with two pickups: a conventional

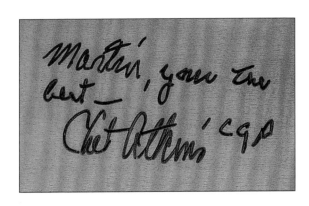

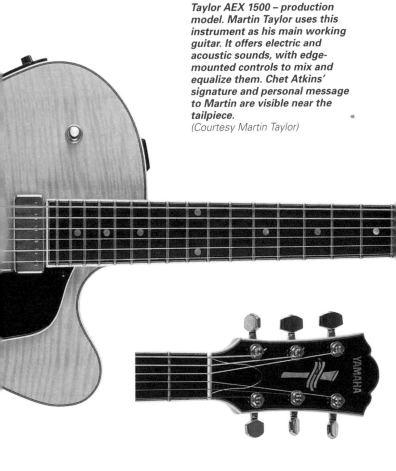

Above and below: Yamaha Martin Taylor AEX 1500 – production model. Martin Taylor uses this instrument as his main working guitar. It offers electric and acoustic sounds, with edge-mounted controls to mix and equalize them. Chet Atkins' signature and personal message to Martin are visible near the tailpiece.
(Courtesy Martin Taylor)

Acoustic Guitars

humbucker in the neck position, and a piezo device to capture the acoustic sound. He worked on detailed plans for the instrument with Martyn Booth of Yamaha-Kemble U.K., and these were eventually submitted to the company's Design Department in Hamamatsu, Japan. There, luthier Jackie Minacuchi built a prototype, which Martin used on his "Artistry" CD (1992) and on subsequent tours. He then sent a list of suggested modifications back to Minacuchi, who responded with a second prototype; Martin has never used this for live dates or recordings, although he has frequently played it at home. After some further changes, Yamaha completed the final, production version of the design, the Martin Taylor AEX 1500; it can be seen opposite, together with the two prototypes.

The Yamaha is now Martin Taylor's main working instrument, providing him with the range of tone-colors he needs for both solo and group work. He has used it on many TV appearances, videos, and CDs, including the "Portraits" album, recorded in Nashville with veteran country music guitarist and producer Chet Atkins. During the sessions, Chet paid tribute to Martin by signing his guitar with the simple inscription: "Your the best" (sic).

Right: Yamaha Martin Taylor AEX 1500 – first prototype. One of only two initial prototypes of the guitar developed by Martin Taylor and Martyn Booth, and hand-built by luthier Jackie Minacuchi. Martin has toured and recorded widely with it. This prototype AEX 1500 is owned by Martin Taylor himself; the other is kept at Yamaha's Design Department in Hamamatsu, Japan.
(Courtesy Martin Taylor)

Left: Yamaha Martin Taylor AEX 1500 – second prototype. This guitar was made after Martin requested some alterations and improvements to prototype No. 1; again, only two identical examples of the revised design were ever built.
(Courtesy Martin Taylor)

The Contemporary Guitar

Since its emergence in the sixteenth century, the acoustic guitar has evolved into many differing forms, and this process continues today, as luthiers combine ideas and designs from various traditions to create new and exciting instruments. The three guitars shown here are all examples of this eclectic approach, and they form a fitting conclusion to this book.

Robert Benedetto's "Il Fioren-tino" is a nylon-strung archtop guitar with strong echoes of classical violin design. The first model in Benedetto's "Renaissance" series, which also includes a similar steel-strung archtop, "Il Palissandro" (The Rosewood), its top is made from aged European spruce, and the back and sides from European curly maple, with a centerpiece of American birdseye maple. The instrument dates from 1994.

Below and bottom right:
Benedetto "Il Fiorentino" 16-inch archtop nylon-strung guitar, 1994. A radical departure from standard archtop design. It is built from European and American tonewoods, with a wood burl veneer on its classical guitar-style headstock. Solid ebony tuning pegs are used as opposed to conventional tuning machines. It features a violin-style bridge, hand-carved from curly maple, and an ebony tailpiece (with abalone inlay), which is attached to the body using cello tailgut.
(Courtesy Robert Benedetto)

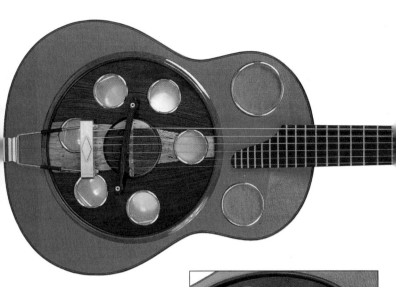

Above and right: Paul McGill resonator guitar. McGill's resonator designs are influenced by Dobros and by the now-rare Brazilian DelVecchio instruments favored by leading players such as Chet Atkins, who also owns a McGill resonator model like the one shown here. The neck and top are fashioned from cedar, the back and sides rosewood, and the fingerboard is made from ebony. (Courtesy Mandolin Brothers, New York)

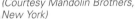

Acoustic Guitars

Paul McGill, a luthier based in Nashville, Tennessee, builds outstanding classical instruments as well as resonator guitars, and this colorful Dobro-type model, made by him in 1995, has a Spanish guitar-style headstock and fingerboard. The resonator cover is decorated with sapwood – the soft wood found directly underneath tree bark. Paul McGill's customers include Chet Atkins, Earl Klugh, Ricky Skaggs, Phil Keaggy, and many other leading names.

The final instrument brings together the traditions of jazz and classical guitar making. Its creator, John Buscarino, calls it the "Cabaret;" its body is based on the designs of the great German luthier Hermann Hauser, but its cutaway and built-in pickup make it especially suitable for fingerstyle jazz performers. One leading British jazz musician, Adrian Ingram, has described it as "the best amplified nylon-string guitar I have ever played."

Outstanding instruments like the

ones seen here – and elsewhere in this book – are proof that acoustic guitar building is currently reaching new heights of excellence. As Don Young of National Reso-Phonic puts it: "People need to realize that right now the guitar industry as a whole, whether it's the individual luthier or some of the bigger companies, are making some of the best guitars that have ever been produced. We're in a very rich period, and I commend all our fellow guitar-makers out there for doing a fine job."

Below and right: Buscarino Cabaret cutaway. John Buscarino designed this instrument to provide "the perfect blend of a traditional classical guitar and an acoustic archtop guitar." He also makes a slightly larger "Grand Cabaret," based on a José Ramirez III model.
(Courtesy John Buscarino)

Part Two

Electric Guitars

After completing the acoustic guitars section of this book it became clear that the section on electric guitars would need to be structured rather differently. Acoustic guitars evolved over hundreds of years, but electrics, which made their first serious impact on the music scene as recently as the 1930s, have developed far more quickly. Only twenty years separate the first-ever mass-produced electric guitar, Electro's innovative but primitive "Frying Pan," from the Gibson Les Paul, a mature design that is still bought and used by thousands of today's players. And other comparatively early instruments, such as Fender's Telecaster and Stratocaster, have also shown remarkable staying power, surviving alongside newer models and retaining the loyalty and affection of countless musicians and audiences since their introduction in the 1950s.

Accordingly, after examining the early years of the electric guitar in Section One, we devote an entire section of the book to these and other classic designs. While our focus is firmly on the market leaders in electric guitar manufacture, Fender and Gibson, we also include key models by other influential makers – and show how all the major companies strove to generate publicity and recognition for their guitars by seeking out leading jazz, country, and (increasingly) pop and rock players as endorsees.

The long post-war run of success enjoyed by Gibson and Fender was followed by a more unsettled climate from the mid-1960s onwards. In many ways this period, which is reflected in Section Three, was a fruitful one for guitar buyers. Those professionals who could afford it were commissioning fine custom instruments from small, independent makers and individual luthiers. Meanwhile, for the impecunious amateur and beginner, factories in the Far East were beginning to offer a bewildering range of guitars looking outwardly similar to "classic" Fenders and Gibsons. The quality of these "copies" has always been highly variable (as many buyers can testify!). Accordingly, they are not represented in detail in our selection of photographs: given the size of the subject, and the limited space available, we have preferred instead to feature a broader selection of original designs.

In the last two decades, there have been more and more of these to choose from, as we demonstrate in Sections Three and Four. The archtop guitar has undergone a resurgence on both sides of the Atlantic, and fine examples by master craftsmen such as Robert Benedetto are included here. We show solid-bodies from Steve Klein, Rick Turner, and Alembic: three Californian makers whose guitars make a bold visual impact to match their outstanding sound. The work of Hugh Manson and other top British luthiers is also documented; and in conclusion we look at one of the few entirely new fretted instruments to have successfully established itself since the advent of the electric guitar itself: Emmett Chapman's Stick.

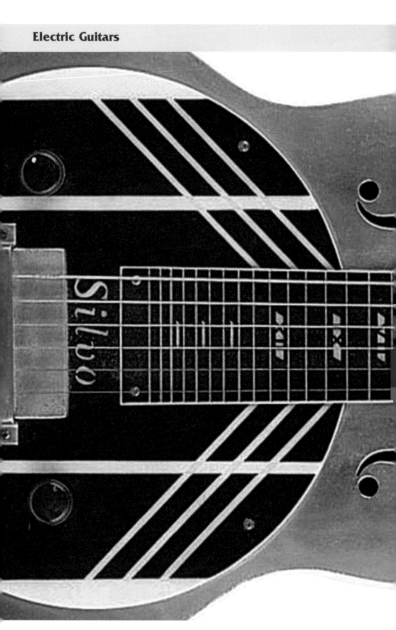

Above and right: National "Silvo" electric lap steel, c.1937. The National String Instrument Corporation, founded in California in 1928, is most famous for its powerful-sounding acoustic resonator guitars. By the late 1930s, however, the company (which moved to Chicago in 1936) had responded to the growing demand for electric instruments with models like this one. It has a nickel-plated body and an "ebonoid" coverplate carrying its pickup assembly. Players with National acoustics could have their guitars converted to electric operation by having a similar "res-o-lectric" unit factory-fitted in place of the resonator. (Courtesy Mark Makin)

SECTION ONE

The Birth of the Electric Guitar

The electric guitar evolved from theoretical concept to practical instrument in only a few decades. A wholly American creation, it was made possible by earlier developments in acoustic guitar design also pioneered in the New World. The most crucial of these was the introduction of steel strings on guitars by late nineteenth- and early twentieth century luthiers. Steel was louder and more durable than the gut traditionally used on European-style classical instruments; but by the 1920s, American designers were starting to exploit the metal strings' magnetic characteristics as well as their acoustic properties. By mounting pickup systems near them and feeding the electrical signals created by their vibrations to amplifiers and loudspeakers, it was possible to produce a more powerful sound than even the biggest or most ingeniously designed acoustic instrument could create. In fact, a conventional, hollow wooden body was not strictly necessary at all – as George Beauchamp and Adolph Rickenbacker were soon to demonstrate with solid bodied guitars like the famous "Frying Pan."

Inevitably, the electric guitar generated a certain amount of initial resistance. Classical purists were quick to dismiss it as barbarous and offensive; and the great Spanish guitarist Andrés Segovia (1893–1987) allegedly branded it "an abomination." But as the 1930s progressed, a growing number of American players took up the amplified instrument. It gave them the opportunity to become true front-line soloists, trading licks with instruments that would once have overwhelmed them; and by the War years, the electric guitar had become widely accepted on the bandstand and in the recording studio.

The Early Years 1930–1945

The electric guitar as we know it emerged during the 1930s, but the principles underlying its operation had been familiar to scientists since the previous century. Discoveries about the nature of electricity and magnetism made by Danish physicist Hans Oersted (1777–1851) and his great English contemporary, Michael Faraday (1791–1867) led to the development of the dynamo and other major technological breakthroughs. They also inspired a number of more eccentric inventions – such as the "apparatus for producing musical sounds by electricity," patented in 1890 by a U.S. naval officer, George Breed.

In his patent specification, Breed describes a method of using magnetism and battery power to create vibrations in wire strings, and explains how his ideas may be applied to the guitar and piano. Instruments using his system required extensive modifications. The guitar shown in the diagram is fitted with a magnet, supported by a brace inside the body. Its strings pass between the poles of the magnet and across a metal bridge, which is wired to a rough-edged conducting wheel housed in a box at the tailpiece. This wheel, turned by a small clockwork motor, is connected, via a contact-spring, to a battery. The other side of the circuit comprises an electrical link between the battery and the instrument's frets, which are wired together.

When the player presses a string against a fret, the circuit is completed. A voltage from the battery passes to the contact-spring; the spinning conducting wheel, brushing against it, causes interruptions in the flow of electricity, creating a charge that is then introduced, via the bridge, into the magnetic field surrounding the strings. This makes the fretted string vibrate, sounding the selected note.

Breed's cumbersome, impractical guitar can have had little appeal to players, who would have been obliged to adapt their technique to master it, as no picking or strumming was possible. However, his instrument appears to be the first documented example of a guitar using electromagnetism, and some of its features – especially the "wrap-around" design for the string magnet – seem to anticipate the work of later pioneers like those discussed in the following pages.

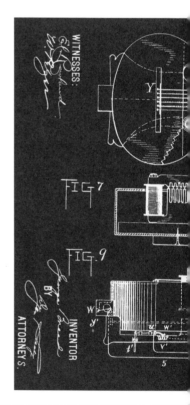

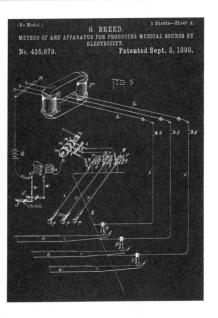

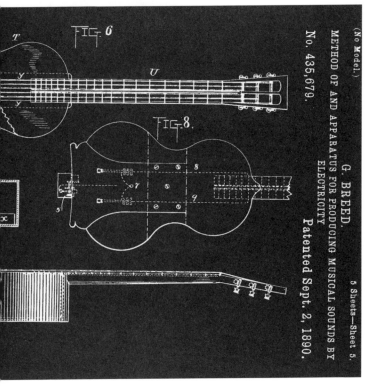

Left and below: Drawings of George Breed's experimental guitar, showing the large magnet around the strings, the clockwork wheel used to create the charge needed to make them vibrate (this is mounted in the box attached to the guitar's base) and details of the wiring.
(Courtesy U.S. Patent and Trademark Office, Washington D.C., and Rickenbacker International Corporation)

George Beauchamp and the "Frying Pan"

The strings of George Breed's guitar were activated by electricity and magnetism, although the instrument still relied on a standard acoustic body to reflect and enhance its sound. But new technology soon opened up more radical possibilities. In 1907, Lee DeForest, invented the triode, a vacuum tube capable of amplifying weak electrical signals, and this component, which provided an output strong enough to be fed to a loudspeaker, later became a key part of the circuitry used in radios and phonographs. The possibilities of electronic amplification also attracted the attention of guitar makers and players seeking to boost the volume

Below: Ro-Pat-In/Electro "Frying Pan" Hawaiian guitar. This is the original prototype model, carved from a single piece of maple by an ex-National employee, Harry Watson (production "Frying Pans" were made of aluminum) and featuring George Beauchamp's innovative pickup design, for which he was granted a U.S. patent in 1937.
(Courtesy Rickenbacker International Corporation)

of their instruments, and by the late 1920s, a few far-sighted designers were working on prototype guitars which were fitted with magnetic pickups, and intended to be connected to amplifier and speaker units.

Among them was George Beauchamp (d.1940), a vaudeville guitarist and co-founder of National Corporation, which was set up in California in 1928 to produce John Dopyera's tri-cone resonator guitars, the most powerful-sounding acoustics on the market. Beauchamp's time at National was stormy, and he was eventually ousted from the board of directors; but since well before his ▶

Below: The "Frying Pan's" headstock shows no company name or decal. Some early production models had "Electro" engraved on them, and later, the familiar "Rickenbacher Electro" nameplate (see pages 22-23) was used.
(Courtesy Rickenbacker International Corporation)

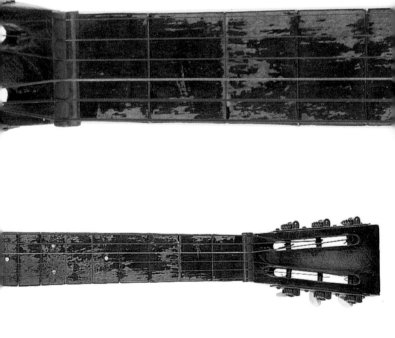

departure, he had been developing his own design for an electric guitar pickup. Its strings passed through two horseshoe-shaped magnets surrounding a coil wrapped around a core plate. The coil assembly was mounted below the strings, and when these were struck, they created a disturbance in the magnetic field around them; this was converted to a current by the coil and fed via an external amplifier to a loudspeaker.

This pickup became the basis for the first mass-produced electric guitar, a Hawaiian model nicknamed the "Frying Pan." To manufacture the instrument, Beauchamp and his supporters formed the Ro-Pat-In Corporation in 1931 (the company's odd name has never been explained). Based in Los Angeles, its directors included Beauchamp, Paul Barth (who

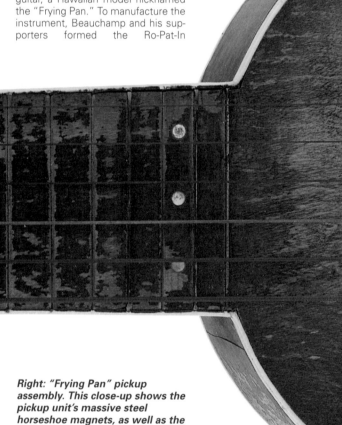

Right: "Frying Pan" pickup assembly. This close-up shows the pickup unit's massive steel horseshoe magnets, as well as the guitar's bridge and (beneath the left-hand magnet) the two screw terminals for the amplifier lead. Later models were fitted with a conventional jack socket.
(Courtesy Rickenbacker International Corporation)

collaborated on the pickup design), and Adolph Rickenbacker – a wealthy, innovative engineer who had manufactured steel bodies and resonators for National, and who was soon to play a crucial role in the subsequent development of the electric guitar industry.

Lloyd Loar and Vivi-Tone

Ro-Pat-In's early models sold slowly, and for some time, other makers remained skeptical about the potential demand for electric instruments. Such conservative attitudes were understandable, particularly at companies such as Gibson, that already had extensive, successful ranges of fretted instruments, and were reluctant to devote time and money to what many players and luthiers still regarded as a gimmick.

However, not everyone at Gibson shared this cautious attitude. Lloyd Loar (1886–1943) had come to work at the firm's headquarters in Kalamazoo, Michigan, in 1919, and was responsible for the design of its highly acclaimed L-5 archtop acoustic guitar, which was launched in 1922. Subsequently, Loar turned his attention to amplified instruments, developing an electric viola and an electric bass in his workshop at Gibson. Unfortunately, the company's management decided not to market them, and in 1924 Loar resigned to pursue his ideas by himself. He eventually set up the Vivi-Tone Company in 1933, making guitars,

Below and right: Vivi-Tone guitar, 1933. This design, made by musician, engineer, university teacher and former Gibson designer Lloyd Loar, was in production for little more than a year. Its innovative features (including the unusual pickup assembly mounted beneath the bridge) were patented by Loar in 1934.
(Courtesy Rick Turner)

mandolins, and (later) an electric keyboard – although his designs brought him little commercial success.

The Vivi-Tone guitar shown here was presented by Loar to his friend Carl Christiansen, and has several remarkable features. The vibrations of its strings are passed from the bridge, via two steel screws, to a steel plate (clamped at one end and floating at the other) with a magnetic pickup mounted below it in a drawer-like compartment. The top of the guitar has no sound-holes, but its back has small f-holes, and is recessed about half an inch (1.27cm) into the body.

American luthier Rick Turner, who owns the instrument, explains that Loar thought of the back as a secondary soundboard – an idea that is currently in favor with a number of modern classical guitar makers. Having played the Vivi-Tone through an amplifier, Rick says that its sound is disappointing, although this may be due to deterioration of some of the internal rubber parts. He suggests that renewing these might be "like putting fresh tires on an old Jaguar," and adds that restoring the guitar could make a great retirement project for him!

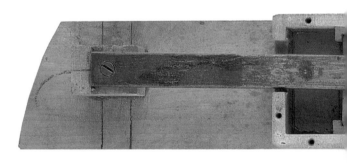

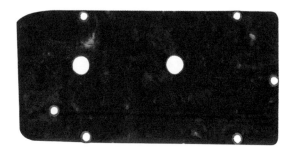

Above: The metal plate that
transfers the string vibrations from
the bridge.

Above: Vivi-Tone – pickup assembly.
This wooden compartment contains
the magnet, coil and pole-piece for
the pickup.

Left: Vivi-Tone – rear view. The
back of the instrument is slightly
recessed, and has small f-holes
carved into it.
(All photographs courtesy Rick
Turner)

Gibson's First Electric Guitars

In the 1920s, Gibson had ignored Lloyd Loar's urgings to introduce electric instruments, and it delayed its entry into the new market until 1936 – 12 years after his departure from the company. Gibson's first electric guitar was a Hawaiian model, the EH-150, which sold for $150 including a matching amplifier, and appeared that January. A few months later Gibson announced an archtop "Electric Spanish" guitar with the same serial number: the ES-150.

By the mid-1930s, Gibson's most popular acoustic archtops (including the L-5, L-7, and L-12) all had 17-inch (43.2cm) bodies, and in 1934 the company had brought out its top-of-the-range Super 400, which was 18 inches (45.7cm) wide. At just over 16 inches (40.6cm), the new ES-150 is more modestly sized, and altogether less visually striking than its more finely finished acoustic counterparts. Perhaps its most remarkable feature is its pickup, an ingenious design by Gibson's Walter Fuller: the unit's bulky magnets are hidden beneath the guitar's spruce top, leaving only the blade-shaped polepiece, the coil cover and the three mounting and adjusting screws visible. The instrument "plugs in" unobtrusively via a jack socket mounted in the tailpiece.

The ES-150 and its pickup are most closely associated with the brilliant jazzman Charlie Christian.

Right: Charlie Christian playing his Gibson ES-150. On the right is the great jazz drummer Gene Krupa (1909–1973), also a member of the Benny Goodman band during the 1930s.
(Courtesy Christian Him's Jazz Index Photo Library)

Left: Gibson ES-150, 1937. The ES-150's top, fitted with X-braces, like the guitars in Gibson's acoustic archtop range, is made from spruce; the back and sides are maple. The Gibson ES-150 is relatively plain and unadorned – when it was first introduced in 1936, it sold for just $72.50.
(Courtesy Lloyd Chiate, Voltage Guitars, Hollywood)

(1916–1942), whose interest in electric guitars was kindled when he met Eddie Durham (1906–1987) – probably the first major jazz player to use an amplified guitar on stage and on record – in the mid-1930s. Soon afterwards, Christian acquired one of the new Gibson models, and in 1939, he shot to fame as a member of the Benny Goodman band, where he pioneered the single-string, saxophone-like soloing style that helped to establish the electric guitar as a front-line jazz instrument. His high-profile use of the ES-150 influenced many other important artists – including his friend and sometime pupil T-Bone Walker (1910–1975) – to play it.

Gibson responded to the success of its first electric archtop by introducing a more finely decorated, 17-inch model, the ES-250, in 1939; this too was used and endorsed by Charlie Christian. Another new guitar, the ES-300, with its distinctive slanting pickup, appeared a year later, and is shown opposite.

Electro:
The Pre-War Years

Ro-Pat-In launched its aluminum "Frying Pan" Hawaiian guitar in 1932; later the same year, it brought out a wooden-bodied "Spanish" model that also used George Beauchamp's "horseshoe" pickup. Both guitars appeared under the "Electro" brand name; in 1934, Beauchamp, Adolph Rickenbacker, and Paul Barth rechristened their company the Electro String Instrument Corporation, and added the Rickenbacker name (misspelt as "Rickenbacher" – see caption on page 269) to their headstock decals.

For the rest of the decade, Electro continued to develop and innovate, introducing Hawaiian and Spanish guitars made of Bakelite, combo amplifiers, and some strikingly futuristic electric violins and basses constructed using plastics and aluminum. The company's wooden instruments often ▶

*Right: Rickenbacker lap-steel, pre-World War II. This chrome-decorated Bakelite Hawaiian guitar has undergone some modifications (including the addition of a Vibrola vibrato unit), but its pre-war status is confirmed by the 1½-inch (3.8cm) width of its pickup magnet. When large-scale production of Rickenbackers resumed in 1946, the size of their magnets was reduced to 1¼ inches (3.2cm). The company also produced seven-, eight- and ten-string lap steels, as well as double-neck models.
(Courtesy Elderly Instruments: photograph by Dave Matchette)*

Left: Gibson ES-300, 1940. Like the ES-250, the 300's body was 17 inches (43.2cm) wide. Its angled pickup provided a brighter tone on the higher strings; post-war models were fitted with a standard-shaped transducer. The instrument's finish, with double parallelogram fingerboard inlays, and a headstock decorated with a crown (soon to become a

familiar feature on later Gibson models), was considerably more elaborate than the cheaper ES-150's.
(Courtesy Elderly Instruments: photograph by Dave Matchette)

had bodies sourced from other manufacturers. The Harmony Company of Chicago built the body for the original 1932 Electro Spanish, and the guitar shown opposite, a rare instrument without a serial number dating from 1937, has a body made by Kay.

The manufacture of products such as the Bakelite lap-steel (also illustrated here) drew on Adolph Rickenbacker's prodigious engineering skills. For a while, he had worked alongside the Belgian-born inventor of Bakelite, L.H. Baekeland (1863–1944); and his later industrial experience included a spell at Hotpoint, where he pioneered advanced injection molding techniques, solving the long-standing problem of sticking and breakage within the mold by the addition of a well-known brand of scouring powder to the plastic mix! John C. Hall, Rickenbacker's present Chairman and CEO, acknowledges the importance of Adolph's technical ability to Electro's success: "If you look back at [his] use of materials, it's quite extraordinary what he achieved." However, Mr. Hall believes that ultimately, the founder's greatest contribution to his firm was probably financial: "He was a pretty wealthy guy, and more than anything, it was his cash that kept National and later Rickenbacker going."

In 1940, George Beauchamp resigned from Electro due to ill health, and died later that year. Adolph Rickenbacker maintained the company's instrument production until 1942, when the Electro factory was obliged to take up war-related work; but in the post-war years, the company would soon resume its major role on the guitar scene.

Right: Rickenbacker archtop, 1937. Only two examples of this model exist at Rickenbacker's headquarters in Santa Ana: this instrument has a body by the Chicago guitar-maker Kay, and the other guitar's body was built by Harmony. Both feature the same distinctive Beauchamp-style pickup assembly.
(Courtesy Rickenbacker International Corporation)

Above: The spelling of "Rickenbacher" (with an "h") on the decal is a misprint that appears on a number of other guitars and amps made by the company from the 1930s until the early 1950s – but not on its printed publicity material. Adolph Rickenbacker anglicized the spelling of his name before 1920, and always signed it with a "k" thereafter.

Left: Rickenbacker combo amplifier, 1930s. Early models like these were often sold with a specific instrument as a "set."
(Courtesy Rickenbacker International Corporation)

*Above and right: Gibson Les Paul
Standard, 1958. An early example
of this classic model, dating from
the year of its introduction. Pre-
1960 Standards are among the
most desirable and valuable of all
Gibson solid electrics.*
(Courtesy Mark Knopfler)

SECTION TWO

The Classic Designs

During the war years, the manufacture of "non-essential" goods was strictly limited, and American instrument makers were obliged to focus much of their energy and manpower on defense-related work. With the end of hostilities, guitar production was scaled up again, but it soon became clear that the market had changed. Demand for electric instruments was outstripping acoustic sales, and long-established companies such as Gibson – whose output in the immediate post-war years was still dominated by labor- and cost-intensive acoustic archtop models – had to adapt quickly to the new situation. Significantly, one of the first innovations introduced by the firm's new General Manager (later its President), Ted McCarty (b.1909), when he took over in 1948, was the introduction of a detachable pickup unit that could "electrify" archtops without extensive modification. Later, McCarty was to preside over Gibson's "golden years" of modernization and expansion – as well as supervising the introduction of its most famous solid-body model, the Les Paul, in 1952.

By contrast, former radio repair man Leo Fender (1909–1991) and his small, California-based company, were relative newcomers to guitar manufacture. Leo himself was not a "traditional" luthier, but a skilled engineer with a firm grounding in practical electronics. His basic, functional solid-body instruments were easy to mass-produce and maintain, with pickup assemblies that simply slotted into place, and necks that could be removed by unscrewing just four bolts. The Fender Telecaster (1950) and Stratocaster (1954) rapidly became accepted as classics, and are perhaps the most profoundly influential of all electric guitar designs.

While Fender and Gibson set the pace for the industry throughout the 1950s and early 1960s, a considerable number of other makers were also catering for the electric guitar boom. This section features a broad cross-section of their instruments, from the exclusive Gretsch White Falcon, with its gold-leaf finish and $600 price tag, to the inexpensive but brilliantly designed hardboard-bodied guitars of Nathan Daniel.

The Solid-Body Electric 1946–1965

In the post-war years, California retained its pre-eminence as a center for electric guitar development. In fact, a number of the main figures in the evolution of the instrument were friends, associates or rivals living within a few miles of the town of Fullerton, just east of Los Angeles. Its residents included Clayton O. Kauffman (known as "Doc"), who developed the Vibrola vibrato unit used on many Rickenbacker guitars; during the mid-1940s Kauffman had a brief business partnership with Leo Fender, making instruments and amplifiers under the K & F brand name at Fender's radio shop in downtown Fullerton. Later

Fender amps and guitars were distributed by F.C. Hall, a businessman and engineer based in nearby Santa Ana. In 1953, Hall bought Adolph Rickenbacker's Electro String Company, re-named it after its founder, and played a central role in its subsequent international success.

A short distance away, in the Los Angeles suburb of Downey, lived Paul Bigsby, a guitar builder, repairer and machinist who was also an expert on motorcycles. It was probably a mutual enthusiasm for bikes that led to his friendship with the famous country guitar player Merle Travis (1917–1983), who had settled in Los Angeles after the war, and was working with Western ▶

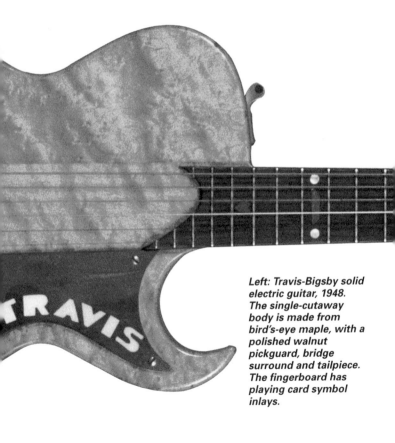

Left: Travis-Bigsby solid electric guitar, 1948. The single-cutaway body is made from bird's-eye maple, with a polished walnut pickguard, bridge surround and tailpiece. The fingerboard has playing card symbol inlays.

Swing bands fronted by Cliffie Stone and Ray Whitley. In 1948, Travis commissioned a solid-bodied electric from Bigsby, and the resultant instrument had several unusual features. All six tuning machines were fitted onto one side of a distinctively carved headstock, and the neck was not glued or bolted at the heel, but extended right through the maple body, whose elegant single cutaway and striking finish made the "Travis-Bigsby" a guitar to remember.

Travis subsequently claimed that the instrument caught Leo Fender's eye at a Cliffie Stone concert in Placentia (only a few miles from Fullerton), that Fender was allowed to borrow it, and that key aspects of its design were later incorporated into Fender's own guitars. Fender denied ever borrowing the Travis-Bigsby, and although the instrument has a few superficial similarities with his famous later models, it seems unlikely that it especially influenced him.

Below: The shape of the headstock (below) and the positioning of the tuning machines are two of the major similarities between the Travis-Bigsby and Leo Fender's guitars. However, such designs were in use in Europe over a century earlier, and are also found on some of the first acoustics made by the Martin company in Nazareth, Pennsylvania. Paul Bigsby later became famous for creating the guitar vibrato that bears his name.

Leo Fender's Early Designs

Leo Fender made his first guitar in 1943, when he and Doc Kauffman collaborated on a crude instrument built from a single block of wood with a bought-in fingerboard attached. It was used as a test-bed for a prototype pickup the two men had developed – a design in which the strings pass through the device's coil, not over it as in conventional designs. This "Direct Sound" pickup subsequently featured on Leo and Doc's "K & F" lap steels, which went into production in 1945. By early 1946, their fledgling company was making about 40 instruments a week, often sold as "sets" with matching K & F amplifiers.

It was at this stage that Fender and Kauffman attracted the attention of Don Randall, the manager of a Santa Ana-based electronic component distribution company, Radio-Tel, owned by local businessman F.C. Hall (see earlier, page 273). Randall ▶

Right: Fender Champion 600 combo amplifier, c.1949. This was the smallest amplifier in the Fender range, fitted with a single 6-inch (15.2cm) loudspeaker, and designed for student or practice use. The Champion 600 was introduced in 1949 as a companion to Fender's "Champion" range of lap steels, and renamed "Champ" in the early 1950s. The example shown here has lost its leather carrying handle, but is still in full working order after 50 years – a tribute to the "extremely rugged construction" mentioned in the original publicity for the amp. (Courtesy Real Guitars, San Francisco)

saw considerable potential in K & F, and persuaded his boss to offer them an exclusive distribution deal. Inevitably, this would have involved the two guitar-makers in considerable expansion; but while Leo Fender was excited by the prospect, Doc Kauff-man did not share his enthusiasm. According to one of Fender's closest associates, Forrest White, in his book *Fender: The Inside Story*, "Doc was apprehensive about investing more money in this as yet unproven venture. Leo said, 'Doc was scared because had a little real estate in Oklahoma which he didn't want to lose, so rather than take the risk, he left.'" However, the dissolution of the K & F partnership was an amicable one, and Leo Fender and Doc Kauffman remained close friends until Doc's death in 1990.

Leo went ahead with the Radio-Tel venture, setting up the Fender Electric Instrument Company in 1946, and developing and manufacturing an extensive range of lap steels and amplifiers over the next few years. But despite the sales deal, his firm had serious financial difficulties. It took the introduction of a revolutionary new product – Leo's mass-produced, solid electric guitar, designed, unlike his lap steels, for the regular "Spanish-style" player – to ensure Fender's survival, as well as its place in history.

Below and right: Leo Fender/Doc Kauffman prototype guitar, 1943. Despite its shape, this is actually a standard "Spanish-style" guitar, not a lap steel. According to Leo Fender, it was hired out to various musicians for concerts during the 1940s – although it cannot have been very easy or comfortable to play. The prototype of 1943 is fitted with a Fender/Kauffman "Direct Sound" pickup (patented in 1948), whose volume and tone control wheels are visible (above right) on either side of the strings. Leo Fender presented the guitar to the Roy Acuff Museum in Nashville, Tennessee in 1965.
(Photograph courtesy John Peden, New York)

From "Standard Electric" to Telecaster

Unlike previous solid wood "electric Spanish" models, the guitar that Fender began to develop in 1949 was specifically conceived as a factory-made instrument, and intended to be as cheap and easy as possible to manufacture and repair. It had a basic, single-cutaway body shape and a bolted-on, detachable neck, as well as two important innovations: a new pickup with individual pole-pieces for each string, and an adjustable bridge to ensure better intonation.

By the end of 1949 two prototypes of the "Standard Electric," as the instrument was initially known, had been made; it was only on the second of these that Leo introduced his soon-to-be famous headstock with all six tuning machines on one side. In Spring 1950, the new model was formally announced by Fender and Radio-Tel; it was renamed the Esquire, and displayed for the first time at that year's National Association of Music Merchants (NAMM) show in Chicago.

Right: Fender "No-caster," 1951. For a short period between Gretsch's complaint and the decision to rechristen its new guitar "Telecaster," Fender simply removed the word "Broadcaster" from the headstock decals (see inset on page 281) – hence the curious nickname for this model. There are few other significant differences between "No-casters" and

Broadcasters. On this example, the bridge/pickup assembly is fitted with a removable metal cover; an accessory (also supplied with later Telecasters) designed to shield the pickup from interference and damage. Most guitarists find it inhibits their playing, and either discard it or use it as an ashtray!
(Courtesy Lloyd Chiate, Voltage Guitars, Hollywood)

Left: Fender Broadcaster, c.1950. This instrument (serial number 0053) was made between the end of 1950 and February 1951, when an accusation of trademark violation from Gretsch forced Fender to change the name of its new model. It is owned by David Gilmour of Pink Floyd. (Courtesy David Gilmour)

279

Many of the earliest Esquires shown to dealers during the following weeks had warped necks, and Don Randall of Radio-Tel urged Fender to remedy this defect by installing metal truss-rods on the instruments. Meanwhile, Leo himself was planning a more fundamental change: the addition of a second pickup, fitted in the neck position. This was incorporated, along with the truss-rod, on the first production run of his new guitar in late 1950.

The extra pickup caused some concern among the sales force, which had been promoting a single-pickup instrument. The solution was to rename the modified two-pickup guitar the Broadcaster (although a number of two-pickup Esquires were also sold) and to delay the introduction of the single-pickup Esquire until the following year. Another snag also befell the new model; in February 1951, the New York-based Gretsch Company complained that the "Broadcaster" name infringed the "Broadkaster" trademark used on Gretsch's drumkits and banjos. Fender's initial response was to remove the word "Broadcaster" from its headstocks, but soon afterwards, it came up with yet another name for its two-pickup electric Spanish guitar: the Telecaster.

Above: Two near-identical headstocks – the Fender No-Caster and the Fender Telecaster – show the omission that earned the former its nickname.

Left: Fender Telecaster, 1952. By 1952, the Telecaster, now selling at $189.50, was becoming an increasingly familiar sight on bandstands throughout the USA. The previous year, Leo Fender had been granted a patent for his revolutionary design. The "butterscotch" finish and black pickguard seen on all the instruments shown here were the only standard color schemes initially available.
(Courtesy Guitar Showcase, San Jose)

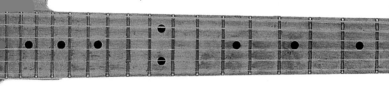

Like the other guitars on the previous pages and here, the Fender Broadcaster has an ash body, and a maple neck with a truss-rod fitted. The bridge allows pairs of strings to be adjusted for length and height, and the nearby "back" pickup (angled to give a cutting treble tone while also preserving lower-frequency response) can be raised and lowered to optimize its output level and sound. The Broadcaster was introduced at a retail price of $169.95.
(Courtesy David Gilmour)

The "Pre-CBS" Telecaster

The Fender Telecaster is a classic design, which has inspired and delighted guitar players for decades. Its appearance and shape have altered relatively little since its introduction – although more fundamental modifications have been made to its internal circuitry. These began as early as 1952, when Leo Fender made an important change to the pickup wiring.

Fender targetted the Broadcaster /Telecaster at the busy professional player of the early 1950s, who would want to take solos, provide rhythm accompaniment, and sometimes even pick out bass lines on his instrument. Accordingly, the original

Tele offered three basic sounds, selected by the switch on the right of the strings: a "rhythm guitar" tone from the neck (or "front") pickup; a bassy timbre created by passing the front pickup signal through a special pre-set circuit; and a harder, more cutting "lead" tone from the back (bridge) pickup, which could be blended with the front pickup by adjusting the lower of the instrument's two knobs (the upper one is a volume control). The 1952 modification removed the "blend" function, substituting a conventional tone control. This meant that players could no longer combine the front and back pickups, and it was not until 1967 that

Right: Fender Telecaster, 1959. This guitar is finished in fiesta red – one of the "custom colors" offered by Fender to Telecaster purchasers. Bright, primary colors were not initially very popular, but soon caught

on in the 1960s. By the time of the CBS takeover, possible options included foam green, candy apple red and daphne blue, as well as sunburst, black, and the original blond. (Courtesy San Diego Guitars)

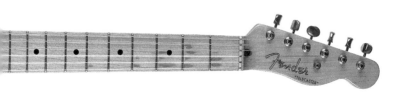

Left: Fender Telecaster, 1954. This example was one of the last 1954 Telecasters to be fitted with a black pickguard. Despite the launch of Fender's three-pickup Stratocaster in Spring '54, Tele sales continued to flourish; the following year, the company's Head of Sales, Don Randall, commented in Down Beat magazine that "Fender is having a hard time keeping up with demand for electric guitars".
(Courtesy Mark Knopfler)

the instrument was reconfigured in its "modern" form, offering a choice of front, back, or front and back pickups. At this time, the "bassy" circuit was finally abandoned; thanks to the popularity of the bass guitar – another Fender invention – it had become an anachronism.

Between 1951 and 1965 (the date when Leo Fender sold his company to CBS; see later, page 360) several changes were made to the Telecaster's neck shape, and in 1959 the original all-maple neck was replaced by one with a rosewood fingerboard. There were also cosmetic changes to the instrument; a white pickguard was introduced in 1954, and soon afterwards, alternative body finishes began to be offered (at a five percent surcharge) – at first in any color of the player's choice, and later, in a range of specified "custom colors." A mahogany-bodied Telecaster was introduced in 1963, but discontinued two years later.

The Stratocaster – Another First for Fender

Leo Fender was not a man to rest on his laurels, and after launching the Telecaster and Esquire, he quickly turned his attention to new projects. His groundbreaking Precision Bass Guitar appeared in 1951, and his next "electric Spanish" design, the Fender Stratocaster, has proved to be one of the most innovative (and widely copied) instruments of all time.

The "Stratocaster" name, with its image of high-flying modernity, was probably coined by Don Randall, previously General Manager at Radio-Tel, and then President of Fender Sales Inc., which took over distribution of Fender products in 1953. As Randall explains in Richard R. Smith's book *Fender: The Sound Heard 'Round the World*, "The Stratocaster's introduction was market driven. And without minimising Leo's invention, it was a ▶

Left: Fender Telecaster, 1965. Leo Fender sold his company to CBS in January 1965, but it was some time before the new owners made any changes to the design of their products. This superb 1965 guitar has the same overall specification as a "pre-CBS" instrument.
(Courtesy Lloyd Chiate, Voltage Guitars, Hollywood)

Below: Fender Stratocaster, 1957. In 1956, according to guitar expert A.R. Duchossoir, Fender started using alder instead of ash for Stratocaster bodies, although no changes were made to their size or contours. The model shown here has its rarely seen metal bridge cover attached. The Strat's "synchronized tremolo" bridge was a major selling point; however, not all players favor vibratos, and the unit's controlling arm can easily be unscrewed and removed, as it has been here.
(Courtesy Room 335, Rose-Morris, London)

composite of ideas from many players." Customer feedback from Telecaster owners had revealed some areas of dissatisfaction, especially with the instrument's body, which some of them found bulky and awkward. Meanwhile, other man-ufacturers were busily introducing rival solid guitars, and Fender needed an innovative new model of its own.

The response from Leo and his team was to create a radically different double cutaway shape for the Stratocaster, with "comfort contouring" on the back and at the point where the player rests his or her picking arm. The "Strat" would also have three pickups, and a patented vibrato system ("tremolo" in Fender nomenclature) combined with an innovative bridge setup allowing all six strings to be adjusted separately for length and height. (This addressed another weakness in the Telecaster, whose double bridge saddles did not permit precise intonation.) Among the Fender staffers who contributed to the design were Freddie Tavares, a skilled musician and craftsman who joined Fender in 1953, and George Fullerton, who had worked with Leo since 1948, and subsequently became his business partner and one of his closest friends.

The Stratocaster was introduced in 1954 with a fanfare of publicity, proclaiming it "years ahead in design – unequalled in performance." This judgment would quickly be echoed by its first players, including leading names from country music, blues and – a little later – rock and roll.

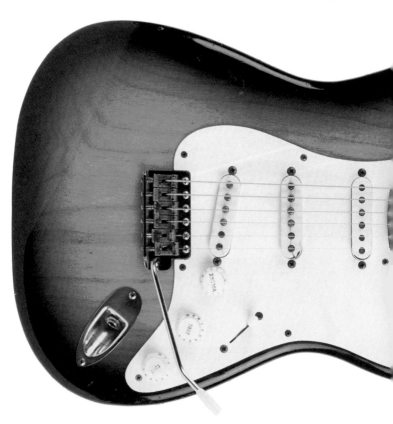

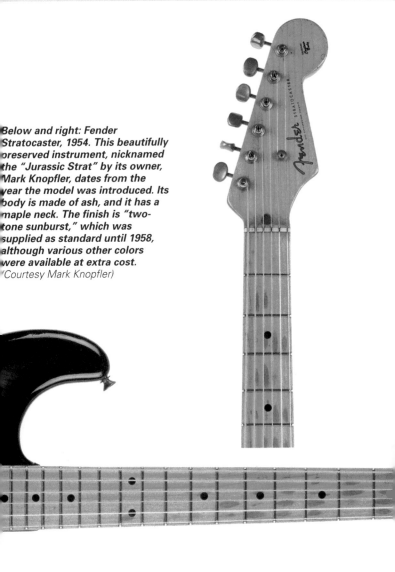

Below and right: Fender Stratocaster, 1954. This beautifully preserved instrument, nicknamed the "Jurassic Strat" by its owner, Mark Knopfler, dates from the year the model was introduced. Its body is made of ash, and it has a maple neck. The finish is "two-tone sunburst," which was supplied as standard until 1958, although various other colors were available at extra cost. (Courtesy Mark Knopfler)

The "Pre-CBS" Stratocaster

The first Stratocasters were sold for $249.50 (with tremolo) and $229.50 (without it). Like the Telecaster, the original Strat had an ash body and an all-maple neck; this was replaced in 1959 by a maple model with a rosewood fingerboard. The guitar was given a sunburst finish as standard, with custom colors, and eventually a range of Fender's "standardized" optional finishes, available at extra cost. In 1957, a deluxe Strat with gold-plated hardware was launched; confusingly, this good-looking model had a "Blond" finish of the kind that was standard on the Telecaster and Esquire.

Fender's "years ahead in design" claim for the Strat was certainly justified; in fact, some of the instrument's musical possibilities were not fully exploited until over a decade after its appearance. The tremolo/bridge unit, developed especially for the guitar and patented by Leo Fender in 1956, was able to produce much more dramatic effects than the gentle pitch fluctuations favored by most early Strat players. Unlike some other vibratos, it was able to keep the strings fairly well in tune after being used, and this encouraged a more extreme use of its capabilities by 1960s and '70s musicians, notably Jimi Hendrix.

There was also more to the Strat's electronics than may have been intended by its designer. The pickups

Below: Fender Stratocaster, 1961. From Buddy Holly onwards, the Strat has been associated with many major names in pop and rock music. This "fiesta red" *model belongs to Mark Knopfler, and is the instrument he used on his band Dire Straits' first major hit, Sultans of Swing, in 1979.* (Courtesy Mark Knopfler)

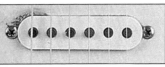

Above: The Stratocaster's pickups (like the Telecaster's) use "Alnico" (aluminum, nickel and cobalt) magnets. Their coils were given 8,300 or more turns of wire in the early years of Strat production.

Above: Fender Stratocaster, 1958/60. Another Strat with a famous owner: it was formerly the property of Alvin Lee, guitarist and singer with Ten Years After. The group's bluesy playing was one of the highlights of the 1969 Woodstock music festival, and their hits included Love Like A Man (1970). The guitar's neck dates from 1958, its body from 1960.
(Courtesy Room 335, Rose-Morris, London)

were selected by a three-position switch, below which were three knobs: an overall volume control, and individual tone controls for the neck and middle pickup. (The bridge pickup was wired straight to the volume knob.) When the switch was used in its three standard settings, only one pickup at a time could be activated; but guitarists soon learned how to balance it between these positions to give combinations of neck-and-middle and middle-and-bridge pickups, creating unexpected and distinctive tone-colors. Surprisingly, it was many years before Fender fitted a five-position switch to make these sounds easier to obtain.

Stratocaster sales took a brief downturn in the early 1960s, but the instrument's longer-term popularity was unaffected. Today its only serious rival as the most sought-after of all solid electric guitars is the Gibson Les Paul, the origins and development of which are featured on the following pages.

Les Paul and Gibson

L es Paul, born in 1916 in Waukesha, Wisconsin, was already a skilled guitarist by his teens. After achieving early fame as an acoustic player, he became attracted to the possibilities of the electric guitar during the 1930s. His musical abilities were paralleled by a strong interest in electronics; in the late 1940s, he was one of the first performers to use overdubbing on his recordings, and the subsequent hit singles he made with his wife, singer/guitarist Mary Ford, often featured double-tracking, "speeding-up," and other novel tape effects.

A few years earlier, the "Wizard of Waukesha's" curiosity about technology had led him to make a significant breakthrough in electric guitar design. In 1941, using facilities borrowed from the Epiphone company in New York, he constructed an experimental instrument that would later become famous as "The Log." After cutting up an old ▶

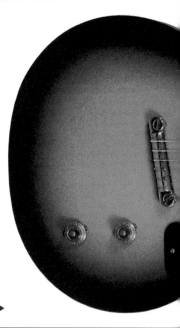

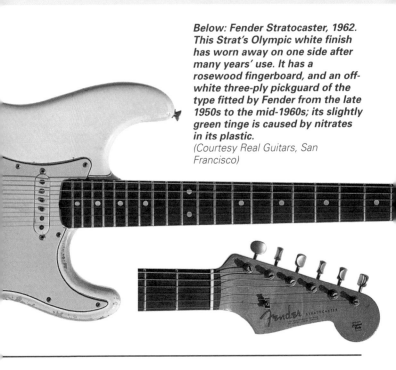

Below: Fender Stratocaster, 1962. This Strat's Olympic white finish has worn away on one side after many years' use. It has a rosewood fingerboard, and an off-white three-ply pickguard of the type fitted by Fender from the late 1950s to the mid-1960s; its slightly green tinge is caused by nitrates in its plastic.
(Courtesy Real Guitars, San Francisco)

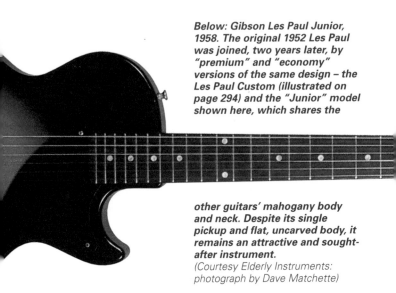

Below: Gibson Les Paul Junior, 1958. The original 1952 Les Paul was joined, two years later, by "premium" and "economy" versions of the same design – the Les Paul Custom (illustrated on page 294) and the "Junior" model shown here, which shares the

other guitars' mahogany body and neck. Despite its single pickup and flat, uncarved body, it remains an attractive and sought-after instrument.
(Courtesy Elderly Instruments: photograph by Dave Matchette)

Epiphone archtop body, he reassembled it with a slab of solid pine in its center. This block of wood carried two home-made pickups, a bridge and a vibrato tailpiece, and the guitar was completed with an old Gibson neck and fingerboard. "The Log" proved to have remarkable sustain, and was also impervious to the acoustic feedback that dogged many hollow-body electrics; but despite Les Paul's efforts in the following years, he was unable to persuade anyone to manufacture it commercially.

By the early 1950s, however, the industry was more receptive to the idea of solid guitars. Foremost among the leading manufacturers eagerly developing rivals to the Fender Telecaster was Gibson, with a carved-top prototype solid that the company's President, Ted McCarty, showed to Les Paul – then at the height of his fame as a recording artist – in about 1951. The exact role that Les played in the guitar's evolution is a matter of debate (he has always maintained that it was entirely his brainchild), although he was certainly responsible for the original tailpiece, and had some input into later modifications. He also agreed to endorse the guitar, and the Gibson Les Paul went on sale in 1952 priced $210.

Right: Les Paul pictured with "The Log" – the remarkable instrument put together by the great guitarist to explore the possibilities of solid body design. It is now on display at the Country Music Hall of Fame in Nashville.
(Photograph Courtesy Jon Sievert, San Francisco)

*Below: Gibson Les Paul, 1952. This "gold-top" model is
the earliest version of the Les Paul. It has two Gibson P-90
pickups (often nicknamed "soapbars" because of their
shape) and a trapeze-style bridge/tailpiece designed by
Les Paul himself. As on most Gibson electric guitars, the
pickups on the Gibson Les Paul "gold top" have individual
volume and tone controls, and are selected by the switch
on the top left of the body.*
(Courtesy Guitar Showcase, San Jose)

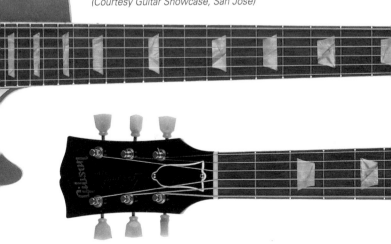

The Evolution of the Gibson Les Paul

Unlike the Fender Telecaster and Stratocaster, the Gibson Les Paul underwent substantial changes to its hardware and electronics throughout the 1950s. Ironically, the first of these was the removal of the trapeze bridge/tailpiece that had been Les Paul's major contribution to the design. In 1953, it was replaced with a simpler "stud" or "stop" bridge/tailpiece attached directly to the top of the guitar. The following year, Gibson introduced its "Tune-O-Matic" bridge, invented and patented by Ted McCarty, and allowing individual string adjustment; this was incorporated onto a new model, the

all-black Les Paul Custom, and subsequently fitted to the original instrument (which was later named the Les Paul Standard).

Gibson then launched another pair of Les Pauls; in contrast to their predecessors, the "Junior" (1954) and "Special" (1955) had flat, uncarved tops, but retained the simple "stop" bridge/tailpiece. The Junior had a single pickup, while the Special featured two.

The next and most important alteration was to the pickups on the two top-of-the-line models. The Les Paul's P-90s, like all previous guitar pickups, had single coils, which can

Below: Gibson Les Paul Custom, 1959. The Les Paul Custom, nicknamed the Black Beauty because of its finish, was introduced in 1954
(Courtesy Lloyd Chiate, Voltage Guitars, Hollywood)

Above: Gibson Les Paul Special, 1956. This two pickup Les Paul (fitted with black-covered "soapbar" P-90s) has a so-called "TV" or "limed mahogany" finish. The origins of the "TV" name are uncertain; it has been suggested that the instrument's color scheme was designed to stand out on black-and-white television. The guitar has a flat top and a straightforward "stop" bridge/tailpiece.

The proliferation of Les Paul variants can be a considerable source of confusion. The "Custom" is the most expensive member of the family; the "Standard" (which evolved from the original "Les Paul Model") is the regular instrument; the "Special" model comes below it in price and features; while the "Junior" and "TV" occupy the budget end of the range.
(Courtesy San Diego Guitars)

Left: The Les Paul Custom is also known as the "Fretless Wonder" – its fret wire is wider and flatter than the type used on the original Les Paul. By the late 1950s, almost every Gibson Les Paul Custom was being fitted with three humbucking pickups, but this unusual example has only two humbuckers, although it displays all the other regular features of the model, including ultra-low fretting on its ebony fingerboard.

be affected by interference from nearby electrical equipment. In the 1930s, when the first electric guitars appeared, electricity itself was a rarer commodity, and there were fewer problems with this kind of noise. But by the 1950s, far more mains-driven appliances were in use, and buzzing and humming were often clearly audible – thanks in part to the increasingly powerful, higher-fidelity amplifiers and speakers now available to players. In 1954, Gibson engineer Seth Lover (1910–1997) began developing a guitar pickup containing two adjacent coils, wired out-of-phase with each other. This design canceled out ("bucked") stray electrical fields, while producing a richer tone and more powerful output from the strings.

In 1955, Lover submitted a patent application for his "humbucking" twin-coil pickup (it was granted four years later), and from 1957 onwards, humbuckers were fitted to Standard and Custom Les Pauls. While some players still favor the single-coil P-90s, it is Seth Lover's humbuckers that are responsible for the distinctive "Les Paul sound," familiar from countless rock and blues records. Replicas of both transducers are currently made by several specialist pickup manufacturers.

Above and below: Gibson Les Paul Standard, 1960. The original Les Paul model was officially renamed the Les Paul Standard in 1958, when its distinctive golden finish was replaced by the sunburst coloring seen here. The instrument's top is maple, with mahogany back and sides and a rosewood fingerboard.
(Courtesy Real Guitars, San Francisco)

From Les Paul to SG

In the late 1950s, Gibson decided to make radical alterations to its Les Paul guitars. The changes started with the Junior and TV models, which were relaunched with double cutaways in 1958; the Special followed suit a year later. These modified instruments retained the 1¾-inch (4.4cm) thickness of the original design, and also continued to carry Les Paul's endorsement – at least for a while. The musician's contract with Gibson was drawing to a close; over the next few years, his name gradually disappeared from the company's headstocks and catalogs,

and the "Les Paul" range was eventually given a new classification: "SG" (for "solid guitar").

The thick-bodied double cutaway design (illustrated opposite, far right) proved to be only an intermediate stage. In 1960, the Les Paul Standard was the first guitar to adopt what became known as the "classic" SG shape, with its much thinner profile and sharp-horned cutaways. The following year, this slimline style was introduced on the Custom, Special, Junior, and TV models, and the old, single cutaway Les Paul went into (temporary) retirement. However, the

Below and right: Gibson Les Paul/SG Standard, 1961. An early example of the first SG model, which still carries Les Paul's name on the headstock (bottom). It has a mahogany body, a rosewood fingerboard, and two humbucking pickups, as well as a "Tune-O-Matic" bridge and the Gibson vibrato unit described above. (Courtesy Lloyd Chiate, Voltage Guitars, Hollywood)

Standard, Junior, and Custom were not officially given the "SG" name until 1963.

SGs were intended to satisfy Gibson players who found the 1950s-style Les Pauls too heavy; but the instruments' mass had been crucial to their distinctive sustain, and the thin-bodied SGs had a very different sound. Another significant change was the inclusion of a vibrato unit on some SG models. The earliest type (seen on the 1961 Les Paul/SG Standard opposite) had a hinged arm that was pulled from side to side; this was replaced by a Vibrola unit with an up-and-down action. SG pickup configurations corresponded to those on the Les Pauls; humbuckers were used on the Standard and Custom SGs, and single-coil P-90s on the Specials and Juniors. The SG was Gibson's first attempt at a slim, streamlined solid body design, and it has retained its popularity for 40 years. Leading players who have used it include Angus Young of AC/DC, Tony Iommi of Black Sabbath, and the late Frank Zappa.

Below: Gibson SG Special, 1961. The first stage in Gibson's redesign of the Les Paul line was the introduction of this "intermediate" body shape, featuring a double cutaway but retaining the same thickness as the original Les Paul models. The Special was available in this form for about two years from 1959; in 1961 it was given the thinner, contoured SG body with its sharp-horned cutaways.
(Courtesy Mark Knopfler)

Above: Gibson SG Standard, 1964. By the time this instrument was made, Les Paul and Gibson had ended their endorsement agreement, and his name had disappeared from the SG range. The vibrato unit on the guitar is the newer up-and down model, but the pickups and overall construction remain unchanged. *(Courtesy Real Guitars, San Francisco)*

The SG Special, Melody Maker and SG Junior

Sales of the old Les Paul range had been declining in the late 1950s, but Gibson's promotional literature was upbeat about the prospects for its replacement – the "ultra-thin, hand contoured double cutaway" SG design. One advertisement described the new, distinctive shape as "an exciting new approach to the solid body guitar" and quipped that it was "a solid success with players."

In fact, SGs were fairly modest sellers, due in part to the overall shift in public tastes towards folk-style music in the first years of the decade. This was not a matter of great concern to Gibson; as a highly acclaimed manufacturer of both acoustic guitars and of electric instruments, its diversity – and sheer size – seemed to be a guarantee of its continuing success. By 1966, the company was the largest guitar maker in the world, occupying 250,000 square feet (23,225m²)of man-ufacturing space; and its output had

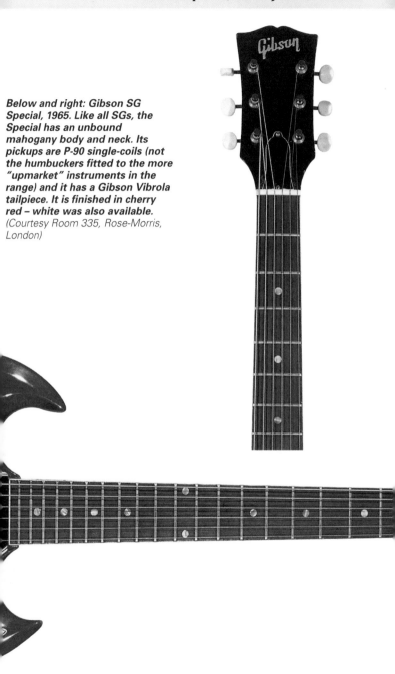

Below and right: Gibson SG Special, 1965. Like all SGs, the Special has an unbound mahogany body and neck. Its pickups are P-90 single-coils (not the humbuckers fitted to the more "upmarket" instruments in the range) and it has a Gibson Vibrola tailpiece. It is finished in cherry red – white was also available. (Courtesy Room 335, Rose-Morris, London)

expanded to include not only its own instruments, but also the less-expensive Epiphone and Kalamazoo lines. (See pages 318-321 for the history of Epiphone's assimilation by Gibson/CMI).

Gibson understood the importance of keeping its more basic models within the reach of beginners and younger players. In 1959, it launched the Melody Maker solid-body guitar, priced at only $99.50 for a single pickup version in full or 3/4 sizes (a twin pickup instrument was also available). In its original form, the Melody Maker bore a close resemblance to the Les Paul Junior (see page 291), but the example shown here dates from 1964 – two

years after the introduction of a double cutaway. In 1967, the Melody Maker underwent some more sub-stantial changes, acquiring an "SG" shape and also appearing in three-pickup and twelve-string configur-ations.

The third guitar shown here is an SG Junior – like the Melody Maker, a direct descendant of the Les Paul Junior. It acquired its SG-style body in 1961, but its electronics were essentially unchanged from its Les Paul days, with a single P-90 pickup fitted close to the bridge for a harder, punchier tone. Its vibrato, previously an additional extra, became a standard feature in 1965, and the instrument remained in production until 1971.

Right: Gibson SG Junior, 1967. This SG Junior has a single P-90 pickup, surrounded by a black plastic pickguard – a new design brought in during 1966. The SG Junior's bridge is a non-adjustable unit with factory-set string compensation, rather than the "Tune-O-Matic" type found on the SG Custom and Standard.
(Courtesy Rod & Hank's, Memphis)

Below: Gibson Melody Maker, 1964. One of the most distinctive features of the Melody Maker is its narrow headstock. This does not appear on the Les Paul Junior from which it took so many other characteristics, but can be found on the Epiphone Olympic (see pages 318-321), another Gibson-made solid introduced in 1960. The Melody Maker's single pickup was specially designed for the model, but later appeared on a number of cut-price "Kalamazoo" guitars manufactured by Gibson in the late 1960s.
(Courtesy Guitar Showcase, San Jose)

The Fender Esquire, Jazzmaster and Jaguar

In 1950, the single-pickup Esquire had been announced as Fender's first "electric Spanish" guitar (see pages 278-281); but after the company decided to launch the dual-pickup Broadcaster/Telecaster instead, the Esquire's debut was delayed until the following year. One curious result of the company's indecision over the specifications for the Esquire and Broadcaster is the presence of a routed-out space for the "missing" neck pickup on production Esquires. This cavity is concealed beneath the guitar's pickguard.

In most respects, the Esquire's design and finish are identical to the Telecaster's. It has a simplified version of the Tele tone-circuitry, with a three-position switch that can provide a preset "bassy" sound, and allow the instrument's rotary tone control to be used or bypassed. The Esquire continued in production until 1970; the model illustrated here dates from 1957.

The previous year, Fender had launched two smaller-size electric guitars aimed chiefly at beginners, the Musicmaster and Duo-Sonic; but its next premier model was the Jazzmaster, which appeared in 1958. It featured new pickups, a shape designed to fit the contours of the player's body even more snugly than the Stratocaster, and a "floating" vibrato system that could be disabled.

Right: Fender Jaguar, 1962. The Jaguar's has 24-inch (61cm) scale length (1½ inches [3.8cm] shorter than the Jazzmaster, Stratocaster, or Telecaster). Like the Jazzmaster, the Fender Jaguar features a floating vibrato and elaborate pickup switching options. It also has a string mute (positioned between the back pickup and the bridge) designed to make playing effects involving string damping easier to perform.
(Courtesy Real Guitars, San Francisco)

Left: Fender Jazzmaster, 1960. The body and headstock are finished in "daphne blue," and the pickguard is imitation tortoiseshell. The Jazzmaster's pickup controls allow the player to switch easily between *pre-set "lead" and "rhythm" tone-colors. On this instrument, the arm controlling the patented "floating" vibrato mechanism has been removed.*
(Courtesy San Diego Guitars)

with a "trem-lok" to allow easy restringing and minimize tuning problems caused by string breakages.

There were initial doubts about the Jazzmaster's look and feel. Leo Fender's friend and colleague Forrest White said that at first sight, it reminded him of "a pregnant duck," and other players were put off by its considerable weight. However, the guitar proved highly successful with 1950s and 1960s pop groups, and later with punk and New Wave artists such as Elvis Costello.

Fender's follow-up to the Jazz-master was its 1962 Jaguar model. It had many similarities to its predecessor, but was fitted with a 22-fret neck that had a shorter scale than previous full-size Fenders, and newly designed pickups incorporating notched metal screening as protection against electrical interference. It was less popular than the Jaguar, and was discontinued in 1974 – although Fender is currently producing a "reissued' version made in the Far East.

The Fender Mustang and Electric XII

The Fender Mustang, introduced in 1964, was designed as a student model. It had a 24-inch (61cm) scale length, but was also available with a 22½-inch (57.15cm) scale, like Fender's other beginners' in-struments, the Musicmaster and Duo-Sonic. Compared to them, however, the Mustang had a much more sophisticated range of features, including yet another new "floating" vibrato system, and the now-familiar sliding pickup switches offering a variety of tone settings.

While the other Fender student guitars are rarely used by serious performers, the Mustang has developed something of a cult following over the years. One of its more recent high-profile devotees was Kurt Cobain of Nirvana, who made it the basis for his "Jag-Stang" – the ▶

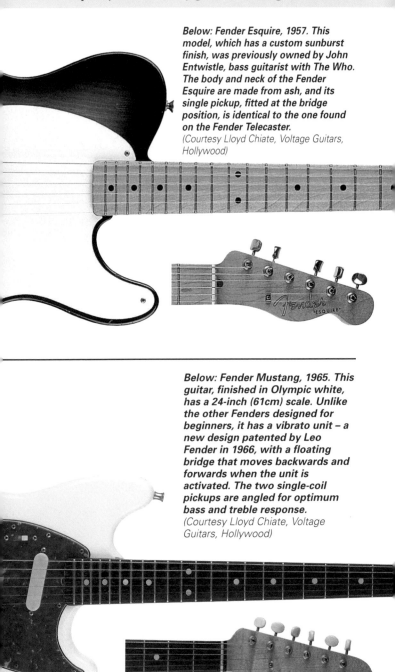

Below: Fender Esquire, 1957. This model, which has a custom sunburst finish, was previously owned by John Entwistle, bass guitarist with The Who. The body and neck of the Fender Esquire are made from ash, and its single pickup, fitted at the bridge position, is identical to the one found on the Fender Telecaster.
(Courtesy Lloyd Chiate, Voltage Guitars, Hollywood)

Below: Fender Mustang, 1965. This guitar, finished in Olympic white, has a 24-inch (61cm) scale. Unlike the other Fenders designed for beginners, it has a vibrato unit – a new design patented by Leo Fender in 1966, with a floating bridge that moves backwards and forwards when the unit is activated. The two single-coil pickups are angled for optimum bass and treble response.
(Courtesy Lloyd Chiate, Voltage Guitars, Hollywood)

custom model that he played from 1993 until his death a year later. In 1996, Fender put a replica of this unusual design into regular production, and it is featured on pages 110-111.

During 1965, The Byrds' Mr. *Tambourine Man* and *Turn, Turn, Turn*, featuring the distinctive tones of Jim McGuinn's twelve-string Rickenbacker, were making a major impact on the charts. The time was right for Fender to capitalize on the sound of the moment with its Electric XII model, which appeared that summer, but had been in development for some months before the CBS takeover in January. The new guitar's pickups were installed as two pairs of staggered units (an idea borrowed from the split-pickup configuration found on Fender's Precision basses

from 1957 onwards). The combined tension of its extra strings made the provision of a vibrato unit impracticable; but Leo Fender's elaborate bridge design ensured that intonation could be precisely adjusted. The Electric XII was not a great success and was withdrawn in 1969. More recently, Fender has introduced another solid-body twelve-string, the Venus XII (also available in a cheaper Squier version endorsed by Crispian Mills of Kula Shaker).

Over a 15-year period, Leo Fender and his team had created an astonishing range of superbly designed guitars. The background to Leo's departure from the company he founded, and the changes brought about by its new owners' more rigid managerial approach, are outlined in Chapter Four.

Right: The Electric XII's distinctive headstock inspired its affectionate nickname – "the hockey stick." A more conventional headstock shape has been used for Fender/Squier's current Venus XII model.

Below: Fender Electric XII, 1966. The Electric XII was one of the last designs developed during the "pre-CBS" days at Fender. Its pickups are switched by the black knob on the top right of the pickguard; they can be selected individually, combined, or fed through a pre-set tone-circuit. This example has a sunburst finish; blond and custom Fender colors were also available. (Courtesy Real Guitars, San Francisco)

Sears and Danelectro

Leo Fender's designs stimulated demand for the electric guitar at all levels. His "flagship" models, including the Telecaster and Stratocaster, attracted professionals and serious players, while his student instruments were priced within reach of reasonably well-heeled beginners – or their parents! But by the mid-1950s, even cheaper electric guitars and amplifiers were readily available, thanks to the buying power and marketing muscle of America's premier sales catalog company: Sears, Roebuck, and Company.

Sears had been selling musical instruments since well before World War I, and in 1954 it launched its first electric Spanish solid-bodied guitars. These carried the Sears "Silvertone"

label, but were actually made by a variety of outside contractors, including Harmony, Kay, and Nathan Daniel, an innovative New Jersey-based designer Daniel (1912–1994) had been Sears' exclusive amp manufacturer since 1948, and his company, Danelectro, also supplied equipment to a number of other leading wholesalers.

The earliest Silvertone solids had poplar bodies; Daniel produced them in single and double pickup versions, and soon afterwards began selling similar models under his own Danelectro trademark. In 1956, he changed the design and construction of his guitars. The second generation of Silvertone /Danelectros still had poplar or pine sides, necks, and bridge blocks, but for

Right: Danelectro U-2, 1957 (serial number 5047). In 1956, Nathan Daniel launched his U-1 and U-2 models – the former has a single pickup, the latter has two. They were the first of his guitars to be built using Masonite, and another unusual feature is the use, on the

U-2, of concentric volume/tone controls, with the two knobs for each pickup stacked on top of each other.
(From the collection of Doug Tulloch, City Guitar, New Bedford, MA: photograph by Doug Tulloch)

Left: Danelectro "Convertible" – early 1960s. As its name suggests, this ingenious guitar is designed to be equally suitable for electric and acoustic playing, with a single pickup fitted across its soundhole. It has the distinctive double-cutaway "Shorthorn" body shape first used by Nathan Daniel for his Danelectros and Silvertones in the late 1950s.
(Courtesy Guitar Showcase, San Jose)

their tops and backs, Daniel started using Masonite – a cheap hardboard material containing wood chips and fiber, mixed with resin. The guitars' finish and hardware were also highly unconventional; their sides were coated with Naugahide (a durable plastic often used on chair-seats), and the metal pickup covers were made from surplus chrome-plated lipstick tubes.

Nathan Daniel fashioned these odd ingredients into strikingly effective designs. One of his Silvertone guitar outfits featured an amp and speaker built into the instrument's case, while his Danelectro and later Coral ranges offered innovative body shapes, the first-ever six-string bass, and even a hybrid sitar guitar. Sadly, his company went out of business in 1969; but there is still considerable demand for his instruments, and since the mid-1980s, Jerry Jones Guitars of Nashville, Tennessee, has been making high-quality reproductions of the Danelectro line. Its work is featured on pages 434-437.

Solid Guitars by Gretsch and Rickenbacker

The Fred Gretsch company of Brooklyn, New York, was a long established and highly respected manufacturer and distributor, famous for its drums and fretted instruments. Gretsch had been making electric archtop guitars since the 1940s, but was initially skeptical to the point of derision about solid-bodies. When Gibson introduced the Les Paul in 1952, Fred Gretsch Jnr. phoned Gibson President Ted McCarty to express his horror at the move, commenting that "now anyone with a band saw can make a guitar."

Nevertheless, only two years later Gretsch launched its own electric solid-bodied guitar, the Duo-Jet. It had some similarities to the Les Paul, but used a different body construction (see caption, page 317) and, like other Gretsch electrics of the ▶

Left: Danelectro Pro 1 – c.1965. The Pro 1 has an unusual "bow-tie" outline not found on any other Danelectros, and is fitted with a single "lipstick-tube" pickup. The model was introduced in 1963, and stayed in production for the remaining six years of the company's life.
(Courtesy Real Guitars, San Francisco)

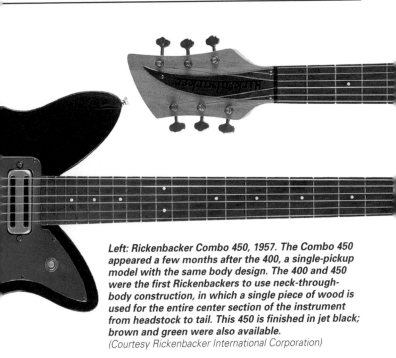

Left: Rickenbacker Combo 450, 1957. The Combo 450 appeared a few months after the 400, a single-pickup model with the same body design. The 400 and 450 were the first Rickenbackers to use neck-through-body construction, in which a single piece of wood is used for the entire center section of the instrument from headstock to tail. This 450 is finished in jet black; brown and green were also available.
(Courtesy Rickenbacker International Corporation)

period, was fitted with pickups made by DeArmond, which had made its early reputation with removable "floating" pickup assemblies for acoustic archtops. The Duo-Jet went through a number of subsequent design changes, eventually acquiring a double cutaway body and a pair of Gretsch's own twin-coil "Filter-'Tron" pickups. The company also produced several other closely related "Jet" models, including the Jet Fire Bird, which first appeared in 1955.

In 1953, Adolph Rickenbacker sold his Electro String Instrument Company to F.C. Hall (founder of Radio-Tel, the original distributor of Leo Fender's guitars), and soon afterwards, work began on a new line of Rickenbacker solid-bodies, named the "Combo" range. The first Combo

guitar emerged a year later, and the instrument on pages 314-315, the distinctively tulip-shaped Combo 450, made its debut in 1957. The 450, and its single-pickup version, the 400, quickly found favor with distinguished jazz musician Toots Thielemans (b.1922), who used them while working with the George Shearing Quintet. The instruments also attracted the attention of the young John Lennon; according to John C. Hall, who has succeeded his father as Chairman and CEO of Rickenbacker, it was the sound of Thielemans playing a "Tulip" that prompted Lennon to visit a Hamburg music store and order a Rickenbacker of his own – although the guitar he eventually acquired was not the 450 but the "thin hollow body" Model 325 he made famous

Right: Gretsch Duo-Jet, 1956. Unlike the Gibson Les Paul, which has a similar body shape, the Duo-Jet is not completely solid, but has a substantial cavity inside its mahogany body. The model is associated with several famous players, notably George Harrison, who frequently used one with The Beatles.
(Courtesy Guitar Showcase, San Jose)

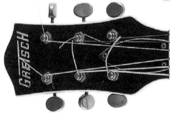

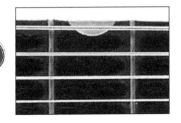

Left: Gretsch Jet Fire Bird, 1965. This 1960s version of the Jet Fire Bird has a double cutaway and two Gretsch "Filter-'Tron" pickups; it retains the body cavity of the original Duo-Jet. The "thumbprint" position markers on the neck (left) are a characteristic Gretsch feature, also found on many of their semi-acoustic models (see pages 350-357).
(Courtesy Eric Schoenberg)

Solid Guitars by Epiphone

Epiphone, like Gretsch, had been a major name in American instrument building for many years. The company was a family business, founded in New York by a Greek émigré, Anastasios Stathopoulo, in 1873, and originally known as the House of Stathopoulo. The Epiphone name came from Anastasios' son, Epaminondas (Epi), who took control of the firm in 1928; under his management, it had excelled in archtop guitar manufacture throughout the 1930s and early 1940s.

Epi's death in 1943 marked the start of a more difficult period for Epiphone, which was eventually sold by the Stathopoulo family. In 1957 it was taken over by Chicago Musical

Instruments (CMI), the parent company of its former arch-rival, Gibson, and for the next 13 years both brands were built at Gibson's headquarters in Kalamazoo, Michigan.

As former Gibson President Ted McCarty explained in an interview for "The Gibson," published in 1996, several existing Epiphone designs continued in production under the new regime. "We shipped the entire factory to Kalamazoo and began making Epiphones in exact accordance with the original plans for those guitars." But McCarty also had other ideas for CMI's new acquisition: "Epiphone…was a useful marketing tool as we could sell the Epiphone line to the newer dealers and keep selling

Right: Epiphone Crestwood, 1962. The Crestwood was the first of the Kalamazoo-designed Epiphone solids; it was launched in 1958 and underwent a number of design changes over the following 12

years. Its two humbucking pickups are smaller and lower in output than those found on Gibson instruments.
(Courtesy Lloyd Chiate, Voltage Guitars, Hollywood)

Left: Epiphone Olympic, 1961. The Olympic was introduced in 1960 – the year after the Gibson Melody Maker with which it shares many similarities. Early versions of both models feature one single-coil pickup mounted in the bridge position, and a characteristic cutaway body with a Les Paul-like outline.
Courtesy Room 355, Rose-Morris, London)

Gibson guitars to loyal Gibson dealers....They were a companion line for Gibson but not an exact copy and fitted perfectly with our plans."

Effectively, McCarty's approach was to make Epiphone instruments a slightly cheaper complement to the Gibson range. He began introducing new Epiphone models soon after the takeover, and some of them had strong similarities to more upmarket Gibson designs. For example, the Epiphone Olympics illustrated here and on previous pages closely resemble Gibson's Melody Maker solid-bodies (see pages 304-305). However, other Epiphones have no direct Gibson counterpart; among these is the Crestwood also shown here, which was probably aimed at would-be Gibson SG owners whose finances could not stretch to the more expensive model.

In 1970, Gibson changed their policy over Epiphone, discontinuing U.S. manufacture of the range and transferring its production to the Far East.

The Hollow-Body and Semi-Solid Electric 1946–1965

Since the introduction of the ground-breaking L-5 in 1922, Gibson had been steadily developing its archtop range; however, its earliest amplified archtops, such as the successful ES-150 (see pages 264-265) were essentially acoustic instruments with added pickups, rather than thoroughgoing electric designs. This was soon to change after World War II, when the company began to adopt a different approach to the construction of these models.

In 1946, Gibson resumed production of the ES-150 and two other hollow-body electrics, the ES-125 and ES-300. The reissued guitars were made from laminated wood, not solid timbers, and their tops were no longer carved, but pressed into shape. There were a number of ▶

Left: Epiphone Olympic, 1966. By 1961, the Gibson Melody Maker had gained a double cutaway, and a year later the same feature appeared on the Epiphone Olympic, which – like its Gibson counterpart – was also available in one- or two-pickup versions, and with a vibrato arm.
(Courtesy Rod & Hank's, Memphis)

Left: Gibson ES-175D, 1965. Unlike the 1961 guitar, this sunburst-finish model is fitted with an original-style trapeze tailpiece. The ES-175 has now become the longest surviving and best-selling archtop in the Gibson catalog.
(Courtesy Mark Knopfler)

reasons for this apparently retrograde step. Carving guitar tops was slow and labour-intensive, and Gibson's new owners, Chicago Musical Instruments (CMI), were keen to increase production levels. Premium-quality tonewoods were scarcer and more expensive than they had been before the war; and, significantly, some designers felt that solid wood was not necessary for a good electric sound. Gibson went on to use laminates for the majority of its post-war archtop designs.

Another departure was the inclusion of cutaways on the company's electric archtop bodies, allowing easier access to the higher reaches of their fingerboards. Gibson used two styles of cutaway: the rounded "Venetian" type found on its first-ever electric cutaway model, the ES-350P, which appeared in 1947;

and the sharper "Florentine" shape used for another new model, the ES-175, that was launched two years later.

The 175 proved to be one of the most important electric archtops ever to come out of Kalamazoo. It was modestly priced ($175), and fitted with a single pickup in the neck position (a dual pickup version appeared in 1953). The 175's deep body and warm, rich sound made it especially appealing to jazz players; Kenny Burrell was among the first major names to use it, and it has subsequently been associated with Joe Pass, Herb Ellis, Pat Metheny, and many others. Over the years, it has also attracted a number of leading rock guitarists (including Steve Howe of Yes, and Mark Knopfler of Dire Straits), and it remains in production today.

*Above: Gibson ES-175, 1958. Its
16-inch (40.6cm) top is made from
laminated spruce; the back and
sides are laminated maple, and
the neck is mahogany. This model
has a humbucking pickup – earlier
ES-175s had been fitted with P-90
single-coil units. The one-pickup
version of the 175 was eventually
discontinued in 1972.*
(Courtesy Mark Knopfler)

*Left: Gibson ES-175D, 1961. The
"D" suffix denotes a double-
pickup model. In 1956, three years
after its introduction, the 175D
gained a new T-shaped tailpiece
(above right, inset) with zigzag
metal tubing on either side.*
(Courtesy Guitar Showcase,
San Jose)

The Gibson ES-5 and L-5CES

The ES-175 was not the only new Gibson archtop unveiled in 1949. The other major design launched by the company that year was its ES-5, a "supreme electronic" version of the acoustic L-5 model, fitted with no fewer than three P-90 pickups.

The ES-5's introduction was a clear indication that Gibson now saw its amplified archtops as true electric guitars, not acoustics with pickups. Mounting a trio of bulky P-90s onto its laminated top inevitably had an detrimental effect on its "unplugged" tone, but provided a remarkable range of electric sounds. Gibson's publicity proclaimed the ES-5 an "instrument of a thousand voices;" its neck pickup gave a warm, "rhythm guitar" timbre, while the other two transducers were positioned to emphasize the middle and treble frequencies. Each pickup had a separate volume knob, allowing the player to mix the sounds together, and there was an overall tone control mounted on the instrument's upper right-hand bout.

Surprisingly, the original ES-5 had no selector switching; and many players must have found its rotary volume knobs awkward to manage when quick changes of sound were required. Gibson's solution was to introduce a modified version of the instrument, named the "Switch-master," in 1955. This offered

Above: Gibson ES-5 Switchmaster, 1957. This version of the ES-5 was designed to make pickup selection and control easier for players. Apart from the four-way switch, fitted to the Gibson ES-5 Switchmaster in place of the master tone control, the only significant difference between the Switchmaster and the original ES-5 is the newer instrument's more elaborate tailpiece.
(Courtesy Mark Knopfler)

Left: Gibson ES-5, 1951. The ES-5's 17-inch (43.2cm)-wide top, as well as its sides and back, are made from laminated maple. Like most Gibson archtops of the period, it was available in a blonde "natural" finish (as shown here) or in sunburst.
(Courtesy Mark Knopfler)

separate volume and tone controls for each pickup, and a four-way lever selecting individual pickups or all three simultaneously.

For lovers of the L-5 who wanted less elaborate electronics, Gibson produced the L-5CES (the C stands for "cutaway") in 1951. This guitar, one of the two "flagships" of the Electric Spanish range (together with the Super 400CES – see below) was among the few post-war Gibson electric hollowbodies to retain a carved solid spruce top. When the instrument first appeared, it was fitted with two P-90 pickups. These were later replaced by Alnico V single-coils, and, in 1958, by Gibson's newly developed humbuckers (see pages 295-296); these can be seen on the instrument at right, which dates from 1961.

The L-5CES has had many devotees among famous jazzmen, among them Wes Montgomery, Oscar Moore (guitarist with the Nat King Cole Trio), and Mundell Lowe.

The Gibson Super 400CES and ES-295

The Super 400 acoustic had been a landmark model for Gibson when it first appeared in 1934. At $400, it was the most expensive guitar the company had ever produced, and it was given an appropriately opulent finish, including gold-plated tuning machines and fine pearl inlays. It was also the largest archtop of its time, with a lower body width of 18 inches (45.7cm) subsequently exceeded only by the Epiphone Emperor (1936) and Elmer Stromberg's 19-inch (48.3cm) Master 400 (1937). Such increased body sizes were a by-product of the constant search for extra acoustic volume and power, and the coming of amplification had, to some extent, rendered them un-necessary. However, this had little effect on the popularity of the Super 400, and in 1951, Gibson introduced a ▶

Below: Gibson L-5CES, 1961. Like the later versions of its acoustic predecessor, this luxury electric hollowbody has a 17-inch (43.2cm) carved spruce top, with maple back and sides. The cherry red color of the model shown here was introduced in 1959, and was only available to customers for two years.
(Courtesy Lloyd Chiate, Voltage Guitars, Hollywood)

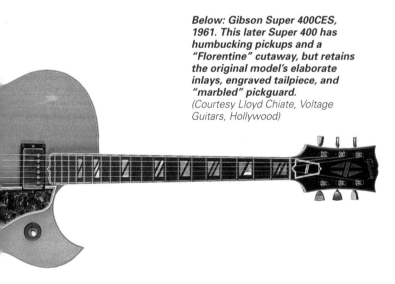

Below: Gibson Super 400CES, 1961. This later Super 400 has humbucking pickups and a "Florentine" cutaway, but retains the original model's elaborate inlays, engraved tailpiece, and "marbled" pickguard.
(Courtesy Lloyd Chiate, Voltage Guitars, Hollywood)

new two-pickup electric version of its classic design. It cost $470, and became once again the highest-priced model in the catalog.

The Super 400CES was launched simultaneously with the L-5CES, and shared its carved, solid-top construction. The natural finish example shown opposite was one of the first Super 400s to be fitted with Gibson's Alnico V pickups, which were beginning to supersede the original P-90 units in 1953. The other, cherry red model, dating from 1961, has humbucking pickups.

The idea of producing electric equivalents of its finest archtop acoustics was a logical and highly lucrative move on Gibson's part. But in 1952, it made a more surprising addition to its electric hollow-body range. This was the ES-295, whose all-gold finish, white pickup covers and distinctive bridge/tailpiece strongly resembled the company's new Les Paul solid, launched the same year. The 295's appearance was also reminiscent of the ES-175, with the same sharp-edged "Florentine" cutaway and "double-parallelogram" fingerboard inlays. The model remained in production for only six years; Gibson felt that its gold-colored body and neck were contributing to its unpopularity with players, and, as A.R. Duchossoir explains in his book *Gibson Electrics – The Classic Years*, the introduction of red and grey ES-295s was briefly considered. However, the idea was quickly abandoned, and no more ES-295s were built after 1958.

Right: Gibson ES-295, c.1952. A striking but relatively short-lived electric archtop. Its combination bridge/tailpiece was "borrowed" from the original "gold-top" solid Les Paul Model, while its body shape resembles the ES-175, and the gold-inlaid engraving on its white pickguard (above, inset) is copied from a Gibson lap steel instrument. Its headstock is shown below. (Courtesy Guitar Showcase, San Jose)

Left: Gibson Super 400CES, 1953. In the words of Gibson's own publicity, the Super 400CES offered "the tonal quality of an acoustic guitar with the advantages of an electric instrument." The Alnico V **pickups seen on this model were invented by Gibson's Seth Lover; they had larger magnets and a higher electrical output than the P-90s fitted to the first Super 400s.** (Courtesy Mark Knopfler)

The First Gibson "Thinlines"

"What would you like in a guitar that we don't already have?" This intriguing question was posed by a Gibson staffer to Hank Garland and Billy Byrd, two of Nashville's leading 1950s session musicians, at a disc jockey convention held in Music City in 1955. During a later interview with *Guitar Player* magazine, Garland recalled that he and Byrd "sat down [with the Gibson executive] and said we'd like an instrument like the L-5, but with a thin body and a bunch of other stuff. He wrote it all down on a piece of paper, and after he went back to...the Gibson factory, they made the guitar and sent us one."

Garland and Byrd were influential and highly respected in country music and beyond it. Byrd was famous for his work with singer Ernest Tubb, Garland had been closely associated with another star vocalist, Eddy Arnold ("The Tennessee Plowboy"), and the two men also had a strong involvement in jazz. The model they inspired, named the Byrdland in their honor, was announced only a few months after their first discussions with Gibson; it went on sale in 1956, and represented an important new direction for the company's archtop line.

While it retained the L-5's carved spruce top and outline, its reduced

Above: Gibson ES-140T (³/₄ size), c.1960. The first publicity shots for the 140 showed it against the outline of an ES-175, and the instrument is effectively a scaled-down, single-pickup replica of that classic design.
(Courtesy Amanda's Texas Underground, Nashville)

Left: Gibson ES-350T, c.1958. A thinline version of Gibson's 1947 ES-350 archtop. It is more than an inch (2.5cm) shallower than the original, and is fitted with two humbucking pickups, a "Tune-O-Matic" bridge and a redesigned tailpiece.
(Courtesy Mark Knopfler)

depth – 2¼ inches (5.7cm) as opposed to the L-5 and Super 400's 3⅜ inches (8.6cm) – gave it a much less bulky feel, particularly for guitarists who preferred to play standing up. It also had a shorter scale length, designed, as Gibson put it, "for the fast action needed in modern playing." The Byrdland was an immediate success, and has proved popular with a wide range of performers, from jazzman Barry Galbraith (with whom Hank Garland subsequently worked and studied in New York) to hard rocker Ted Nugent

Gibson's commitment to "thin-line" bodies was confirmed with the launch of two other 1955 models, the ES-350T and the less-expensive ES-225T. The following year, Gibson issued a thinline version of an already smaller-than-average guitar, the ES-140. This ¾-size instrument had first appeared in 1950; designed, according to Gibson's publicity, "principally for youngsters but ideal for any …guitarist with small fingers," it remained in production until 1968.

Below and right: Gibson Byrdland, 1964. This Byrdland is a 17-inch (43.2cm) archtop with a spruce top, maple sides, and a laminated maple back and neck; the fingerboard is ebony. The original 1956 model had Alnico V pickups and a rounded "Venetian" cutaway. Two years later, the Alnicos were replaced by humbuckers, while the cutaway shape was changed to the sharper Florentine style in 1960. (Courtesy Lloyd Chiate, Voltage Guitars, Hollywood)

The Gibson ES-335

The first thinline archtop models paved the way for an even more radical Gibson design – the ES-335 "semi-solid," introduced in 1958. Its inspiration may have been Les Paul's experimental "Log" guitar of 1941, which had a central wood block supporting its pickups, bridge, and strings (see pages 292-293). The "Log" offered remarkable sustain and practically no risk of acoustic feedback, but had been rejected by Gibson after Paul showed the company the prototype.

The ES-335 featured a refined and improved version of the same basic approach. Outwardly, it looked like a standard thinline archtop, although its double cutaway was an unfamiliar sight on a Gibson instrument. Internally, there were a number of other surprises. The two outer sections of the 335's body were hollow, but at its center was a strip of maple, with glued-in pieces of spruce above and below it. These were cut to

Below: Gibson ES-335TD, 1958.
This beautiful early 335 is unusual
in having no neck binding –
standard models are edged with
single-ply plastic around their
fingerboards. The guitar's other
features – a 16-inch (40.6cm)
laminated maple body, twin
humbuckers with individual
volume and tone controls, and a
three-way pickup selector switch –
are as normal.
(Courtesy Mark Knopfler)

the shape of the instrument's top and back, sealing off its hollow sides. Two humbucking pickups, a "Tune-O-Matic" bridge, and a "stud" or "stop" tailpiece were all mounted on this central section. Their positioning contributed to the guitar's highly distinctive sound, which was modified and enriched by the arched top and the side cavities, but had almost as much sustain and freedom from feedback as a solid-bodied instrument's.

The 335 was an important landmark in electric instrument technology. Its innovative body design was complemented by a slim, comfortable neck with unrivaled access to the top of the scale; all 22 frets could be reached with ease, and the action was as fast and light as a Les Paul's. At a basic price of $267.50 for a sunburst model (natural finish 335s were $15 dearer) it quickly became a best seller, and was subsequently used by a host of leading names in jazz, blues, and rock. Although it has been in continuous production since 1958, many musicians and collectors believe that the earliest 335s are superior to later models. The three examples shown here are so-called "dot" 335s, made before 1962, when Gibson replaced the original fingerboard dot position markers with block inlays.

Right: Gibson ES-335TD, 1959. A sunburst ES-335 from the same early period as the other two instruments. Later, a cherry red finish was available on the model as an optional extra.
(Courtesy Real Guitars, San Francisco)

Left: Gibson ES-335TD, 1959. Both this 335 and its companion on previous pages are nominally "natural finish" guitars. However, their differing shades demonstrate the varying degrees of "blondeness" found from model to model.
(Courtesy Mark Knopfler)

337

"Artist" Guitars

The approach to Billy Byrd and Hank Garland that led to the creation of Gibson's "Byrdland" archtop was not an isolated occurrence. Instrument makers retained close links with their distinguished customers, and fully appreciated the value of an endorsement, or a "signature" model, in boosting sales and generating publicity. Gibson's position as the inventors and premier manufacturers of archtop guitars gave it a special advantage in this area, and during the early 1960s, its President,

Ted McCarty, capitalized on it by commissioning a series of "Artist" hollowbodies bearing the names of leading performers.

One of the first of these was the Gibson "Johnny Smith," launched in 1961. Smith (b.1922), a self-taught guitarist who also excelled as a trumpeter and arranger, had helped to define the "cool jazz" movement with his 1952 album *Moonlight in Vermont*, and was greatly admired as a player and bandleader. A meticulous man, he gave

Below and right: Gibson Johnny Smith, 1963. The Johnny Smith was designed as a true acoustic/electric, and its humbucking pickup and volume control have no contact with its solid spruce top. The instrument's back, sides and neck are made from maple. Gibson continued to produce the guitar until the end of the 1980s.
(Courtesy Paul Leader)

the company precise instructions about the design of his instrument, insisting that its acoustic tone should not be compromised by fitting any pickups or controls directly onto the top. Instead, the Johnny Smith had a "floating" humbucker attached to the end of the guitar's neck, and a volume control built into its pickguard. The single pickup Johnny Smith was joined two years later by a double pickup version; both instruments remained in the Gibson catalog until the 1980s.

Following the success of the Smith guitar and the Gibson "Barney Kessel" archtop that appeared at the same time, McCarty introduced a third "Artist" model in 1962. Developed in collaboration with virtuoso bebop player Tal Farlow (1921–1998), this was a 17-inch (43.2cm), two-pickup instrument with a Venetian cutaway inlaid to resemble a scroll; like the Johnny Smith and Barney Kessel, it featured a "personalized" tailpiece displaying the endorsee's name.

Other archtop makers were also active in producing "signature" guitars. Gretsch's association with distinguished Nashville-based player and producer Chet Atkins (b.1924) is detailed on pages 354-357, while one of rock and roll's earliest heroes, Duane Eddy (b.1938) had an elegant archtop carrying his name designed and made by the New York-based Guild company. A 1962 example of this model is shown below.

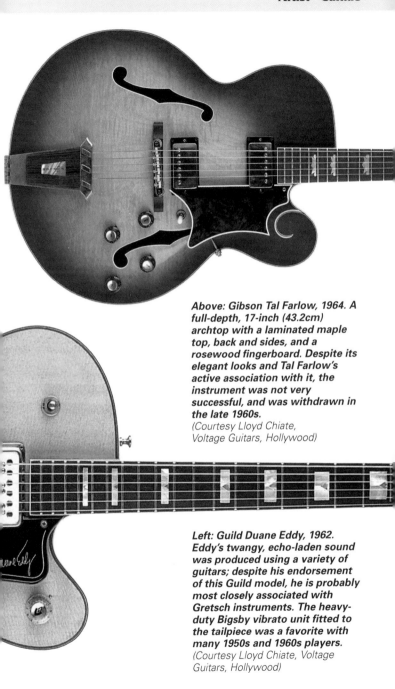

**Above: Gibson Tal Farlow, 1964. A
full-depth, 17-inch (43.2cm)
archtop with a laminated maple
top, back and sides, and a
rosewood fingerboard. Despite its
elegant looks and Tal Farlow's
active association with it, the
instrument was not very
successful, and was withdrawn in
the late 1960s.**
*(Courtesy Lloyd Chiate,
Voltage Guitars, Hollywood)*

**Left: Guild Duane Eddy, 1962.
Eddy's twangy, echo-laden sound
was produced using a variety of
guitars; despite his endorsement
of this Guild model, he is probably
most closely associated with
Gretsch instruments. The heavy-
duty Bigsby vibrato unit fitted to
the tailpiece was a favorite with
many 1950s and 1960s players.**
*(Courtesy Lloyd Chiate, Voltage
Guitars, Hollywood)*

Epiphone Electric Archtops 1951–1963

Most of Epiphone's classic archtop designs were introduced before World War II, and those that remained in production during the post-war period underwent a number of significant changes to their specifications. The first instrument shown here is a very unusual example of this; it is a 1951 version of a lower-price model, the Byron, which made its initial appearance in about 1939. Originally, the Byron was a non-cutaway acoustic; cutaways only began to be used by Epiphone in the late 1940s, and the company normally favored the rounded, Venetian style, as seen on the Emperor guitar also illustrated on pages 344-345. However, this 1951 Byron has a sharper Florentine cutaway, as well as a pickup that appears to have been factory-fitted, although the guitar is not listed as an electric model in any of the standard vintage guitar guides. It retains the relatively small body size, "center-dip" headstock, and single trapeze tailpiece found on its pre-war namesake; during this period,

Below and right: Epiphone Byron, 1951. The Byron, with its relatively small 15³/₈-inch (39cm) width, was at the lower end of the Epiphone range; however, it is a highly attractive instrument with a solid spruce top and a mahogany body. Because of its unusual Florentine cutaway, this model would be worth more than $1,000 to a vintage guitar collector.
(Courtesy San Diego Guitars)

Epiphone only fitted its double-trapeze "Frequensator" tailpiece to higher-end guitars.

The Emperor was the flagship of Epiphone's archtop range, launched in 1936 in direct competition to Gibson's Super 400. In 1952, Epiphone produced an electric cutaway version of the instrument fitted with three pickups, hoping to provide an attractive alternative to would-be Gibson ES-5 purchasers. When Gibson took over Epiphone in 1957, it retained the Emperor's pickup configuration, but made it a thinline model, and later replaced its "New York-style" pickups with its own "mini-humbucker" units. The Emperor was discontinued in 1970.

As well as preserving and adapting designs from the company's earlier history, Gibson introduced a number of entirely new Epiphones during the 1960s. One of the oddest of these was the Professional, which made its debut in 1962. Its double-cutaway body is reminiscent of the Gibson 335, but there is only one pickup, controlled by two standard knobs on the bottom right of the pickguard. The knobs and miniature switches on the opposite side allow the player to adjust volume, tone, and various effects on a separate amplifier unit. This concept was not especially successful, and in 1967 the Professional was dropped from the Epiphone catalog.

Above and above left, inset: Epiphone Professional, 1963. The Professional, in production from 1962–1967, was intended for use with its own amplifier, and the player can control the amp's tremolo, vibrato, and five "Tonexpressor" settings directly from the instrument.
(Courtesy Lloyd Chiate, Voltage Guitars, Hollywood)

Left: Epiphone Emperor, 1961. In contrast to the Byron, the Emperor was the largest and most expensive Epiphone archtop, whose 18¹/₂-inch (47cm) top eclipsed even the Gibson Super 400 for size. This example is fitted with the "mini-humbucking" pickups designed by Seth Lover and used on a number of other "Gibson-Epiphones."
(Courtesy Lloyd Chiate, Voltage Guitars, Hollywood)

The Rickenbacker 300 Series

In 1956, Rickenbacker celebrated its first 25 years in the guitar-making business. The company already had a distinguished track record, and now its new owner, F.C. Hall, was nurturing plans for an exciting and innovative line of electric archtops. Initially known as the Capri series, and later as the 300 series, it was soon to bring Rickenbacker international recognition – and some very famous customers from the world of pop and rock.

The Capri/300 series guitars were designed by Roger Rossmeisl, a German émigré who had previously worked, like his father, at Gibson. Rossmeisl took charge of the wood shop at Rickenbacker's Los Angeles factory, where he developed a variety of single- and double-cutaway, thin- and full-bodied models in an integrated "house style" that made them instantly recognizable.

The range divides into a number of distinct types and classifications, though all Capri/300s share the characteristic sloping Rickenbacker headstock, and are made from maple with rosewood fingerboards. The earliest guitar illustrated here is a natural-finish pre-1958 Deluxe. "Deluxe" Rickenbackers, whether they are single-cutaway "full-body" instruments like this one, or thinner double cutaway designs, all have triangular fingerboard inlays and bound bodies.

After 1958, the company began to use numbers and suffixes for its various Capri/300 models, and the three-pickup single cutaway instrument also shown below, which dates from 1960, was given the designation 375F. (Numbers from 360 to 375 were assigned to Deluxe models, and the "F" stands for [thin] "full-body.") The guitar illustrated below is a

Left and above, inset: Rickenbacker Capri 330, c.1959. A "standard" model (without binding or triangular inlays) in two-tone sunburst. It is slightly deeper than later instruments, which were reduced to c.1¹/₂ inches (4cm) in 1962. Its two pickups are single coil "chrome bar" units made and used by Rickenbacker until the late 1960s.
(Courtesy Rickenbacker International Corporation)

Rickenbacker 330, a "standard" thin hollow-body model with dot fingerboard inlays and no binding.

The 300 series had even more impact on musicians than Rickenbacker's popular Combo range of solid-body guitars. A key factor in this popularity was the instruments' adoption by The Beatles; after John Lennon acquired his Model 325 in Hamburg (see page 317). George Harrison began to use a twelve-string 360, and later, Paul McCartney would frequently be seen with a Rickenbacker 4001 bass. Leading American groups were also attracted to the 300 series, and we shall be looking in more detail at their choice of models in last pages.

Right: Rickenbacker 375F, 1960. A three-pickup thin full-body model incorporating a "vibrola" of the type originally developed by Doc Kauffman for Electro String/Rickenbacker in the 1930s (see pages 272-273). In the 1960s, *this was superseded by a more modern "Ac'cent" unit, while non-vibrato Rickenbackers had their plain "flat" tailpieces replaced with ones bearing the "R" trademark.* (Guitars on these pages courtesy of Rickenbacker International Corporation)

*Left: Rickenbacker Capri Deluxe,
pre-1958. This guitar dates from
before the advent of numerical
classification for Rickenbackers,
but shares the specifications of an
"F" (thin full-body) Deluxe series
instrument. The Capri Deluxe has
a 17-inch (43.2cm) body and is
c.2¹/₂ inches (6.35cm) deep. The
"slash" soundhole found on
Rickenbacker archtops is a
distinctively "European" feature,
first used by the German Framus
company and also made famous
by American archtop luthier
Jimmy D'Aquisto.*

Gretsch – from Electromatic to Double Anniversary

Gretsch's first electric archtop, the "Electromatic Spanish" guitar, appeared in 1940, but no examples or precise specifications of it are known to survive. Nine years later, the company introduced a higher-profile single pickup instrument bearing the same name; this was followed in 1951 by the Electro II – offered in 17-inch (43.2cm) cutaway and 16-inch (40.6cm) non-cutaway versions – and the 16-inch Electromatic, which was available with one or two pickups. In 1954 the Electromatic became the Streamliner, while the cutaway Electro II was renamed the Country Club.

These guitars were relatively straightforward in design. However, despite its rather tentative initial approach to the electric market – and the horrified reaction of its founder's son to the introduction of Gibson's solid-bodied instrument (see pages 314-317) – Gretsch quickly developed a flair for colorful finishes and extra gadgetry. This more adventurous approach could be seen in some of its "Chet Atkins" archtops (see pages 354-357), and was also apparent on

Below and right: Gretsch White Falcon, 1966. The original White Falcon, launched in 1955, had a single cutaway; this double-cutaway version appeared in the early 1960s. It is fitted with two "Filter'Tron" pickups, and its string mutes (the two black pads just above the bridge) are controlled by twin lever switches on either side of the tailpiece. (Courtesy Lloyd Chiate, Voltage Guitars, Hollywood)

the top-of-the-line White Falcon model, which made its first appearance in 1955. An unashamedly ostentatious guitar, with a retail price of $600, it boasted gold sparkle decoration, gold-plated metalwork, and bird and feather engravings on its pickguard and fingerboard position markers. Its later versions incorporated additional features such as stereo circuitry and an ingenious mechanical string "muffler" mounted between the back pickup and the bridge (illustrated opposite).

Gretsch guitars were especially popular with country musicians and rockers, including Hank Garland, Duane Eddy, and the tragically short-lived Eddie Cochran. The company also had a following among several major jazz artists; its 1959 floating-pickup "Convertible" electric/acoustic was endorsed by Sal Salvador, former guitarist with the Stan Kenton Big Band, who had a long association with them.

A year before, Gretsch had celebrated 75 years in the instrument-making business by launching a pair of new electric archtops, the Anniversary (single pickup) and the twin pickup Double Anniversary These models were fitted with the company's new "Filter'Tron" humbuckers (previous Gretsch electrics had used single-coil transducers manufactured by DeArmond) and, at under $200 each, were comparatively inexpensive guitars, "priced for promotional selling" as the company's publicity put it; they remain desirable collectors' items.

Right: Gretsch electric archtop, 1953. Confusingly, Gretsch used the "Synchromatic" headstock label for both acoustic and electric guitars in the early 1950s.
This model is especially unusual because of the position of its *controls; Gretsch electrics of the period normally had three knobs on the lower treble bout and a fourth (master volume) near the cutaway.*
(Courtesy Lloyd Chiate, Voltage Guitars, Hollywood)

Left: Gretsch Double Anniversary, 1961. This later example has "HiLo Tron" single-coil pickups instead of the original "Filter'Tron" humbuckers. The instrument has a master volume control, individual knobs for each pickup volume, and two switches – one to select and combine the pickups, the other to provide different tone settings.
(Courtesy San Diego Guitars)

353

Gretsch and Chet Atkins

In 1954, Gretsch signed an endorsement deal with star Nashville guitarist Chet Atkins – a move that proved to be a vital factor in the company's subsequent success. Atkins (b.1924), a top session musician with a high popular profile thanks to his solo work and TV appearances, was also assistant to the Head of RCA in Nashville, and in 1957, after he became Chief of RCA's Country Division, his career and reputation reached new heights. However, by the mid-1950s he had already played on, arranged, and produced a string of hit records, and was helping to shape what came to be known as the Nashville Sound.

The earliest versions of the first Gretsch Chet Atkins guitar, the 6120, were not entirely to the endorsee's liking when he first tried them. As he explained in *The Gretsch Book* by Tony Bacon & Paul Day: "The [pickup] magnets pulled so strong on the strings that there was no sustain there, especially in the bass." Atkins also had reservations about the styling, which featured a longhorn headstock logo and "Western" fret

Right: Gretsch Chet Atkins Hollow Body (Model 6120), 1959. The instrument's distinctive "amber red" finish was originally combined with a stylized black "G" painted onto its lower bass bout. This, like the Western-style decorations, was removed from later versions. The single-coil pickups whose magnets Chet Atkins complained about were subsequently replaced by Gretsch "Filter'Tron" humbuckers, which are fitted here.
(Courtesy Guitar Showcase, San Jose)

Left: Gretsch Chet Atkins Tennessean, 1963. The first version of the Tennessean, which appeared in 1958, had just one humbucking pickup, but in the early 1960s two single-coil transducers were substituted. **Like all the instruments here, it is fitted with a Bigsby vibrato carrying the Gretsch name – Chet Atkins' preferred choice of unit.** (Courtesy Rod & Hank's, Memphis)

markers (subsequently phased out). However, he soon started using the new model for recordings and live work; it carried his signature on the pickguard, and, as he acknowledged to Bacon and Day, "I was *thrilled* to have my name on a guitar like Les Paul had his name on a Gibson."

Gretsch was equally thrilled to have Atkins on board; his presence had an impressive effect on its sales, and in 1957 a second Chet Atkins guitar, the Country Gentleman, was launched. It had one highly unusual feature for an electric archtop: no

soundholes. Atkins and Gretsch found that sealing the instrument's top helped to minimize acoustic feedback, and the f-holes on most models (including the one shown here) are simply painted on as a *trompe l'oeil* effect.

The Country Gentleman was followed a year later by a lower-priced design, the Tennessean, which was originally fitted with a single pickup; all three instruments remained in production until the 1980s. A Chet Atkins model manufactured by Gibson, the SST, is also featured on pages 398-401.

Left and above, inset: Gretsch Chet Atkins Country Gentleman, 1965. The Country Gentleman has a 17-inch (43.2cm) body (an inch wider than the 6120). On this example, the pickguard does not have the Chet Atkins signature that appears on the other two guitars, though the model name is shown on the metal plate screwed to the headstock. Note the fake f-holes!
(Courtesy Lloyd Chiate, Voltage Guitars, Hollywood)

Above and right: Fender Telecaster, 1967. This guitar is a fairly typical early "post-CBS"

model with a maple fingerboard and new, bolder headstock decal. (Courtesy Rod & Hank's, Memphis)

SECTION THREE

The Evolving Electric

The mid-1960s were turbulent times for the electric guitar industry, with takeovers at Fender and subsequently at Gibson, and the departure of Leo Fender and Ted McCarty from the companies they had led since the 1940s. These two famous figures left a vacuum that their more business-oriented successors found it hard to fill, and for a number of years, both Fender and Gibson seemed in serious danger of losing their way. Many of their new instruments were failing to appeal to players, and Fender suffered increasing complaints from customers about quality control and standards of construction.

Alongside this disenchantment with current models was a growing reverence among musicians for earlier, "vintage" designs, as well as a desire for guitars that offered extra performance and personalized features. Some leading rock and jazz performers chose to have their instruments tailor-made by pioneering companies such as Alembic in San Francisco. Others took a "customizing" approach, combining and modifying existing components to make hot-rodded hybrids like the "Superstrats" first created in the 1970s by (among others) Grover Jackson and Eddie Van Halen.

Gibson and Fender (both of which acquired new, forward-looking and quality-conscious management teams in the 1980s) eventually responded to players' requirements by opening their own custom shops, reissuing accurate, lovingly made replicas of older models, and offering fresh and exciting additions to their instrument ranges. They and other major U.S. firms also manufacture lower-priced ranges of their own under licence in Japan, China, Korea, or Taiwan; a move that provides effective competition against the flood of Far Eastern imports that once posed such a severe threat to their livelihood. These policies have led to a proliferation of high-quality instruments at every price level; as one of the United Kingdom's leading luthiers, Hugh Manson, observes: "There's probably never been a better time to buy a good guitar."

359

A Changing Climate 1965–1980

Fender's takeover by New York-based broadcasting and entertainment conglomerate CBS (Columbia Broadcasting System) was announced officially on January 5, 1965. For a total purchase price of $13,000,000, CBS had acquired the company's entire manufacturing and sales operation. Don Randall, formerly President of Fender Sales, became Vice-President and General Manager of the new Fender division of CBS; Leo Fender was given a research and development consultancy, but took no further part in running his old business, and did not retain an office at its Fullerton headquarters.

Leo had been in poor health during the previous year, but the precise reasons for his decision to sell remain uncertain, although he knew that hi[s] firm needed a substantial injection o[f] capital. CBS was able to provide it, bu[t] also brought a "big business" approac[h] to Fender management and produc[t] develop-ment, which was soon to prov[e] damaging to the health and reputatio[n] of its new subsidiary.

Under the new régime[,] workmanship and quality control wer[e] sometimes markedly inferior; the ter[m] "pre-CBS" began to be used by player[s] to differentiate instru-ments produce[d] after 1965 from those made while Le[o] Fender himself was still in charge. Als[o] a number of post-CBS designs simpl[y] did not measure up to the company'[s] previous high standards. In 1966, [a] disagreement over a line o[f]

Right: Fender Telecaster Custom, 1967. The Custom Tele, which first appeared in 1959, has a bound body and an attractive sunburst finish. "Blonde" (as on the Bigsby-equipped guitar on pages 362-363) remained the sole finish on Standard Telecasters until 1974. *(Courtesy Mark Knopfler)*

Left: Fender Telecaster Thinline, 1971. The Thinline retains the standard Tele shape, but its bass side has a hollow cavity and sports an f-hole. When the instrument was introduced in 1968, it was fitted with single-coil pickups; but from 1971 these were replaced by humbuckers (as shown here) designed by Seth Lover, who had left Gibson to work for Fender in 1967. The Fender Telecaster Thinline remained in production until 1978.
(Courtesy Dave Peabody)

transistorized amplifiers led to the resignation of Manufacturing Operations Director Forrest White, who felt they were not worthy of the Fender name; and less than three years later, Don Randall himself decided to leave.

However, the change of management did not have an immediate effect on Fender instruments. Early CBS Telecasters look and sound little different from their pre-1965 counterparts, and it was not until well after the takeover that any significant changes to the company's classic designs began to be made. In 1967, the Telecaster was rewired to remove its bass boost circuit and allow two-pickup operation (see pages 282-285), and, the following year, a "new" Telecaster variant, the Thinline, was launched. This combined a half hollowed-out body with the standard Tele pickup configuration, neck, and body shape, and remained in production until the late 1970s.

The New Fullerton Plant and the Post-CBS Stratocaster

By 1966, CBS-Fender had a new 120,000 sq. ft. (1,115m2)factory, built adjacent to their original premises in Fullerton, and providing the latest and best in manufacturing facilities. As plant manager Forrest White observed in his book *Fender: The Inside Story*, its pristine, dust-free environment and stylish office furnishings were "quite a departure from what we had been used to." (Conditions in the older buildings had been much more spartan – even Leo Fender's personal research and development area, used for crucial tests and experiments on amplifiers, pickups, and other components, had occupied only a single workbench in a vacant room.)

The extra space and capacity were badly needed now, as CBS-Fender was widening its areas of ▶

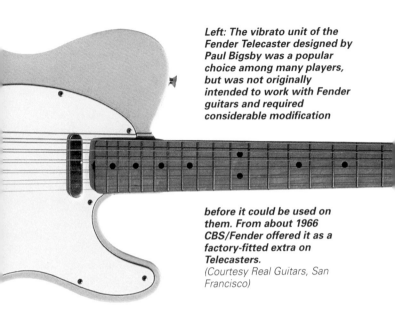

Left: The vibrato unit of the Fender Telecaster designed by Paul Bigsby was a popular choice among many players, but was not originally intended to work with Fender guitars and required considerable modification

before it could be used on them. From about 1966 CBS/Fender offered it as a factory-fitted extra on Telecasters.
(Courtesy Real Guitars, San Francisco)

Left: Fender Stratocaster, 1969. Curiously, Leo Fender never registered his company's distinctive "Fender" and "letter F" trademarks – an omission that CBS corrected in 1967. As a result, both this blonde Strat and the blue model on

pages 364-365 display the ® symbol on their decals.
All these Stratocasters feature the enlarged headstock introduced within a year of the CBS takeover. A smaller headstock design, similar to the original, appeared in 1981.
(Courtesy Room 335, Rose-Morris, London)

operation – becoming involved in semi-acoustic guitar production (see pages 366-369), banjo-making, electric organ building, and, as mentioned earlier, solid-state amplification. None of these new ventures had been prompted by Leo himself, and one of the few substantial ideas he offered the company during his five-year term as a consultant – an ingenious design for a guitar string bender – was rejected by CBS as uncommercial.

The Stratocasters coming off the new production lines at Fullerton had slightly larger and differently shaped headstocks than their pre-CBS counterparts. This apparently minor modification is felt by many players and collectors to spoil the instrument's looks – and, as many of them have commented, it was possibly done to permit the use of a larger name/model decal! (See photos on pages 362-363 and below.) Another cosmetic change took place after 1968, when Fender abandoned the use of three-coat nitro-cellulose finishes on its instrument bodies, substituting polyester, which is easier to apply during mass production. In his exhaustive guide to the Stratocaster, guitar expert A.R. Duchossoir explains that while the original nitro-cellulose process involved just three coats of lacquer, the high-gloss "thick-skin" method that replaced it covered the wood with up to 15 layers of polyester – not only changing the instrument's appearance, but giving it a radically different feel in the player's hands. "Thick-skin" finishes can be seen on both the 1969 Strats shown on these pages.

Right Fender Stratocaster, 1966. This example has a dakota red custom finish; dakota was Fender's medium red custom coloring, lighter than the popular "candy apple red" but darker than "fiesta." The enlarged, post-CBS headstock has a "transitional" decal; the "Fender" and "Stratocaster" lettering are smaller and less bold than on the other two instruments shown here.
(Courtesy Amanda's Texas Underground, Nashville)

Left: Fender Stratocaster, 1969. This elegant model has a sonic blue finish – the lightest shade of blue offered by Fender during this period. The 1969 list price for a custom color Strat was

$367 – 5 percent greater than the cost of a "standard" instrument. (Courtesy Stephen Strachan; photographed at Voltage Guitars, Hollywood)

Fender in the Late 1960s and 1970s

Fender was certainly not short of new guitar models during the early CBS period. One of the first (and least successful) of these was the Marauder, a four-pickup solid launched in 1965 and available for less than a year. It was followed, in 1968, by the Bronco, a single-pickup, double-cutaway instrument whose body bore a close resemblance to the pre-CBS Mustang (illustrated on pages 308-309). Both steeds survived in the company catalog until the 1980s.

A more surprising departure fo the company was its introduction of number of acoustic and semi-acousti guitars in the mid-1960s. In fact, Le Fender himself had previously show interest in this area, hiring Roge Rossmeisl (the designer of the classi Rickenbacker electro-acoustics – se pages 346-349) in 1962, and workin with him over the next two years on range of five acoustics – includin even a nylon-strung classical mode Rossmeisl stayed on after Leo departure, and was responsible fo

Below and right: Fender Coronado II Wildwood II, 1968. Wildwood finishes were available in a variety of colors; this one (number II) is green, gold, and brown. The Coronado was Fender's first semi-acoustic; designed by Roger Rossmeisl (formerly of Rickenbacker), it was made in one- and two-pickup configurations, and there was also a twelve-string version. (Courtesy Rod & Hank's, Memphis)

many of CBS-Fender's later flat-top acoustic and archtop electric guitars, including the Coronado, which debuted in 1966.

Coronados, along with several other post-CBS Fender instruments, were available for a time either in standard finishes or in five shades of "Wildwood" – a beechwood injected, while still growing, with special dyes that created distinctive colorings. Wildwood (not itself a Fender product; it had been developed in Scandanavia) was used on a number of the company's solid-body models, but was probably most effective on acoustic or semi-acoustic designs such as the Coronado II shown opposite.

Right: Fender Bronco, 1977. Like its two-pickup cousin, the Mustang, the Bronco was chiefly intended for the student market, at whom CBS-Fender also aimed new products

The Coronados had considerable merits, but the guitar-purchasing public associated Fender too closely with solid electrics such as the Telecaster and Stratocaster to accept them. Sadly, the same fate was to befall Fender's most attractive and underrated semi-acoustic, the Starcaster, which dates from 1975. A thinline model, fitted, unusually for Fender, with humbucking pickups (the "Fender sound" is invariably associated with single-coil units, although humbuckers were available on a number of its post-CBS guitars), the Starcaster might have provided an effective challenge to some Gibson and Gretsch semi-acoustics. However, it never sold in large numbers and was withdrawn in 1982.

such as the smaller, lighter transistorized amplifiers launched in 1967 despite the disapproval of many old Fender employees.
(Courtesy Rod & Hank's, Memphis)

Left: Fender Starcaster, c.1976.
Unusually for a Fender, the Starcaster
has five control knobs – individual
volume and tone for each pickup, plus
a master volume. The pickup selector
switch on the upper treble bout is not
the original component.
(Courtesy John Firth)

Gibson's "Modernistic" Guitars

In the 1950s, Fender had shaken up the guitar-making establishment with its bold solid-body designs. Gibson had responded with the Les Paul, a highly effective instrument, but clearly the product of a maker with roots in traditional lutherie. For some critics, the Les Paul was simply not radical enough, as Ted McCarty, the firm's former President, admitted in an interview for "The Gibson" in 1996. "Other guitar makers [were saying] that Gibson was a fuddy duddy old company without a new idea in years. That information came back to me, so I said we would shake 'em up if that's what they thought." McCarty quickly commissioned sketches for some brand-new designs, and the resultant drawings and specifications were to form the basis for some of the wildest looking instruments in Gibson's history.

The most celebrated of these models, all of which had bodies made from African korina wood, was the Flying V, whose extraordinary shape derived from a tongue-in-cheek idea of McCarty himself. A few were produced in 1958, but the V was soon

Right: The headstock of the Gibson Flying V.

Below: Gibson Flying V, late 1970s. A reissue of Ted McCarty's wild design, which first appeared in 1958. Most later Flying Vs like this one are made from mahogany, not korina wood, and are fitted with conventional "stop" tailpieces instead of the V-shaped metal plates found on the originals.

The Gibson Flying V makes a wonderful visual impact, but its radical shape makes it extremely difficult to play while sitting down.
(Courtesy Paul Evans)

discontinued, although it was to make frequent reappearances in the Gibson catalog from the mid-1960s onwards. Its real fame came after its adoption by bluesman Albert King (1923–1992); later, it was a favorite with many hard rock and heavy metal players, notably Andy Powell of Wishbone Ash.

The second of McCarty's "modernistic" guitars (as they were described in company literature), the Explorer, had an angular body shape with dramatically extended upper treble and lower bass bouts, and shared the same electronics as the Flying V. Original examples of it are very rare, and no more than 40 1958-vintage examples are thought to have been built. The Explorer design then went out of production until 1975, when the model was reissued in a mahogany-bodied version.

The third guitar in the series, the Moderne, has a bizarre, myth-laden history. Its design was certainly blueprinted and patented in 1958, but despite persistent rumors to the contrary, was probably never actually produced at all! The version shown below is one of a limited edition of 500 Modernes issued by Gibson in 1982; the guitar had never been revived.

Right: Headstock of the Gibson Moderne "reissue."

Below: Gibson Moderne "reissue," 1982. No original 1958 Modernes have ever been discovered – although Ted McCarty suggests, in his interview for "The Gibson," that up to four prototypes may have been constructed for a trade show in New York. The limited-edition replica of the Moderne was made using the original plans for the guitar; its body, like that of the original Flying V and Explorer, is made from African korina wood.
(Courtesy Room 335, Rose-Morris, London)

The Gibson Firebirds

Gibson's "modernistic" guitars had proved too advanced for their time; but Ted McCarty continued his quest for a contemporary-looking solid-body model to provide serious competition for Fender. In the early 1960s, he decided to seek inspiration from a distinguished outsider: Ray Dietrich, a leading Detroit-based automobile designer famous for his work with Chrysler and Packard, who had never previously been involved with musical instruments. Dietrich was invited to submit sketches for a new-style guitar body, and his ideas were eventually realized as the Gibson Firebird.

The original Firebird featured a reverse body shape, with its treble wing or "horn" larger than the one on its opposite (bass) side, and a "six-tuners-in-a-row" headstock, of the type first adopted by Gibson on the ill-fated Explorer, oriented the "wrong" way round. The tuning machines themselves were banjo-type units with their buttons facing downwards, not sideways. The new guitar had a "neck-through-body" construction, and was made from mahogany; its pickups were the mini-humbuckers previously designed for Gibson's Epiphone line by Seth Lover. Four Firebird instruments, available in basic sunburst or, like their Fender competitors, in a range of custom colors, were launched in 1963; the model name was suggested by Ray Dietrich, and he also contributed the bird sketch visible on the pickguards

Below and right: Gibson Firebird VII (reverse body), 1965. The three-pickup Firebird VII has a mahogany center section, with the instrument's two wings glued onto either side. Other models in the series, which was introduced in 1963, are fitted with single or paired mini-humbucking pickups. Among the optional finishes available to customers were kerry green, frost blue, or polaris white. (Courtesy Lloyd Chiate, Voltage Guitars, Hollywood)

of the guitars illustrated here.

The Firebirds were competitively priced (from $189.50 to $445 for a top-of-the-line Firebird VII like the one illustrated here), and certainly lived up to the claims of Gibson's publicity, which described them as "revolutionary in shape, sound and colors." However, they met the same resistance as the Flying V and Explorer, and also provoked a complaint from Fender, who claimed that the design infringed their patents. This was denied by Gibson, and no action was ever taken; but the dispute was probably a factor in Ted McCarty's decision, made during 1965, to modify the Firebirds' appearance and construction, and drop the reverse body shape. The line survived only four more years before being discontinued, but like several other "radical" Gibson solid-body models, Firebirds have grown in popularity since their initial appearance, and the company has produced numerous reissues and replicas of them in recent years

Gibson in the Late 1960s and 1970s

The Firebirds were the last major new electric models introduced by Ted McCarty, who left Gibson in 1966 after 16 years as its President. Two years later, the company changed hands; its new owner was Norlin Industries, which derived its name from Maurice Berlin of CMI (Gibson's former owners) and Norton Stevens of ECL Industries, the incoming purchasers. The Norlin régime at Kalamazoo brought about some major changes in working practices, design, and marketing – focusing on high volume production in an increasingly competitive market, and transferring the construction of Epiphone instruments to the Far East, where manufacturing costs were much lower.

For some time, CMI had used Epiphone as a lower-cost "companion brand," and many Epi models were, to ▶

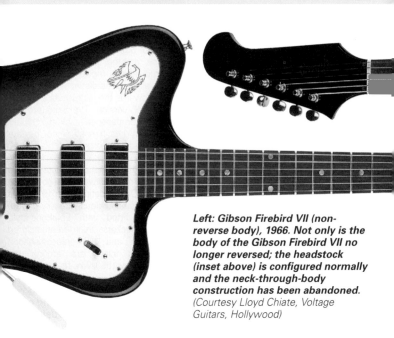

Left: Gibson Firebird VII (non-reverse body), 1966. Not only is the body of the Gibson Firebird VII no longer reversed; the headstock (inset above) is configured normally and the neck-through-body construction has been abandoned.
(Courtesy Lloyd Chiate, Voltage Guitars, Hollywood)

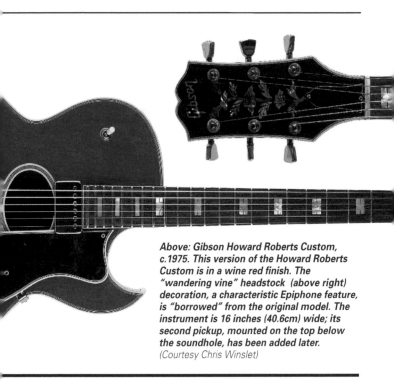

Above: Gibson Howard Roberts Custom, c.1975. This version of the Howard Roberts Custom is in a wine red finish. The "wandering vine" headstock (above right) decoration, a characteristic Epiphone feature, is "borrowed" from the original model. The instrument is 16 inches (40.6cm) wide; its second pickup, mounted on the top below the soundhole, has been added later.
(Courtesy Chris Winslet)

put it crudely, slightly downmarket copies of standard Gibson designs. However, on one occasion in the 1970s, this process was put into reverse, when a fine Epiphone instrument, the Howard Roberts Custom semi-acoustic (developed in collaboration with Roberts [b.1929], a distinguished jazz player), was reintroduced as a Gibson! The rebranded guitar was launched in 1974, and is shown below; five years later, Gibson produced another Howard Roberts model, the Fusion, this can be seen on page 403.

The late 1960s and 1970s also saw several additions to familiar Gibson lines. A few short-lived new SGs appeared, and after Les Paul renewed his endorsement deal with the company in 1967, there was a rash of new and reissued models bearing his name, some of them with special on-board electronics. Among these is the Les Paul Signature illustrated here – a thinline archtop bearing little family resemblance to regular solid-body Les Pauls, although its distinctive coloring is a nod towards the instrument's earliest "gold-top" version. The Signature has the low impedance pickup circuitry favored by Les himself since the late 1960s, and a three-position "vari-tone" switch.

The third instrument on these pages is a more conventional gold-top: a Les Paul Deluxe dating from 1971. This attractive (and obviously heavily-played) guitar is fitted with Epiphone-style mini-humbuckers; their cream-colored mountings and the trapeze-shaped fingerboard inlays are among the guitar's many 1950s-like features.

Right: Gibson Les Paul Deluxe, 1971. The Deluxe was available in red or blue "sparkle" as well as in this distinctive gold finish. Its mini-humbucking pickups provide *a less powerful, thinner sound than the full-size units found on 1960s Les Pauls. The model remained in the catalog until 1982.* (Courtesy San Diego Guitars)

Left: Gibson Les Paul Signature, c.1974. The Signature was first produced in 1973; despite its hollow-body design, it retains a characteristic deep Les Paul-style cutaway on the right of the neck. Its low-impedance pickups are thought to offer greater clarity and superior frequency response; *however, they require extra circuitry to make them compatible with standard high-impedance guitar amplifiers, and the Signature incorporates two separate outputs, offering low- and high-impedance signals.* *(Courtesy Rod & Hank's, Memphis)*

Alembic – Realizing Musician's Dreams

An "alembic" is defined in the dictionary as "anything that refines or purifies;" more specifically, it was the vessel in which medieval and Renaissance alchemists com-bined base metals as they sought to transmute them into gold. A different kind of alchemy is practiced at Alembic, Inc., of Santa Rosa, California, which produces fine instruments for some of the world's most outstanding performers. Its General Manager, Mica Wickersham, explains that the company name (with its distinctive trademark, shown above right), "has become for us a symbol of purity – and one of our primary goals is purity of sound."

Alembic was founded in 1969 by Mica's parents, Ron and Susan, who are still at the helm of the business. Ron, an electronics engineer, had a background in broadcasting, and subsequently became closely involved with the development of multi-track recording systems, while Susan was a successful artist. Their new company shared premises near San Francisco with the city's legendary rock group, the Grateful Dead, and was responsible for much of the band's sound technology – including its innovative PA system, and the "active" pickups used by bassist Phil Lesh, and guitarists Jerry Garcia and Bob Weir.

In 1974, after several years combining electronics and instrument design with studio management and live recording work, Alembic decided to focus solely on making guitars, basses, and pickups. From the start, its instruments were strikingly different from those

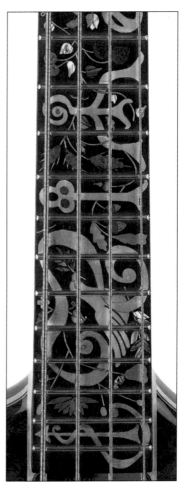

Below and right: Alembic 25th Anniversary Sterling bass, 1997. This limited-edition instrument (only 25 were made) commemorates 25 years of bass building at Alembic. (Users include the great jazz-rock player Stanley Clarke, who bought his first Alembic in 1972.) Susan Wickersham (who designs the body shapes of all Alembic instruments) was responsible for the selection of woods and other materials for the guitar. Its metal parts are sterling silver, its top and back are made from 15-year old Brazilian burl rosewood (highly prized by luthiers for its sound, and now a protected species), and the neck is maple and ebony. (Courtesy Alembic, Inc.)

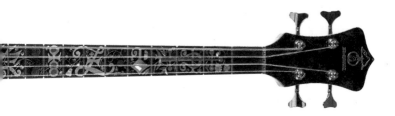

of more mainstream manufacturers. While standard electric guitar pickups are "voiced" to create a dis-tinctive tone-color that cannot be substantially modified, Alembic transducers deliver a clean, high fidelity response that musicians then tailor to their needs by the use of active on-board filters, whose roll-off characteristics are carefully chosen to sound "natural" and musical. The result-

ant range of sonic possibilities gives players a uniquely versatile tool with which to realize their ideas. As Ron Wickersham puts it: "Rather than handing a musician something and saying, 'We have this great inspiration, and if you take our instrument, you'll be famous just like somebody else,' we do the opposite; the musician is free to come to us, and we don't try to talk him out of his dream."

Below: Alembic Series I twelve-string, 1978. The top and back are made from figured purpleheart (the body has a mahogany core), and the neck is maple and purpleheart, with an ebony fingerboard. The large, knob-shaped headstock is also found on Alembic's eight-string basses.
(Courtesy Alembic, Inc.)

Right: Alembic prototype, 1971. A "one-off" instrument made for John "Marmaduke" Dawson, guitarist with the New Riders of the Purple Sage, and a close associate of the Grateful Dead. In these early days, the company was effectively a "custom shop," and formal model designations did not yet exist (see pages 384-385 for an Alembic made soon after this period).
(Courtesy Real Guitars, San Francisco)

Guitars for Rock Stars

Speculation and myth often surround claims that particular instruments were once the property of famous players. However, there is no doubt about the provenance of the two models shown here and over the page, both of which are known to have belonged to major figures in the world of 1960s and 1970s rock.

The Alembic Series II dates from 1972, and was custom-made for English rock musician Greg Lake (b.1948) – best known as a bassist, but also an accomplished six-string player. Lake first came to fame with King Crimson in 1969, before becoming a member of the hugely successful progressive rock trio Emerson, Lake and Palmer (ELP). The body of his

Alembic has an African zebrawood top and back with a maple core; the front and back veneers on the headstock are coco bolo, and the "through" neck is made from layers of maple, purpleheart and cherry wood. The instrument features Ron Wickersham's active pickup circuitry (see pages 90-91), and the side of its ebony fingerboard is fitted with illuminating LEDs. The beautiful mother-of-pearl inlays are the work of Ron's wife Susan.

The Rickenbacker 360/12 is particularly significant: currently owned by Lloyd Chiate of Vintage Guitars in Hollywood, it was the guitar played by Jim (now Roger) McGuinn of The Byrds on the group's classic singles *Mr. Tambourine Man* and *Turn, Turn, Turn* (1965).

Right: Alembic Series II, 1972. When this guitar was made for rock star Greg Lake, model names had only just been introduced at Alembic, and there was considerable variation between individual instruments. Lake's Series II is slightly thicker than more recent examples, and its electronic circuitry is mounted on *the right of its body (later Alembics have their electronics split between both body halves). It has recently been given a new finish, which has been carefully tinted to match the original coloring.*
Inset pictures: Details of the Alembic Series II's headstock and neck inlays.
(Courtesy Alembic, Inc.)

McGuinn (b.1942) first heard Rickenbacker twelve-strings on The Beatles' early records (see pages 316 and 348), and purchased this 360/12 in 1964, after seeing George Harrison using one in the movie *A Hard Day's Night*. The following year, The Byrds were formed (the band also included David Crosby and Chris Hillman), and their distinctive sound, strongly featuring McGuinn's new twelve-string, quickly brought them critical and commercial success on both sides of the Atlantic.

In 1966, the 360 was returned to Rickenbacker for some modifications; surviving paperwork shows that an extra pickup, a new nut, and a "pickguard with special wiring" were fitted. Roger McGuinn was photographed using the instrument onstage before and after these changes; he subsequently bought several other Rickenbackers, but this model was the first and most famous of his twelve-strings.

Unusual Electrics

The first guitar on these pages is a Kapa Continental – a copy of Fender's Jazzmaster/ Jaguar design, but produced by a homegrown American company, rather than one of the Far Eastern competitors that were soon to have such a devastating effect on U.S. manufacturers. Kapa, based in Maryland, was in business between 1966 to 1970; it also produced a twelve-string version of the Continental, fitted, like the model shown here, with a vibrato unit.

The guitar shown on page 389 dates from 1968, and its "cresting wave" double cutaway, single pickup, overall shape and finish are identical to those on a Rickenbacker Combo 425. However, it carries the Electro label; Electro String was, of course, Rickenbacker's original manufacturing company, and for some years, the Electro marque was retained for instruments sold directly to teaching ▶

Left and above: Rickenbacker 360/12, 1964. The 360 is "officially" a two-pickup instrument; Roger McGuinn's guitar acquired its extra pickup and additional circuitry during a factory refit in 1966. Like all Deluxe Rickenbackers, it has triangular fret markers and a bound body. Note the ingenious "compact" headstock design, which disguises the six extra tuning machines by fitting them with their tuner buttons facing downwards.
(Courtesy Lloyd Chiate, Voltage Guitars, Hollywood)

Left: Kapa Continental, late 1960s. This model has an unusual blue-green finish. Its body shape and (especially) its vibrato unit are strongly reminiscent of the Fender Jazzmaster and Jaguar – although, unlike them, the Kapa is fitted with a zero fret.
(Courtesy Amanda's Texas Underground, Nashville)

studios, usually as part of a beginner's "outfit" that also included an amplifier and case. As John C. Hall, Rickenbacker's Chairman and CEO, explains: "Electro guitars were made in the same factory as Rickenbackers, and a lot of the models are the same [as] Rickenbacker models – except that they were not buffed out and polished to the same degree, in order to keep the cost down." Occasionally, though, an Electro instrument would be out-of-stock when required; then an equivalent, finely polished Rickenbacker, like the one opposite, would have its original logo replaced, and be sent out as an Electro.

C.F. Martin & Company, of Nazareth, Pennsylvania, is justly famous for its fine flat-top acoustic guitars; however, the firm's strong association with this particular type of instrument has meant that its occasional forays into archtop, electric, and bass production have never been especially successful. The Martin EM-18 illustrated below, was part of a range of solid-body guitars introduced in 1979, which remained in the catalog for only four years. Significantly, its headstock (whose scrolled shape is reminiscent of the earliest nineteenth century Martin acoustics) bears the company's initials rather than its full name. It is an attractive and versatile instrument, with two humbucking pickups, coil selector and phase switches, and a maple body with walnut laminates. The E series also featured some models with active electronics.

Right: Electro ES-17, 1968. The superb sheen on this Fireglo-colored instrument betrays its origins as a relabeled Rickenbacker. John C. Hall, the company's CEO, points out that the "conversion" process could also work the other way:

"Through the years, many people have taken Electro guitars, buffed them out, and put Rickenbacker nameplates on them – but [the instruments] didn't leave the factory as Rickenbackers".
(Courtesy Rickenbacker International Corporation)

Left: CFM EM-18, c.1980. Martin's
E series included two other six-
string guitars, as well as a pair of
basses. The instrument shown
here has a mahogany neck and a
rosewood fingerboard; its

pickups and "Badass" bridge
(designed to improve sustain)
were bought in from other
manufacturers.
*(Courtesy Amanda's Texas
Underground, Nashville)*

Innovation and Tradition – 1980 to the Present

Leo Fender's departure, in 1965, from the company that bore his name did little to dampen his subsequent creativity. However, the terms of his consultancy contract with CBS meant that he could do no guitar design work on his own account until 1970, and it was two more years before he launched his next business venture, Tri-Sonics, later renamed Music Man. Leo's partners in the firm were both ex-Fender employees: former General Manager Forrest White; and Tom Walker, who had been a key figure in Fender sales. Another Fender "old-timer," George Fullerton, came to work for Music Man in 1974.

Leo Fender could probably have had considerable success by turning out replicas of his classic Telecasters and Stratocasters at Music Man, but he had no intention of retreading old ground. As George Fullerton ex-plained in a 1991 *Vintage Guitar* magazine interview with Willie G. Moseley, "What Leo tried to do…was to make [guitars] that didn't look like the legendary instruments he'd designed at Fender, and he wanted these newer

brands to be improve-ments on his earlier designs. In a lot of ways, he had his work cut out for him, but he felt like his later designs were the best he'd ever done." New features on Music Man guitars included Leo's first humbucking pickups (fitted to the Music Man Sabre illustrated here), a redesigned bass headstock with one tuning machine positioned opposite the other three, and active electronics similar to those pioneered by Alembic a few years earlier.

Despite the high quality of these instruments, Music Man's success was limited – due, in part, to growing disagreements between the three principal shareholders. In 1980, Fender and Fullerton left to set up another company, G & L (the initials stand for "George and Leo"). They were joined by Dale Hyatt, whose association with Leo dated back to 1946; he became G & L's Director of Marketing and Distribution.

The new venture saw the last flowering of Leo Fender's genius for guitar design; he worked at G & L until his death in 1991, developing many of his ideas at the workbench shown on this page.

Above: Leo Fender's office, G & L Musical Instruments, Fullerton, California. The office and desk have been preserved exactly as Leo Fender left them on the day before his death. His test equipment, including an oscilloscope and multimeter (with a

bottle of Listerene antiseptic mouthwash beside it) is within easy reach. On the back wall behind the chair is another bench holding the guitars he was working on, and a door leading to a small inner room.
(Courtesy G & L Musical Instruments)

Left: Music Man Sabre I, late 1970s. This model, which first appeared in 1978, features two humbucking pickups. Its body outline is slightly reminiscent of a Stratocaster's, but there is no vibrato unit.

Music Man guitars, basses, and amplifiers were actually manufactured by CLF Research, the Fullerton-based company set up by Leo Fender after the CBS takeover.
(Courtesy Rod & Hank's, Memphis)

Leo Fender, George Fullerton, and G & L

G & L maintains Leo Fender's innovative approach to guitar design, as well as the hands-on production methods he always favored. Johnny McLaren, the current Plant Manager, explains that Leo "was fascinated by the mechanics of the manufacturing side," and always keen to purchase the finest and most advanced equipment for guitar making. Since the company's formation in 1980, as many of its components as possible have been produced at its own factory in Fullerton, California; those that have to be bought in come from manufacturers with established traditions of excellence. For example,

the cloth-wrapped wire used in some instruments is made by Gavitt Wire & Cable of Massachusetts, which once supplied pioneering automobile builder Henry Ford.

G & L also draws more direct inspiration from its founders. George Fullerton, Leo Fender's partner in the company, lives nearby, and continues to work as a consultant, and Leo's own drawings and notes still provide Johnny McLaren with valuable guidance. "Every time we've had problems here I can go back to Leo's file cabinet and get the exact numbers. Everything's there – it's picture perfect."

George and Leo's approaches to

Right: G & L S.500, 1998. This example is finished in "cherry burst." It has a hard rock maple neck (with rosewood fingerboard) and a body of alder. Like the Legacy, it is fitted with a Dual

Fulcrum tremolo unit, but its "whammy bar" has been removed for this photograph.
(All pictures courtesy G & L Musical Instruments)

Left: G & L ASAT Junior (limited edition), 1998. The ASAT (named after the U.S. Air Force's Anti-Satellite Missile) has an overall shape similar to a Telecaster's. This model, one of a limited edition of 250, has hollow side chambers and a solid center. Its body and neck are mahogany, and its fingerboard ebony. The Magnetic Field pickups, with their fully adjustable pole pieces, provide a warm, rich sound and a high electrical output.

guitar making were complementary. Leo could not play the instrument, although he loved music; while George, an accomplished performer, often contributed to the more artistic aspects of a design. Leo excelled at the mechanical and engineering sides, and never lost his enthusiasm for developing fresh ideas. John C. McLaren, Johnny McLaren's father, whose company, BBE Sound, now owns G & L, paints a vivid picture of Leo on holiday with his second wife, Phyllis: "To please [her] he went on these cruises. They'd be invited to sit at the captain's table...and Leo'd be sitting there drawing new pickups. Then, at the next port, he'd fax them back to George Fullerton!"

One such design, the "Magnetic Field" pickup, is featured on the ASAT Junior illustrated pages 392-393. Another important innovation from Leo Fender's G & L years is the Dual Fulcrum tremolo fitted to two of the instruments shown here. Even the Legacy model, produced post-humously as a tribute to Leo's life and achievements, is largely based on his own ideas and drawings.

Below and right: G & L Legacy, 1998. The Legacy has three G & L Alnico V single-coil pickups in a Stratocaster-type configuration, with a five-way selector switch. The guitar's body is alder, and the neck is maple. Leo Fender's patented Dual Fulcrum tremolo features two pivoting points anchored into brass inserts in the instrument's body. It gives a smoother feel than earlier units, and permits notes to be bent up as well as down.
(Courtesy G & L Musical Instruments)

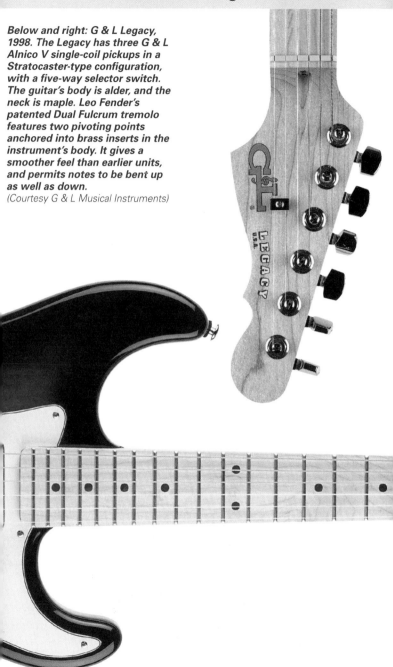

Gibson in the Early 1980s

The 1970s had been a confusing and increasingly troubled period for Gibson. Its guitars were never short of exposure: in fact, leading performers on both sides of the Atlantic were helping to make the Les Paul one of the dominant instruments of contemporary rock. Yet the models favored by these players often dated from the 1950s, and more recent Les Pauls, despite the variety of styles they appeared in, were judged by some musicians to be inferior to their predecessors in sound, feel, and appearance.

Many other Gibson solid bodies were also launched during the decade, but few seemed to catch on, or retain their place in the catalog for

any length of time. Meanwhile, at the lower end of the market, cheap and increasingly proficient Far Eastern copies of Gibson's classic designs (and, of course, Fender's Telecasters and Stratocasters) were successfully circumventing the patent laws and doing substantial damage to the original manufacturers' worldwide sales.

In 1974, Norlin, Gibson's parent company, moved the bulk of its electric guitar production from Kalamazoo, Michigan (where the firm had been based since it was founded in 1902) to a new plant in Nashville, Tennessee. Only acoustic and some top range semi-acoustic Gibson designs continued to be made at

Right: Gibson Les Paul Standard, 1989. An example of Gibson's output soon after its takeover by the new management team. This model is a very attractive reissue of a 1958-style Les Paul Standard, *with a "vintage sunburst" finish. The model has a maple top and a mahogany body, and its trapeze-style fingerboard inlays closely match those of the original.*
(Courtesy Mark Knopfler)

Left: Gibson Sonex 180 Deluxe, 1981. *The Sonex line comprised three instruments, all with the same body shape, but offering a variety of pickup configurations and finishes. This is the most basic model, with two humbucking pickups and standard, passive circuitry.*

The Sonex 180 Deluxe's body is made of Masonite, the hardboard material also used by Nathan Daniel on his Danelectro guitars. The model was manufactured for only three years, between 1981–84.

(Courtesy Rod & Hank's, Memphis)

Kalamazoo. Ten years later, the original factory was closed permanently, and all instrument manufacture transferred to Nashville. The idea behind these changes was to rationalize and reduce costs, but difficulties and poor sales continued, and in 1985, Gibson was put up for sale. Like CBS, which disposed of Fender during the same period (see pages 410-413), Norlin clearly felt that the guitar building business held no future for it; and there were plenty of industry pundits and dealers who believed that Gibson itself might soon cease to exist.

However, the following year, Gibson was bought by a new management partnership headed by Henry Juszkiewicz, who has been its President ever since. His shrewd and capable management has succeeded in re-establishing the company at the forefront of the musical instrument business, and some of its outstanding current designs, displaying a fine blend of tradition and innovation, are featured on the next four pages.

Gibson – Under New Management

In the years immediately following their takeover, Henry Juszkiewicz and his team focused on producing and marketing Gibson's classic models, and the company's current catalog includes SGs, Les Pauls, 335s, and many other well-established in-struments. There are also Custom and Historical ranges, and a small number of highly decorated Art Guitars – among them an Elvis Presley Super 400, and a special version of B.B. King's ES-355, "Lucille," made to celebrate the great bluesman's 70th birthday (see pages 404-405 for a standard "Lucille").

More recently, though, Gibson has been developing some impressive new designs – notably the Hawk Series, launched in 1993 with the three-pickup Nighthawk model. Designed by J.T. Riboloff, the ▶

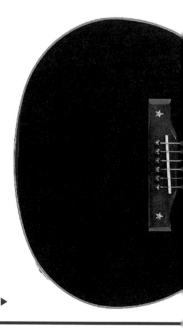

Left: Gibson Les Paul Custom, 1982. The Custom was one of the first of the Les Paul models to be reissued in 1968. The new version was fitted with only two humbucking pickups, but a third was frequently available as an option. This model is in the original ebony finish that gave the instrument its nickname "Black Beauty."
(Courtesy Rod & Hank's, Memphis)

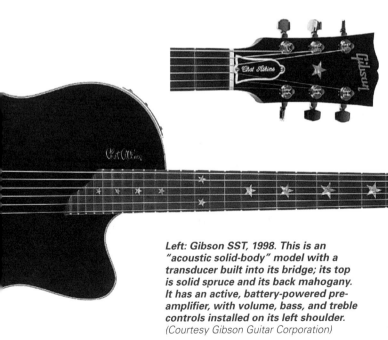

Left: Gibson SST, 1998. This is an "acoustic solid-body" model with a transducer built into its bridge; its top is solid spruce and its back mahogany. It has an active, battery-powered pre-amplifier, with volume, bass, and treble controls installed on its left shoulder.
(Courtesy Gibson Guitar Corporation)

company's Head of Research and Development, this instrument offers a remarkably wide range of sounds, thanks largely to its coil-tap switch, which doubles as a tone control knob. When this is pulled up, the guitar's neck and bridge humbuckers are converted to single-coil operation, providing a thinner, Stratocaster-like timbre that can be quickly changed back to a warmer, twin-coil tone as necessary. The Hawk family includes various different versions of the Nighthawk, as well as the twin-pickup BluesHawk, which appeared in 1995.

Among the many leading players currently associated with Gibson is Chet Atkins, who first collaborated with the company in 1982 to produce his innovative nylon-strung Standard CE (Classical Electric) – designed for fingerstyle playing without the risk of acoustic feedback. The relationship

has continued to flourish under the new management (at one time, Chet and Henry Juszkiewicz had houses in the same Nashville street), and Gibson now manufactures its own versions of the Chet Atkins Country Gentleman and Tennessean archtops, originally developed and made by Gretsch (see pages 354-357). The model shown on pages 398-399 is the SST – a steel-strung adaptation of Atkins' CE.

The third instrument on these pages, a double-cutaway LPS, revives the body outline found on the "intermediate" 1959–1961 style Les Paul featured on pages 298-301 – although its electronics have been updated, and its "tangerineburst" finish gives it a strikingly contemporary look. The model is also available in lemonburst, blackburst, and a range of solid colors.

Right: Gibson Nighthawk DSNH, 1998. This sunburst-finish Nighthawk has two Gibson M-Series humbuckers in the neck and bridge positions (the bridge pickup is slanted (opposite page, inset) and a high-output single-coil transducer in the middle. There is

a five-position pickup selector switch mounted below the volume and tone/coil-tap controls. The Nighthawk's shape is slightly reminiscent of the Les Paul's, but with a wider body, deeper cutaway and an extended scale length.

Left: Gibson LPS, 1998. The example shown here has a figured maple top, a mahogany back and rosewood fingerboard, and all-gold hardware. Unlike similar instruments from other **manufacturers, it features a fitted neck (instead of a bolt-on type) for improved rigidity and sustain.** *(Instruments courtesy Gibson Guitar Corporation)*

The Jimmy Page Les Paul, "Lucille," and the Howard Roberts Fusion

One of the key figures behind the popularity of the Gibson Les Paul over the last 30 years is Led Zeppelin guitarist Jimmy Page – a virtuoso player with precise and demanding requirements for his instruments. When Gibson collaborated with Page to produce a Signature Model Les Paul, the new design was based on the musician's own customized 1959 LP Standard, and incorporated a number of special features. The company's Quality Control Supervisor, Francis Johns, explains that Page "wanted to try and achieve a guitar that felt like it had [already] been played, and was 'broken in.' The neck is unique: it's actually thinner in the center than it is at the top – Jimmy Page shaves his own guitars down to get this feel." The electronics are also unusual: the two humbucking pickups were specially designed for the instrument (the bridge unit is the highest output transducer Gibson has ever made), and the control circuitry offers coil-tapping, phasing, and series/parallel switching – as described in the caption. The Jimmy Page Les Paul is currently Gibson's most expensive production model; Page has given permission for only 2,200

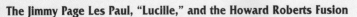

Right: Gibson B.B. King Lucille, 1998. "Lucille," like her close relation, the ES-355, has stereo circuitry (the output from each pickup can be sent to a separate channel or amplifier) and a six-position rotary "Varitone" switch, visible just left of the volume and tone controls, which provides a selection of pre-set sounds. The instrument's body is laminated maple, with a solid center block; the fingerboard inlays are pearl.
(Instruments courtesy Gibson Guitar Corporation)

Left: Gibson Jimmy Page Les Paul, 1998. This special model has a bookmatched figured maple top, gold hardware, and an elegant "light honeyburst" finish – but its sophisticated electronics are not so easily visible. Each of the four control knobs on the Jimmy Page Les Paul (above left) can be pulled up to
obtain additional effects: the tone control for the "rhythm" (neck) pickup switches the circuitry into series or parallel, while the other knobs offer coil tapping for each pickup, and put the two transducers in or out of phase with each other. Jimmy Page's signature can be seen on the pickguard.

instruments to be built.

Bluesman B.B. King (b.1925) is another great guitarist closely associated with a specific Gibson model. Early in his career, King played a Fender Telecaster or a Gibson ES-5, but since the early 1960s he has used a succession of ES-355s, all of which have had the same famous nickname, "Lucille." In 1980, Gibson introduced a production "B.B. King" model, and since 1982, King has officially endorsed the instrument, which was later renamed "B.B. King Lucille." Unlike the original 355, the

Below: Gibson Howard Roberts Fusion, 1998. The "Fusion" has a number of unique features – including its unusually positioned volume and tone controls, its reshaped cutaway, and the distinctive tailpiece, which permits the player to adjust the angles of individual strings via the *six rotary controls at its base. This unit, used in conjunction with the instrument's standard Gibson "Tune-O-Matic" bridge, allows a remarkable degree of control over string height, intonation, and position.*
(Courtesy Gibson Guitar Corporation)

"B.B. King" has no f-holes; the sealed top helps to avoid feedback at high playing volumes.

Jazz musician Howard Roberts (1929–1992) had his first "signature" guitar made by Epiphone in 1965; later this was reissued under the Gibson marque (see pages 376-379). A new Howard Roberts model, the Fusion, appeared in 1980; it is a semi-solid design with a laminated maple body and neck and two humbucking pickups. Its distinctive "six-finger" tailpiece was added in 1990.

Made In Kalamazoo – The Heritage Range

Gibson's departure from Kalamazoo, Michigan, in 1984 did not end the long history of guitar making there. A number of the company's employees decided to resign rather than make the 500-mile (800km) move to Nashville, and three senior ex-staffers – plant manager Jim Deurloo, plant superintendent Marv Lamb, and J.P. Moats (who had been in charge of wood purchasing, repairs, and custom orders) – made plans to continue fretted instrument construction in the town. Together with former Gibson accountant Bill Paige, they acquired premises and machinery from their previous employers, and set up their own business, Heritage Guitars Inc., in April 1985.

The firm's workforce was drawn from ex-Gibson craftsmen who, like the four founder/owners, had chosen to remain in Kalamazoo. Their collective skill and experience is reflected in the superb quality of Heritage's output, which includes electric and acoustic guitars as well as mandolins and banjos. The company is steeped in the Gibson/Kalamazoo tradition: its headstock logo, "The Heritage," is an echo of "The Gibson" trademark used on its predecessor's pre-war instruments; and a number of

Above: Heritage Prospect Standard, 1998. The Prospect, introduced in 1991, is a 15-inch (38.1cm) semi-hollow design with a laminated curly maple top and back, and a mahogany neck. The instrument has a body depth of 1¹/₂ inches (3.8cm), and is fitted with two humbucking pickups. It is available in three standard colors, almond sunburst (as shown here), antique sunburst, or natural.

Left: Heritage H155, 1998. Like the other models in Heritage's H150 series, the H155 has a solid, carved body with a maple top, and two humbucking pickups.

Bottom: Heritage H155 headstock. The guitar's cutaway shape and pickguard design (left) are subtly different from those on the instrument that inspired it, the Gibson Les Paul. The guitar is finished in opaque blue. *(Instruments courtesy Barnes & Mullins Ltd.)*

its models are strongly influenced by classic Gibson designs. However, Heritage instruments such as the "signature" guitars developed in collaboration with leading players like Johnny Smith, Roy Clark, and Alvin Lee invariably offer significant new refinements. The "Alvin Lee" has an ES-335-like body combined with a special three-pickup system, featuring two humbuckers and a single coil transducer; while the "Johnny Smith," a reworking of the jazzman's classic electric/acoustic "floating pickup" design (see page 340) has delighted its creator, who personally signs every example.

All Heritage's full-body semi

acoustics, including the "Sweet 16" illustrated below, are fitted with solid wood tops (many post-war Gibson semis are made with laminates); and a wide variety of custom options is available across the company's entire range – from personalized inlays and special finishes to alternative pickups by EMG or Seymour Duncan. This combination of expert craftsmanship and extensive customer choice – at highly competitive prices – has already brought Heritage considerable prestige, and after less than 15 years in business, it seems likely to succeed in its stated aim of creating "the collectible guitar of tomorrow."

Below: Heritage Sweet 16. 1998. As suggested by its name, this is a 16-inch (40.6cm) wide model – a genuine "semi-acoustic," with a depth of 2³/₄ inches (7cm). The pickguard carries the volume control (bottom, inset) and supports the "floating" pickup, which does not touch the solid spruce top. (Pickups installed directly onto the top inevitably compromise an instrument's acoustic sound.) The back and sides of the guitar are made from curly maple, and the inlays on the headstock and ebony fingerboard are mother-of-pearl. (Courtesy Barnes & Mullins Ltd.)

Fender in the 1980s and 1990s

The year 1980 marked the fifteenth anniversary of CBS's takeover of Fender, and as the decade began, its managers were faced with serious difficulties. The overall economic climate was bleak, Far Eastern imports were damaging sales, and substantial investment was needed to update tools and machinery. The company's reputation as a manufacturer of high quality instruments was also suffering – a situation exacerbated by a sometimes exaggerated reverence for "pre-CBS" Fenders among many players. Such attitudes may not always have been fair, but it was a fact of life that while "an older [Fender] guitar was not necessarily better, most of the better guitars were old," as Richard R. Smith comments in his book *Fender: The Sound Heard 'Round the World.*

The following year, CBS made a serious effort to solve Fender's problems, hiring two senior executives from Yamaha's U.S. musical instruments division, John C. McLaren and William Schultz, to lead a new management team. They made substantial progress, replacing worn-out plant at the Fullerton factory, bringing in new models, and – in a radical and far-sighted move – launching a range of lower-priced

Below: Fender 40th Anniversary Stratocaster, 1994. The Stratocaster, launched in 1954, is one of the most popular of all electric guitar designs – and certainly the most imitated. This "special edition" commemorative model, made at Fender's U.S. factory, features a "40th Anniversary" decal (bottom, inset) on its headstock, and an appropriate slogan (above) on its neck plate!
(Courtesy Amanda's Texas Underground, Nashville)

Japanese-made Fender guitars. These included "reissues" of classic older designs, and were initially sold only in Japan and Europe; however, they soon appeared in the U.S. as well, giving a generation of impecunious young American players its first chance to own a "real" Strat or Tele.

Despite these achievements, however, CBS eventually decided to withdraw from the guitar industry. In 1985, it sold Fender to a consortium headed by Bill Schultz – who, like his former colleague John McLaren (now closely involved with G & L – see pages 392-395) was highly regarded by Fender personnel. In *Fender: The Inside Story,* Forrest White quotes company veteran Freddie Tavares as saying that "he thought Bill was the one who could restore [the firm] to its former position as king of the hill." Tavares' faith was justified; Fender has prospered under Schultz's leader-ship, and the proof of its renaissance lies in the range of excellent instruments it now produces – from the fine guitars made at its new factory and Custom Shop in Corona, California, to the cheaper models manufactured in Mexico and Asia.

Right: Fender "The Strat," 1980. This model was an attempt by CBS/Fender to regain some lost ground with players and collectors. It has gold hardware, its headstock – finished in candy-apple red, like the body – is smaller than previous CBS designs (compare it with the 1969 Strat on pages 362-365), and the neck is attached to the instrument with four bolts, abandoning the less stable three-bolt system introduced in the early 1970s. "The Strat" was launched at the NAMM (National Association of Music Merchants) show in 1980, and remained in the catalog for three years.
(Courtesy Amanda's Texas Underground, Nashville)

Left and above: Fender Telecaster
Custom (made in Japan), c.1985.
The Telecaster Custom made its
first appearance in 1959; this
reissued version was made for
Fender in Japan, and sold at a
lower price than U.S.-made

Fender instruments. Like the 1959
model, it has a sunburst finish, a
bound top and back, and a
rosewood fingerboard. The
Schecter bridge unit, with its six
individual saddles, is not original.
(Courtesy Nick Freeth)

413

Reworking The Classics

Telecasters and Stratocasters are now firmly established as classic guitars, but the profiles of some other Fender models are more dependent on particular musical trends, or identification with specific players. The Mustang, for example, was introduced in 1964 as a student instrument, but underwent a change of image after its adoption by Nirvana frontman Kurt Cobain (1967–1994). Cobain also admired the Fender Jaguar, and when he collaborated on a personalized guitar with the company's Custom Shop luthier Larry Brooks, he combined cut-up photographs of the two models to create a hybrid – naming it, appropriately, the Jag-Stang, and using the first version on Nirvana's 1993 tour dates. As

Cobain explained in Fender's *Frontline* magazine, the Jag-Stang represents his attempt "to find the perfect mix of everything I was looking for." A second example was completed shortly before his death, and Fender subsequently obtained the agreement of his estate to manufacture the instrument, which is shown on pages 416-417.

Kurt Cobain's desire to "tailor" a guitar to his tastes and needs is nothing new. In the 1970s, Schecter Guitar Research of Los Angeles was already producing high quality replacement parts (including alternative pickups, bridges, vibrato units,and other hardware) for standard instruments like Strats and Teles. The company also operates a highly

Right: Rickenbacker 355/12JL, late 1980s. A limited edition guitar featuring reproductions of John Lennon's distinctive artwork and signature (top right, inset). It is one of Rickenbacker's full-size "Thin Hollow Body" instruments, with a 15¼-inch (38.7cm) body width (Lennon's ¾ size 325 was only 12¾ inches [32.4cm]

wide) and three pickups. The "355" serial number denotes a vibrato model, although one was not fitted to this special instrument. Unlike "Deluxe" Rickenbackers, the fingerboard has position dots, not "triangle" inlays, and the neck and body are unbound.
(Courtesy Rickenbacker International Corporation)

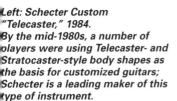

*Left: Schecter Custom
"Telecaster," 1984.
By the mid-1980s, a number of
players were using Telecaster- and
Stratocaster-style body shapes as
the basis for customized guitars;
Schecter is a leading maker of this
type of instrument.*

*Special features and refinements
on this hand-made Schecter
"Telecaster" include special
pickups and an improved, fully-
adjustable bridge assembly (also
fitted to the Japanese Telecaster
shown on pages 412-413).
(Courtesy Mark Knopfler)*

regarded Custom Shop service, which can build almost any combination of neck, body shape, and electronics to players' exact specifications. The Schecter "Telecaster" seen on pages 414-415 was made for Mark Knopfler in 1984. It has been featured on many of his recordings, notably the classic Dire Straits number *Walk of Life*; and he invariably uses it when he plays the song live onstage.

Another model illustrated (page 415) is one of Rickenbacker's limited edition Artist series, the 355/12JL, commemorating John Lennon's close association with the company's instruments. It differs in some respects from the guitar actually used by Lennon with The Beatles – he played a ¾ size model 325, fitted with a vibrato unit – but features Lennon's signature and one of his cartoons on its pickguard, and is a fitting tribute to a musician who played a key role in popularizing Rickenbacker's classic designs.

Charvel, Grover Jackson and the "Soloist"

During the late 1970s, a new generation of virtuoso American guitarists was beginning to emerge. It included Eddie Van Halen (b.1957), born in Holland but brought up in California, who gave his surname to the powerful rock band he formed in 1973 with his brother Alex. Van Halen's debut LP appeared five years later, and Eddie quickly gained a reputation as a lightning-fast, intensely dramatic soloist who demanded the utmost from his instrument. Unsurprisingly, he and artists like him found basic Stratocasters and other off-the-shelf models inadequate for their high-octane playing, and were obliged to turn to custom shops and individual craftsmen to obtain "axes" that answered their needs.

By the end of the decade, Eddie Van Halen was using stripped-down, ▶

Below: Fender Jag-Stang, 1997 (left-hand model). This example, made by Fender Japan, is finished in sonic blue (like the second of the two Custom Shop Jag-Stangs made for Cobain himself – the other was red). It has a humbucking pickup at the bridge, and a single-coil unit in the neck position. The vibrato tailpiece and bridge are very similar to the Mustang's; the Jaguar influence can be seen in the shape of the bass (right) side of the body. (Courtesy Amanda's Texas Underground, Nashville)

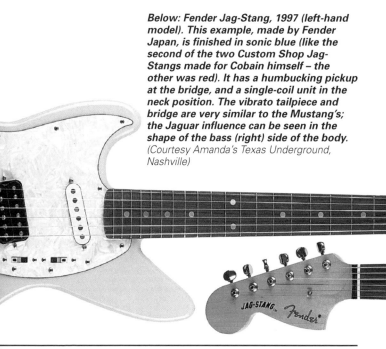

Left: Jackson SLS, 1998. The Soloist Superlite is about 25 percent thinner, and therefore considerably lighter, than the original Soloist. Its body and neck are mahogany, with a slightly contoured flamed maple top and a bound rosewood fingerboard. The pickups are made by Seymour Duncan. (Courtesy Akai/EMI Guitar Division)

417

single-pickup guitars with Strat-shaped bodies and powerful vibratos. One source for these hybrids was Charvel Manufacturing – named after Wayne Charvel, who had run a repair and customizing business in Azusa, California, but had sold it in 1978 to his former employee, Grover Jack-son. The company's mission to provide musicians with instruments that exactly matched their require-ments was enshrined in one of its early catalogs, which stated that "Charvel Mfg. believes very strongly in individual tastes....[there are] absolutely no color or design limitations." However, in 1980, Jack-son was approached by another leading Californian rock player, Randy Rhoads, to build a hot-rodded "Flying V"-style guitar, and was, according to Jackson/Charvel expert Robert Lane, "hesitant to use the Charvel logo on [it] because of its wild shape and contours." The problem was quickly solved: "Grover simply signed his last name on the headstock, and the first Jackson was born!"

Rhoads had recently become lead guitarist for British heavy rocker Ozzy Osbourne, and his high-profile use of the new V-shaped solid led to substantial demand for Grover Jackson's instruments. The following year, Jackson launched a hugely successful new model, the Soloist; it combined a so-called "Superstrat" shape with the neck-through-body design (first seen on Les Paul's "Log" – see pages 292-293) used on the custom Rhoads instruments.

Two Jackson Soloists are featured here, together with a KV1 – the company's most recent take on the V shape.

Right and Bottom right: Jackson Soloist SL1, 1998. The Soloist has a recognizably Stratocaster-like shape, although the horns that form the cutaways have been considerably extended. The instrument's neck section, which runs through the center of the body, is maple; the "wings" on either side are poplar. It is fitted with two Seymour Duncan humbucking pickups, and a Floyd Rose vibrato unit that allows dramatic detuning effects.
(Instruments courtesy Akai/EMI Guitar Division)

Below: Jackson KV1, 1998. The "King
V," Jackson suggests in its publicity,
is "a guitar only those with a certain
edge to their personality can
understand" – and it is endorsed by
one of the most powerful players on
the current heavy metal scene, Dave

Mustaine of Megadeth. It shares the
neck-through-body construction
(inset) of the other instruments
shown here, and has Seymour Duncan
pickups. This model is made from
poplar, but the guitar is also available
in korina wood.

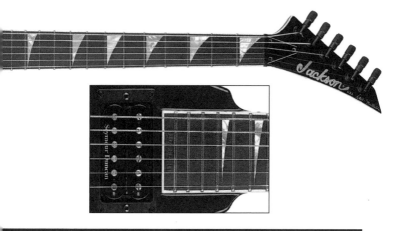

Jackson's Custom Models

Sadly, Randy Rhoads, who commissioned the first Jackson guitar, died in a flying accident while on tour with the Ozzy Osbourne Band in 1982. However, his advocacy of Grover Jackson's instruments encouraged many other hard rock and heavy metal players to adopt them. Among those to do so was his replacement in the Osbourne band, Jake E. Lee, who played Charvel "Strats"; star endorsees for the company's own-name guitars include Phil Collen of Def Leppard and Anthrax's Scott Ian.

The Rhoads guitar remains in Jackson's catalog in a variety of configurations and finishes. In 1995, it received a startling "makeover" when the radically reshaped Roswell Rhoads made its debut. As its name and space age appearance suggest,

this instrument was inspired by events in Roswell, New Mexico, where a UFO and its crew of aliens are alleged to have crashed in 1947. Its fingerboard inlays are modeled on another mysterious manifestation – the "crop circles" that sometimes appear in English cornfields. The standard Roswell Rhoads is produced in black or midnight blue, but is also available with custom "interference" finishes, in which the guitar's color seems to change depending on the angle from which it is seen. The special aluminum version illustrated was made in 1996.

Although its founder is no longer directly associated with the firm (he left in 1989), Jackson maintains the tradition of offering an extensive range of choices on made-to-order instruments. The models illustrated

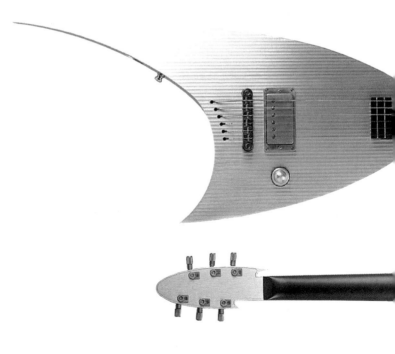

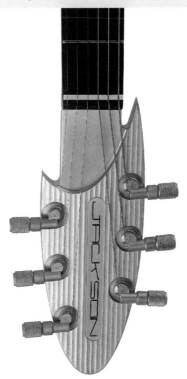

Below: Jackson Custom Shop Roswell Rhoads, 1996. This remarkable guitar has a body and headstock (right) made from aircraft-grade aluminum alloy. The neck is maple, with an ebony fingerboard, and the "crop-circle" inlays (above, inset) are mother-of-pearl. The instrument is fitted with a single high-output humbucking pickup made by Tom Holmes, and its locking tuning machines were made by Bill Turner of LSR Tuners in Chino, California.
(Courtesy Akai/EMI Guitar Division)

here are reworkings of its standard guitars; but the Jackson custom shop can also provide flamboyant graphic finishes, special inlays, and other extras, and offers to build its clients "almost anything they can dream up."

Jacksons have a bold, outrageous quality that makes them ideal and highly sought-after instruments for rock playing. The company ack-nowledges that its designs are not for everyone, but remains strongly committed to the original and daring approach it has pioneered over the last two decades. As it states in a recent catalog, "our goal is not to try and appeal to every last guitar player on earth, but rather to offer the most unique and individually styled instruments in the world."

Right: Jackson Custom Shop "Telecaster," 1998. This 1990s version of the Tele would have caused some raised eyebrows at Leo Fender's workshop! The Jackson Custom Shop Telecaster has three humbuckers, a Floyd Rose vibrato unit (the "whammy bar," which would be inserted into the socket on the right of the bridge, has been removed for this photograph), and a locking nut to improve tuning stability when using it. Note the reversed headstock, with the tuning machines facing away from the player.

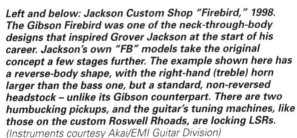

Left and below: Jackson Custom Shop "Firebird," 1998. The Gibson Firebird was one of the neck-through-body designs that inspired Grover Jackson at the start of his career. Jackson's own "FB" models take the original concept a few stages further. The example shown here has a reverse-body shape, with the right-hand (treble) horn larger than the bass one, but a standard, non-reversed headstock – unlike its Gibson counterpart. There are two humbucking pickups, and the guitar's tuning machines, like those on the custom Roswell Rhoads, are locking LSRs.
(Instruments courtesy Akai/EMI Guitar Division)

Klein Electric Guitars

Californian luthier Steve Klein's electric guitars look strikingly unconventional, but their appearance is far from being a visual gimmick. These headless instruments are designed to provide optimum balance and ease of playing, and are favored by a long list of famous musicians, including Bill Frisell, Andy Summers, Henry Kaiser, Kenny Wessel (guitarist with Ornette Coleman), and Lou Reed.

Klein, who started making guitars while still in high school in 1967, is based in Sonoma, about 30 miles (50km) north of San Francisco. He is also renowned for his acoustic instruments, and the bodies of his BF-96 and DT-96 electrics are shaped to support the player's right (or striking) arm in the same way that the upper bout of an acoustic does. Unlike some guitars, they are not neck- or body-heavy, and do not constrict the performer's arm movements by having to be held in position. The design also benefits the left (or fretting) arm, which is given easier access to the higher reaches of the neck by the gently sloping body shape that replaces a conventional cutaway.

Since 1995, the electric division of

Above: Klein DT-96, 1997. Basswood or alder is used on the DT-96; and this basswood example is fitted with a Novax "Fanned Fret Fingerboard System" (an option on all Klein electrics). Invented by luthier Ralph Novak, its fret positioning "fans out" from the 12th fret to provide better overall intonation than is possible with standard horizontal frets.

Left: Klein BF-96, 1997. The BF- and DT-96 shown here have identical electronics – two Seymour Duncan humbuckers in the neck and bridge positions, and a Seymour Duncan single-coil transducer in the middle (various custom options are also available) but their bodies are made from different woods.The BF-96 is made from swamp ash – a tree that remains immersed in water for several months of the year. The timber used to make the guitars is taken from the lowest, most waterlogged part of the trunk, and the BF-96 is somewhat heavier than its alder or basswood DF-counterpart. It is also produced in a version with hollowed-out cavities inside its body.
(Courtesy Klein Electric Guitars)

Steve Klein Guitars has been run by Steve's friend and colleague Lorenzo German, who builds the BF- and DT-96 models (as well as a Klein electric bass) with the assistance of a small staff. However, the third guitar illustrated here, an earlier, custom model known as "The Bird," offers a sharp contrast to the ergonomic perfection of these more recent designs. Described by Lorenzo as "the Anti-Klein guitar," it is heavy, not so comfortable to play – but, as he says, "an amazing art-piece." "The Bird" was com-missioned by W.G. "Snuffy" Walden, who had met Steve Klein in Colorado, but left for England with his band, the Stray Dogs, before the instrument was completed. The two men subsequently lost touch; but a few years ago, Steve discovered that Snuffy Walden had returned from overseas and become a leading Los Angeles-based musical director, providing music for major TV shows such as *Roseanne*, *Thirtysomething* and *The Wonder Years*. Snuffy has now seen the guitar, but has yet to take delivery of it!

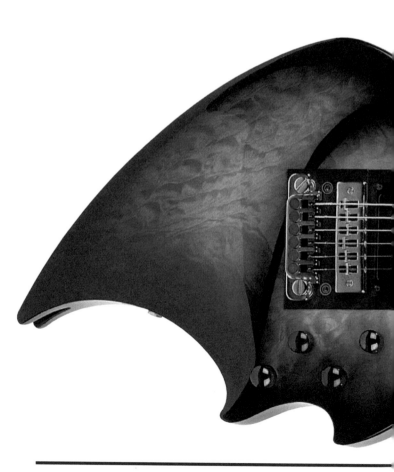

Below and right: Klein "Bird" custom, early 1970s. This guitar has a highly unusual shape, although, as Steve Klein comments, "It's patterned after a Les Paul, believe it or not! The critical points are where your [right] arm rests, and you can see a Les Paul shape in it." The metal decorations are solid bronze – which adds considerably to the instrument's weight – and its original strap (not shown here) was made from a camel harness! The modular pickup and bridge units can easily be removed and replaced.
(Courtesy Klein Electric Guitars)

Rick Turner's "Pretzel" and Model 1 Guitars

Rick Turner, one of America's most creative and respected luthiers, designs and builds his guitars in the Monterey Bay-side city of Santa Cruz. He came to California in 1968, having previously worked as a musician and instrument repairer on the East Coast – where he played guitar in Boston coffee houses, and backed the leading Canadian folk duo Ian and Sylvia. Rick subsequently joined a New York-based rock band, and continued his musical career as a guitarist and bassist after moving west; but by 1969 he had decided that his ambitions lay in electric instrument making.

Rick built his earliest electrics, including the "Pretzel" shown right, entirely by hand. Their design was tailored to what could be achieved with a minimum of tooling; as he explains, the Pretzel was "the first instrument where I ran the neck all the way through the body, and added wings onto the side. It was an easy way to attach the neck, and ideally suited to hand building. I think the only electric tool I had at that time was maybe an electric drill."

During this period, Rick became one of a group of highly talented engineers and craftspeople associated with the Grateful Dead. This

Right: Rick Turner "Pretzel," 1969. This hand-made guitar, with the carved-out body shape that gives it its nickname, shares some of the characteristics of early Alembic instruments. Like the Alembics, the "Pretzel" has a

neck-through-body construction – an alternative to gluing in or bolting on the neck, first used by Rickenbacker in the 1950s before being taken up by Gibson and a number of other manufacturers.

Below and bottom, inset: Rick Turner Model 1, 1998. The original Model 1 went out of production in 1981, but Rick Turner started making it again in 1990. Rick describes the instrument as an attempt to combine a Fender-style neck with a Les Paul-style body, providing a sound that gives "the warmth of a Les Paul, but with a bit more definition." The Model 1 has a Honduras mahogany body and a laminate maple/purple-heart neck, and the rotating humbucking pickup fitted in the "sound-hole" can be complemented by a range of other transducer and electronics options.
(Instruments courtesy Rick Turner Guitars)

team eventually coalesced into Alembic, Inc. (see pages 380-393) a company of which he was a co-founder and stockholder. After playing a key role in the design of Alembic's early instruments, he left the company in 1978 to start his own guitar-making business.

Rick's first post-Alembic guitar, the Model 1, caught the attention of Fleetwood Mac's Lindsey Buckingham while it was still on the drawing board. Buckingham ordered one of the new instruments, and Rick delivered an early prototype to him in 1979, during Fleetwod Mac's rehearsals for their *Tusk* tour. He recalls that "after [Lindsey] had been playing the guitar for about two hours, he yelled to his guitar tech, 'You can leave the Strats and the Les Pauls and the Ovations at home – this is all I need!'" Buckingham has used the Model 1 ever since, and it has been featured on many Fleetwood Mac videos and recordings.

Rick Turner's Renaissance and Model T Guitars

As a luthier, Rick Turner is especially interested in what he calls "the big fuzzy grey area between pure acoustic and pure electric. That's where most of what I do is done." Good "acoustic" sound is notoriously hard to obtain from amplified instruments (especially in noisy, unpredictable onstage settings), and even the finest acoustic guitars will give disappointing results when used with unsuitable added-on pickups. Rick's researches have convinced him of the need for an acoustic/electric that can provide what he calls an "optimum platform" for its pickup, and his "Renaissance" models are conceived as fully integrated systems – with instrument, transducer, and electronics all designed to operate together effectively.

Right: Rick Turner Renaissance, 1998. The instrument shown here belongs to San Francisco Bay Area musician, broadcaster, writer, and Grateful Dead expert David Gans. Designed to provide a high quality amplified acoustic sound, the Renaissance has a solid cedar top, and a mahogany center section with cavities on either side. Its bolted-on neck is maple, with a rosewood fingerboard, and it uses a coaxial pickup system developed by Rick Turner, with a pre-amplifier designed by Highlander Audio – a specialist transducer company which he co-founded in the late 1980s. The instrument's volume and tone controls are visible on its left shoulder.

▶ *(Courtesy Rick Turner Guitars)*

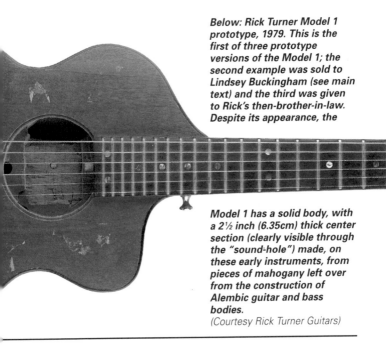

Below: Rick Turner Model 1 prototype, 1979. This is the first of three prototype versions of the Model 1; the second example was sold to Lindsey Buckingham (see main text) and the third was given to Rick's then-brother-in-law. Despite its appearance, the

Model 1 has a solid body, with a 2½ inch (6.35cm) thick center section (clearly visible through the "sound-hole") made, on these early instruments, from pieces of mahogany left over from the construction of Alembic guitar and bass bodies.
(Courtesy Rick Turner Guitars)

The Renaissance has many electric-style features, including a solid, Gibson 335-type center body section with hollow cavities on either side, a bolt-on neck, a slim, fast-playing fingerboard, and a deep cutaway. But other aspects of its construction – the braced, solid wood top, the overall shape and light weight – are typical of an acoustic instrument. Rick Turner recognizes the guitar's "hybrid" status by designating it an "ampli-coustic," and he produces it in different configurations – there are standard six-string, twelve-string, baritone, and nylon-strung versions.

Rick Turner has a refreshingly straightforward attitude to the complex process of creating a new instrument. He describes it as "being like a slot machine – but instead of three or four windows there may be twenty or thirty, and each one c those represents something in portant in the design. And wha happens is that ideas pile up in th wheels behind the windows, an every now and then I can pull th lever, and the windows will all com up cherries – and I've got a new guita design!" Rick certainly hit the jackpc with his Model T (shown below which won the "Best of Show" priz for "retro" guitars at the 1996 NAMN (National Association of Musi Merchants) show. Its appearance wa inspired by the oddly-shaped range c guitars and mandolins manufacture by the Chicago-based Kay compan from the late 1920s until the mic 1930s, although these did not hav the Model T's Formica covering. Ric says the instrument epitomize "taste carried to its absolut extreme!"

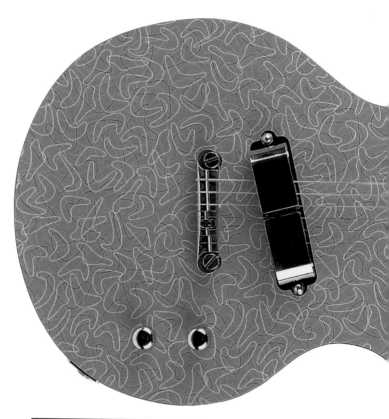

Right: The maple neck of the Model T contains two graphite bars for additional sustain. The guitar has standard volume and tone controls, but these can be bypassed via a push-pull switch on the tone knob, which sends the pickup output direct to the amplifier.

Below: Rick Turner Model T, 1998. The Model T has a Formica-laminate top and back (in a pattern Formica have named "Rosetta Boomerang"), and a Honduras mahogany body core. The Model T's pickup is a modernized version of the "horseshoe" design patented in the 1930s by George Beauchamp and used on many Electro and Rickenbacker guitars (see pages 256-259).
(Courtesy Rick Turner Guitars)

Jerry Jones Guitars

Nashville-based luthier Jerry Jones is dedicated to recreating the classic Danelectro, Silvertone, and Coral electric guitar designs of Nathan Daniel (see pages 50-51). Jerry, who was born in Jackson, Mississippi, has been making guitars in Music City since the early 1980s. He started out by producing a line of self-designed custom models, but a visit from a customer with a damaged Silvertone soon led to a change in direction. Jerry had always been interested in Nathan Daniel's instruments, and as he explains, "This was the first time I ever really got to have one in my shop for repairs. I sat down and thought,

'This is more like the kind of guitar that I would build for myself – rather than one of the custom guitars I was

Right: Jerry Jones Shorthorn, 1998. A more conventional double-cutaway design, available in two-or three-pickup versions. The attractively shaped white pickguard of the Shorthorn closely resembles the ones fitted to Nathan Daniel's Silvertone guitars (manufactured for the Sears company in the 1950s and 1960s). As Jerry Jones' catalog puts it, "They don't make 'em like they used to – so we do!"

Left and below: Jerry Jones Longhorn six-string bass, 1998. In 1956, Nathan Daniel was the first guitar maker to produce a six-string bass; he introduced the double-cutaway "Longhorn" shape seen here in 1958, using it for six- and four-string basses. Jerry produces his own versions of these models, as well as the "guitarlin" (a standard six-string with the Longhorn shape); he has also developed a Longhorn doubleneck, combining six-string guitar and six-string bass.
(Courtesy Jerry Jones Guitars)

building for other people.' So I [decided] I'd just make myself one." Jerry started work on his prototype instrument (shown opposite) in 1984, but put it aside when another client commissioned a Danelectro-style Longhorn six-string bass from him – an event which, in Jerry's words, "opened up the opportunity to make a whole line of [Daniel-inspired] guitars." The prototype remains unfinished, but is still used regularly for testing pickups.

Like Nathan Daniel, Jerry builds his guitar tops and backs from Masonite, and covers their sides with vinyl. However, he has replaced their V-shaped truss rods with a more modern, adjustable design, and now makes their necks out of maple, not poplar. He also uses high-technology CNC (computer numeric control) systems to carve out bodies and

necks – this speeds up production, enabling him and his four employees to complete 16 guitars a week.

Jerry relishes the simplicity and unpretentiousness of Nathan Daniel's instruments, and remembers their creator with admiration. In 1991, he visited Daniel in Hawaii, and recalls the fascination of "being able to sit down and talk to him about all this stuff – it was just incredible." He is uncertain about the origins of the Danelectro's distinctive shape, but comments that "if that design had been drawn out on a napkin in some diner back in the 1950s, I'd love to have that napkin!"

Right: Jerry Jones prototype, 1984. This unfinished instrument was Jerry's first attempt at a Danelectro-style guitar.

Above: Construction of the prototype closely follows Nathan Daniel's original design; a solid block of wood runs down the center of the body to the bridge, which is supported by another block (the two pieces of wood combine in an inverted "T" shape), and the guitar's two side sections are hollow.

Below: Jerry Jones N1 G3, 1998. A single-cutaway guitar fitted with three "lipstick-tube" pickups (Jerry also makes twelve-string and baritone models with the same body shape). The top and back are Masonite (hardboard), and the internal center and bridge blocks are poplar. The headstocks on Jerry Jones guitars retain the classic "Coke-bottle" shape of the Danelectro originals. Such instruments are available in a variety of standard and custom colors.
(Instruments courtesy Jerry Jones Guitars)

Guitars by Hugh Manson

The southwest of England's peaceful rural environment has attracted a number of leading British luthiers. One of the most distinguished of these, Hugh Manson, has lived and worked in the village of Sandford, near Exeter, for the last 12 years. He makes a wide variety of guitars, from the "Classic" range of Tele- and Strat-style six-strings (sold at his music stores in Exeter and Plymouth) to custom models for famous players such as Martin Barre from Jethro Tull and Led Zeppelin's John Paul Jones.

Hugh built his first guitar at the age of 14, and has been a professional luthier for the last two decades. His success did not come overnight: as he explains, "First you have to get a foot in the door, and until you get a name it's very difficult." One guitar design that helped to establish his reputation, the Kestrel electric, originally sold for under £300, but currently fetches well over double that amount on the second-hand market. Hugh now produces about 35 handmade instruments a year, with a delivery time of 12 to 15 weeks, and has a preference for more unusual commissions; his output includes

Below and right: Hugh Manson seven-string archtop guitar, 1998. This "neck-through-body" guitar was designed for a jazz player, who wanted a richer, more "hollow" sound than a typical rock instrument provides. Hugh Manson achieved it by building several air chambers between its flamed maple front and poplar sides. The five-piece neck is made from maple and American black walnut, with an ebony fingerboard. There is a Christian piezo-electric transducer (with a pre-amp designed by Hugh) built into the bridge saddles, providing a more "acoustic" sound that can be combined with the output from the Kent Armstrong humbucking pickup via a "pan" control on the body. The extra bass string extends the instrument's compass by a fifth.
(Courtesy Hugh Manson)

"mandolas, mandolins – everything with frets or without frets on. I made Cliff Richard's electric sitar, and I've made three-necks, four-necks, things with lights on, things with smoke coming out of them....That's really what I do, and what I want to do. I don't like to make the same guitar day in, day out."

One of the advantages of Hugh Manson's rural location is its proximity to high quality, sustainable sources of timber, and he chooses and matches the woods for his instruments with as much care as any acoustic luthier, commenting that "the art of making electric guitars is tailoring the wood to the sound." The three instruments seen here – a standard solid-body, a hollow-chambered jazz archtop, and a highly unusual eight-string model – display very different approaches to this crucial task, but share the striking visual appearance and superior playability that are hallmarks of all Manson electrics. Some of Hugh's more exotic guitars, including a double- and a triple-neck, are featured on pages 472-475.

Right: Hugh Manson Classic S, 1998. While its overall body shape is familiar, the "S" offers a number of special features, including Seymour Duncan pickups – a humbucker and two single-coils – and a vibrato unit designed by Trevor Wilkinson (currently working with Patrick Eggle Guitars in Birmingham, see pages 442-445).The front of the Classic S is Canadian quilted maple, and its back and sides are swamp ash. Bird's-eye maple is used for the neck, which has a rosewood fingerboard.
(Courtesy Hugh Manson)

Right and bottom right: Hugh Manson eight-string electric, 1988. The guitar's added top and bottom strings are both tuned to A (three octaves apart), and the triangular decorations on its body were all carved by hand.
The neck of the eight-string electric features inset LEDs (light-emitting diodes), connected to a power supply via a network of wires that run through tiny holes drilled through the body.
(Courtesy Paul Evans)

Patrick Eggle Guitars

In 1990, a young guitar maker from the English Midlands, Patrick Eggle, was displaying his wares at a local trade fair. He had only a small number of instruments on show, but one of the visitors to his booth, Andrew Selby, was so impressed with their quality and originality that he decided to set up a company to manufacture them. Just a year later, the new firm, Patrick Eggle Guitars, launched a production version of the model Selby had seen at the fair. This instrument, the Berlin, quickly established itself

as a modern classic, and it is currently used by a string of major players, including Tony Iommi of Black Sabbath, Big Country's Bruce Watson, Bill Nelson, Midge Ure, and Ali and Robin Campbell of UB40.

By the mid-1990s, the company was producing up to 2,000 electrics, acoustics, and basses a year; but more recently, it has undergone a fundamental reorganization, moving from its original home in Coventry to smaller, newly converted premises in Birmingham. It has also rationalized

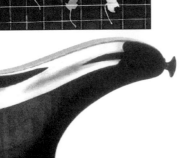

Left: The Patrick Eggle Custom Berlin Pro is fitted with two Seymour Duncan humbuckers (an Alnico Pro II in the neck and a Custom Custom at the bridge) and has a Fishman VS50 piezo system built into its bridge/vibrato unit. This provides an acoustic-type tone that can be mixed in with the other pickups.

Below: Patrick Eggle Custom Berlin Pro, 1998. The Berlin is available in a variety of configurations, and with a 22- or 24-fret fingerboard. The instrument has a maple top (finished in "Adriatic Burst") and a mahogany body; its hardware (including the distinctive Spertzel Trimlok locking tuning machines seen bottom left and right) is finished in gold, and its "falling maple leaf" fingerboard inlays (above left, inset) are abalone. (Courtesy Patrick Eggle Guitars)

its range of models, and now makes only electric guitars – various versions of the Berlin, as well as the Anniversary, Legend, Vintage Classic, and the new Fret King range (shown on pages 446-449). These are built using tools and equipment taken from the firm's old Coventry plant – including a neck profiler converted from a machine for making rifle butts!

Sales Director Peter Goalby welcomes the changes, while acknowledging that Patrick Eggle Guitars has had to face "a lot of tears and a lot of heartache" to reach its present, impressive level of success. The company now employs a much smaller staff than the 30-strong workforce once based in Coventry, currently produces about 20 to 25 instruments a month, and is recognized as one of the UK's most successful guitar manufacturers.

Patrick Eggle himself left the business in 1994, although he remains on excellent terms with his former colleagues, and has visited the new factory in Birmingham. Peter Goalby explains that "Pat never wanted to be involved in a manufacturing situation. He's a designer, and he designed what became a world-class guitar – and you don't do that every day".

Right: Patrick Eggle Berlin Legend, 1998. This model is based on a Limited Edition guitar endorsed by Big Jim Sullivan – a famous British session player who for many years was the guitarist in Tom Jones' backing band. It has a lightweight swamp ash body with a highly figured maple top, a maple neck, and an ebony fingerboard. The pickups are Seymour Duncan "Live" humbuckers, and the vibrato unit (as on the Custom Berlin Pro) is a VS100 unit designed by Patrick Eggle Guitars' Creative Director, Trevor Wilkinson (see page 446).

Left: Patrick Eggle Berlin Pro HT, 1998. The Pro HT is the fixed-bridge, non-vibrato version of the Berlin. It features the same electronics as the Custom model, but without the Fishman pickup. The Berlin's circuitry is designed for maximum versatility and convenience. Its upper knob is a volume control, while the lower knob is a three-position rotary switch, allowing the pickups to be used in single-coil or humbucking modes, or as humbuckers via a special electronic filter providing a rich, bluesy sound.
(Courtesy Patrick Eggle Guitars)

Eggle's "Fret King" Esprit Range

Patrick Eggle Guitars' most recent additions to its range are the "Fret King" Esprit models, a trio of strikingly shaped solid-bodies launched in late 1998. They were designed by the company's Creative Director, Trevor Wilkinson – an influential name in the electric guitar world, famous for the widely used vibrato unit that bears his name. He explains that the Esprits, his first project for Eggle, are aimed at "people who are wanting something a little different from a Strat," and there is certainly nothing run-of-the-mill about these distinctive and reasonably priced new instruments.

The Esprits' shape suggests a cross between a Fender Jazzmaster and a Gibson Firebird, or perhaps one of the Gibson "modernistic" guitars developed in the late 1950s (see pages 370-373). All three models have reversed headstocks, with six-in-line tuning machines facing away from the player, but non-reverse bodies. Like the original "modernistics" (the Explorer and the Flying V) the Esprits are made from korina (sometimes known as limba) wood – a mahogany-like African timber first used for lutherie by Gibson in the early 1950s.

The new range offers a variety of pickup configurations. The Fret King Esprit 1 (not illustrated here) and Esprit 3 are fitted with Gotoh-made replicas of the classic Gibson single-

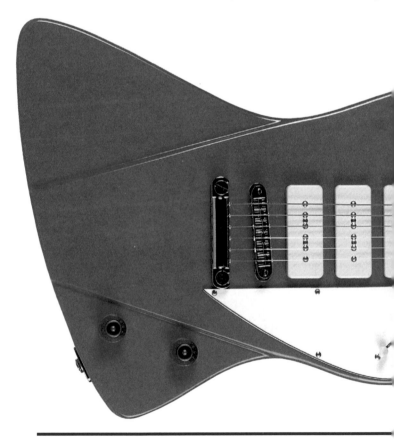

Right: Patrick Eggle Fret King Esprit 5, 1998. The top-of-the-range Esprit, it is fitted with two humbucking pickups. These guitars' distinctive, Gibson-like shape is complemented by the use of "Tune-o-Matic"-type bridges and "stop" tailpieces similar to those found on the Firebird, Explorer, and other classic Gibson models. The instrument shown here has a natural finish; a wide variety of other colors are available.

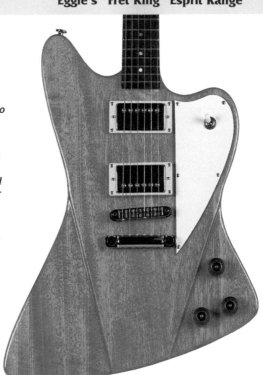

Left and below: Patrick Eggle Fret King Esprit 3, 1998. This coral red Esprit features three replica P-90 pickups (made by Gotoh, who also supply the Fret Kings' tuning machines, bridges, and tailpieces).
(Instruments courtesy Patrick Eggle Guitars)

coil P-90 "soapbar" pickup. (This vintage transducer, originally fitted to a wide range of classic Gibson guitars, from the ES-5 and ES-175 to the Les Paul and the Firebird, is as popular as ever; another version of it can be seen on the Paul Reed Smith "McCarty Soapbar" model featured on pages 470-471.) By contrast, the top-of-the-range Esprit 5 has two humbucking pickups, wired to a three-way coil-tapping switch in the same way as Patrick Eggle's Berlin models. This arrangement allows a wide range of tonal variation, including useful approximations of Strat-type single-coil sounds.

The three Fret King Esprits are an ingenious combination of "retro" features and contemporary design, and were awarded the "Best Guitar of the Show" accolade when they were displayed at the 1998 Frankfurt Music Fair. The Fret King range will soon be augmented by two new models designed by Trevor Wilkinson, the Corona and the Country Squire.

Right: Incomplete body for Patrick Eggle Fret King Esprit 3, 1998. This laguna blue model has not yet had its fingerboard, pickups, or hardware installed, although the holes for the control knobs, bridge, and tailpiece have been drilled, and the pickup and selector switch areas routed out.

The Fret King Esprits have korina bodies and necks (with mahogany as an alternative option) and rosewood fingerboards.
(Courtesy Patrick Eggle Guitars)

Electric Guitars by Robert Benedetto

Robert Benedetto, of East Strouds-burg, Pennsylvania, is recognized as today's finest archtop luthier. In the last 30 years, he has designed instruments for many leading players, from Johnny Smith and Chuck Wayne to Andy Summers and Earl Klugh, and a recent commission from the great American jazz guitarist Kenny Burrell (b.1931) has given him particular pleasure. As Bob explains, "In 1966, I bought my very first jazz guitar album, [Kenny Burrell's] *Man at Work*. He instantly became a great inspiration, [and] I felt strongly that someday I would make him a guitar. Imagine my excitement when I received a phone call from Kenny 30 years later: 'Bob, I'd like to talk with you about making me a guitar'. Wow, I'm living my dream!"

The original plan was for ▶

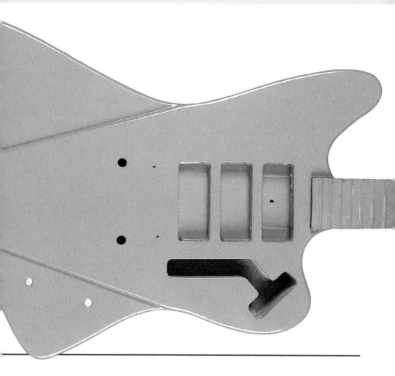

Below: Benedetto custom "Kenny Burrell" model (prototype), 1998. This 17-inch (43.2cm) model (16-inch and 18-inch sizes are also available) has a top of select European spruce, a back and sides of select, highly flamed European maple, and a three-piece neck of flamed American maple. Its tapered body is 2⁵/₈ inches (6.7cm) deep at the neck, gently broadening to 3⁷/₁₆ inches (8.7cm) at the tailpiece. The inlay motifs are abalone, and Kenny Burrell's name is engraved in a mother-of-pearl ribbon on the headstock.

(Courtesy Robert Benedetto; photograph by John Bender)

Benedetto to build a single, custom instrument for Burrell, but it was subsequently decided to produce a limited edition "Kenny Burrell" model, incorporating a number of special features developed by its two creators. The guitar has a tapered body depth (widening from neck to tailpiece) which, in Kenny Burrell's words, makes it "the most comfortable [instrument] you'll ever play," and is fitted with a single Benedetto B-6 pickup. Kenny first used the prototype in public at The Chinery Collection and Smithsonian Institution's "Blue Guitar" concert in June 1998. His response to Bob Benedetto's craftsmanship is simple and heartfelt: "You made my dreams come true."

Benedetto is the most prolific independent maker of seven-string archtops, and the example shown here was custom-built for one of the instrument's finest exponents, jazz guitarist Jimmy Bruno. It has a Benedetto B-7 humbucking pickup fitted directly onto its top, but retains an excellent acoustic sound; its volume and tone controls are positioned near the edge of the top to prevent them interfering with vibrations from the bridge.

On "Il Colibri" (The Dove), Bob has again been at pains to maximize the guitar's acoustic tone, using an arched construction for the top and back, and leaving openings around the two pickups for the sound to escape. This beautiful instrument, made for guitarist Carl Trollinger, also features fine mother-of-pearl and abalone inlays on its headstock, fingerboard, and tailpiece.

Right and below right: Benedetto seven-string, custom-built for Jimmy Bruno, 1995. All the woods used on this 16-inch guitar are American: its top is Sitka spruce, its back and sides flamed Big Leaf maple, and its fittings ebony. The "Jimmy Bruno" inlay on the tailpiece is mother-of-pearl. The finish is Benedetto's signature honey blonde color. The instrument's medium-high string action (preferred by Bruno) contributes to its powerful acoustic and electric sound.
(Courtesy Jimmy Bruno)

Left: Benedetto "Il Colibri," 1995. The body and neck are made from American bird's-eye maple (grown in the northeastern U.S.A.) and the ebony tailpiece is veneered with exotic wood burl, which is also used for the pickguard and headstock. The instrument has an ebony fingerboard, two humbucking pickups, and Schaller machine heads with mother-of-pearl buttons.
(Courtesy Carl Trollinger)

Rosendean Guitars

Having a guitar custom-made is not dissimilar to being measured for a Savile Row suit. Every contour of the instrument, and every aspect of its look and feel, can be precisely tailored to a player's needs, with results that combine comfort and elegance with the highest quality and durability. Trevor Dean, whose one-man company, Rosendean, is based in the southern English town of Woking, has been building custom guitars professionally since 1989. His best-known client is the distinguished British jazzman John Etheridge, who commissioned the six-string Black Ruby model seen below. Etheridge is a hard-working player with a vigorous playing style, and the Black Ruby is designed to withstand a good deal of wear and tear. Its back and sides are made from black-eyed Persian larch, giving exceptional lightness and strength, and Trevor has protected the edges of the body with plastic binding. The instrument also offers an impressive range of tones, and its six-way control circuit and special high-pass filters ensure that, in Trevor's own words, there is always "treble to burn."

The seven-string version of the

Right: Rosendean Black Diamond, 1998. The Black Diamond is an 18-inch (45.7cm) hollow-body archtop designed for both acoustic and electric playing. It has a pine top, and a back and neck made from maple. Its fingerboard is ebony; the headstock and pickguard are waxed Brazilian rosewood, and the body bindings are maple, ebony, and satinwood. The Rosendean Black Diamond's natural blonde finish, nickel-plated hardware, and abalone dot markers all contribute to its simple, but elegant appearance; its owner, Stewart Cockett, wanted it to look more like a 40-year-old vintage model than an obviously new guitar.

*eft: Rosendean Black Ruby
John Etheridge Signature
Model, 1996. The Black Ruby is a
semi-solid design, with seven
nternal compartments. Its body
s 16 inches (40.6cm) wide, with
a top carved from bear-claw
pine, and back and sides of
ranian larch (a material that has* seldom, if ever, previously been
used for guitar making). Trevor
Dean fits Kent Armstrong
pickups to all his instruments;
this model features five single-
coil units, which were hand-
built to his specifications.
*(Instruments courtesy Trevor
Dean)*

Black Ruby bears a family resemblance to the Etheridge model, but has a mahogany back and sides, wooden bindings, and a single neck pickup. Its owner asked for a brass tailpiece covered in wood; Trevor normally uses nickel tailpieces like the one on the Black Diamond archtop (page 453) made for musician Stewart Cockett. In a recent article published in *Jazz Guitar International*, Stewart recalls how, while the instrument was being built, he would call at Trevor's workshop every week to check on its development. "From November 1997 the guitar progressed quickly... Eventually the neck was fitted and I could sit [it] on my knee and get a sense of its size and balance. I was impatient to hear it, but weeks of finishing and polishing were still to come before strings went on and we heard how it would sound." The completed guitar proved to be well worth the wait. Stewart describes it as "quite fantastic," and charac-terizes its tone as "full, smooth, evenly balanced and totally inspiring...[it] will stimulate a whole new musical direction for me."

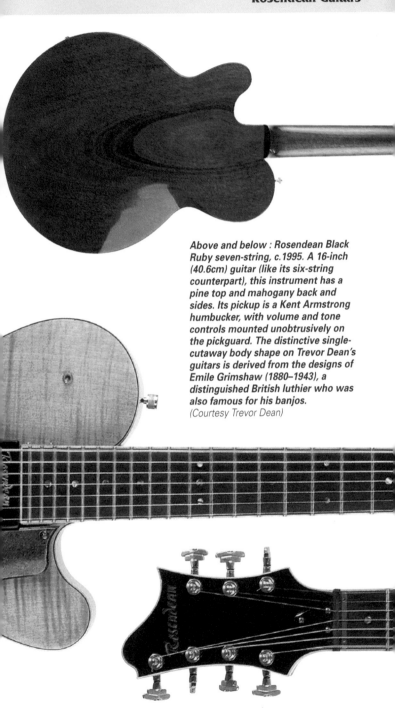

*Above and below : Rosendean Black
Ruby seven-string, c.1995. A 16-inch
(40.6cm) guitar (like its six-string
counterpart), this instrument has a
pine top and mahogany back and
sides. Its pickup is a Kent Armstrong
humbucker, with volume and tone
controls mounted unobtrusively on
the pickguard. The distinctive single-
cutaway body shape on Trevor Dean's
guitars is derived from the designs of
Emile Grimshaw (1880–1943), a
distinguished British luthier who was
also famous for his banjos.*
(Courtesy Trevor Dean)

Mark Knopfler's Pensa Guitars

Custom-designed guitars by Rudy Pensa are played by an impressive list of world-famous performers, including Mark Knopfler, Eric Clapton, and Lou Reed. His instruments, created in the workshop of his music store on West 48th Street in Manhattan (his base since the 1980s), originally carried the Pensa-Suhr label, and it was John Suhr, described as Rudy's "repair guru," who was responsible for building the model that first brought the two men international attention. This guitar – Pensa-Suhr No. 001 – was commissioned by Mark Knopfler, and its design evolved from a drawing made on a napkin while he and Rudy were having lunch! The finished instrument (illustrated here) debuted in 1988 during Dire Straits' appearance at Nelson Mandela's 70th birthday concert (broadcast live throughout the world at a time when the future President of South Africa was still in prison) and Mark Knopfler has gone on to use it for many other major performances and recordings. It features EMG pickups, a Floyd-Rose bridge, and a beautiful one-piece top made from quilted maple. Mark, who possesses a wide range of vintage electrics, confirms that the Pensa-Suhr is something special: "[It] enables me to play with a lot more power than a Strat, and it's more flexible. I've got more range on it than most other guitars." He also owns

Right: The headstock of the Pensa-Suhr (seen from the back).

Below: This instrument (No. 001) is sometimes referred to as the "Flame Maple," due to its distinctive one-piece top. The neck is also made from maple, with a Brazilian rosewood fingerboard, and the rest of its body is made from mahogany. The bridge pickup is an "'85" EMG humbucker, with two SA humbuckers in the middle and neck positions. The guitar also features an EMG SPC Presence tone boost, activated by pulling on the master tone control.
(Courtesy Mark Knopfler)

several other Pensa-Suhrs, including a synthesizer-guitar built to control his Synclavier system, and a black model, dating from 1987, and fitted – like Pensa-Suhr No. 001 – with EMG pickups.

In 1990, John Suhr and Rudy Pensa parted company; Suhr spent the next few years working for Fender's Custom Shop, and has recently started his own lutherie business. Meanwhile, Rudy Pensa has continued to design superb electric instrument for Mark Knopfler

and other distinguished customers. In 1993, Knopfler took delivery of a new Pensa solid-body which has a flamed koa top and three single-coil pickups made by Lindy Fralin, a pickup designer and manufacturer who specializes in creating vintage-sounding transducers for Tele-caster- and Strat-type guitars. Mark's most recent Pensa, dating from 1996, also uses Fralin pickups, but this model features active circuitry, as well as a shorter, Gibson-style scale length.

Right: Pensa Custom, 1996. Another of Mark Knopfler's Pensas, also sporting a flamed maple top and mahogany back. The pickups are by Lindy Fralin

(with active electronics) and, unlike the other instruments shown here, the guitar is fitted with a "stop" tailpiece.
(Instruments courtesy Mark Knopfler)

Left: Pensa Custom, c. 1993. The Lindy Fralin-designed pickups on this model, also made for Mark Knopfler, are "'54s," designed to recreate the sound of an early Fender Stratocaster (the Strat was first introduced in 1954). The instrument has a flamed koa top, and a mahogany back.

Hybrids and Curiosities

The earliest electric guitars were conceived as working tools rather than props or art objects, but performers quickly recognized the instrument's visual and theatrical possibilities. Onstage, it could be posed with as well as played, used suggestively or aggressively, and even smashed up to excite an audience. It was also comparatively simple to make solid-bodied electrics in unusual shapes and finishes. One of the first artists to feature such instruments was rhythm and blues star Bo Diddley (b.1928), who commissioned the Gretsch company to build him several guitars with oblong bodies, and at least one covered in fur! Billy Gibbons and Dusty Hill of ZZ Top followed in Diddley's footsteps with their automobile- and Texas-shaped instruments, and a number of heavy metal guitarists favor even more outlandish custom designs.

However, the "Betty Boop" guitar shown here takes the concept of decorative bodywork several stages further. It was made in about 1984 by Johnson of Los Angeles for Earl Slick, best known as the guitarist on David Bowie's *Young Americans* and *Station To Station*. Betty herself probably has

Below and right: Johnson "Betty Boop" guitar, c.1984–85.
Building an electric guitar in the shape of a cartoon character is a remarkable feat of design and engineering – though it is hard to imagine any player using the "Betty Boop" as a regular

working instrument!
Betty is fitted with a single humbucking bridge pickup and vibrato system, and she can currently be seen at Real Guitars, San Francisco, where this photograph was taken.
(Courtesy Gary Brawer)

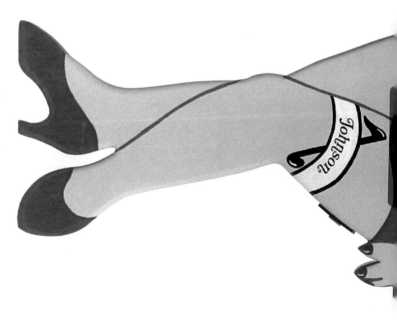

rather different tastes in music – her cartoon films, originally made by animator Max Fleischer, sometimes featured guests like Louis Armstrong, Cab Calloway, and Rudy Vallee – but she seems to have survived her transformation from celluloid into wood and steel remarkably well. Other Johnson creations include guitars shaped like spaceships and machine-guns.

The Fisher "Saturn V," with a rocket-style body that owes its inspiration to NASA, was commissioned by Memphis-based blues guitarist Eric Gales. Eric signed his first recording contract at the age of only 15, winning the "Best New Talent" category in *Guitar World* magazine's Readers' Poll only a year later. He has subsequently made a number of highly acclaimed albums, and his two brothers, Eugene and Manuel, are also talented players.

The third instrument on these pages is a Gibson guitar harp dating from 1993. It was designed by Roger Giffin, an English luthier who was in charge of Gibson's Los Angeles-based Custom Shop for five years, and later worked for its Research and Development department. Giffin now runs his own successful lutherie business in California's San Fernando Valley.

Right: Fisher "Saturn V", c.1994. This guitar has two humbucking pickups and a vibrato unit incorporating tuners for each string – these can be seen at the base of the tailpiece. Eric Gales' name is inscribed on the right-hand side of the body.
This "Saturn V" is a left-hand model. Both Eric Gales (for whom the instrument was made) and his two guitar-playing brothers, Eugene and Manuel, are left-handers.
(Courtesy Rod & Hank's, Memphis)

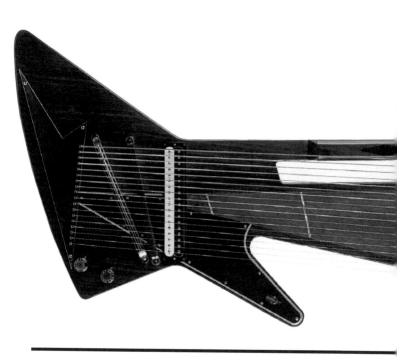

*Left: Gibson guitar harp,
1993. There are 18 strings,
attached to a headstock
that is almost two feet
(61cm) wide. Although the
basic outline resembles
the angular solid-body
guitar designs introduced
by Gibson in the late
1950s, there is no
fingerboard, and the
instrument is much closer
to a harp than a guitar. It
is fitted with a single,
specially extended
Seymour Duncan Zebra
pickup.*
*(Courtesy San Diego
Guitars)*

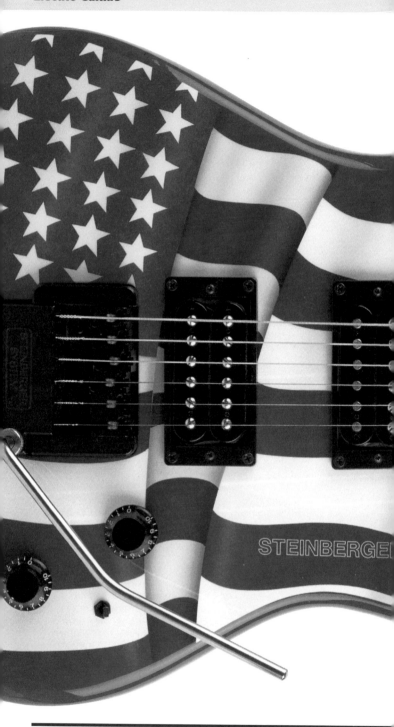

STEINBERGE

SECTION FOUR

Today and Tomorrow

Like its acoustic counterpart, the electric guitar has suffered occasional periods of reduced popularity, but its survival has never been seriously threatened. Even synthesizers and samplers have failed to supplant it; in fact, a number of manufacturers now produce MIDI controllers that permit signals derived from guitar strings to trigger synth modules, with varying degrees of success. Other electronic innovations have proved more popular with players – like the piezo-electric pickup systems fitted to the Patrick Eggle Custom Pro (pages 442-445) and the Parker Fly (pages 468-469), which offer a useful approximation of acoustic guitar tone that can be combined with the instrument's "regular" sound. The use of stereo for guitars is also gradually growing, although the need for a pair of amplifiers and speakers onstage still deters some musicians (and their roadies!).

Stereo circuitry comes into its own on Emmett Chapman's Stick (see pages 476-477), the pickup of which allows bass and melody strings to be routed to individual audio channels on a mixing desk, where they can be processed separately before being panned into place. Such sonic flexibility is only one small aspect of Chapman's remarkably versatile design; and today, more than 25 years since the Stick's introduction, there seems little doubt that this distinctive new member of the electric guitar family is here to stay.

Alongside such innovative recent instruments, later pages in this book include other unashamedly "retro" models paying respectful homage to the great designs of the past and their creators. Paul Reed Smith's McCarty Soapbar solid (pages 142-143) is a tribute to the former Gibson President, who has acted as a consultant for PRS; and we conclude by featuring Jerry Jones' superb revival of Nathan Daniel's 1960s sitar guitar alongside a striking modern reworking of the century-old "harp guitar" concept by another leading contemporary luthier, Steve Klein.

Left and below: Steinberger solid-body, with "American Flag" artwork by Jan Lawrence, 1997. U.S. designer Ned Steinberger pioneered the concept of "headless" guitars; the tuners on instruments like this one are located on the bottom edge of the bridge/tailpiece.
(Courtesy Rod & Hank's, Memphis)

Towards the Future

It is now three decades since Alembic co-founder Ron Wickersham fitted custom electronics into instruments owned by two leading San Francisco Bay area musicians – Grateful Dead bassist Phil Lesh, and singer/songwriter/guitarist David Crosby (who still uses the Guild twelve-string containing his original Alembic pickup). Since then, some of the approaches Ron pioneered have become standard practice among guitar and electronics designers; but back in the late 1960s, many performers were still struggling to find high performance equipment that could stand up to the rigors of rock playing. As his daughter Mica (now Alembic's General Manager) explains, "Probably the main driving force to make the instruments the way they were was the musicians themselves. Jack Casady [of Jefferson Airplane], Phil Lesh and David Crosby were very articulate at describing their frustrations, and my dad is a very good listener; so he could understand exactly what the problems were and help to solve them."

When guitarists and bass players came to Ron Wickersham wanting lower noise levels, increased dynamic range and wider tonal variation from their instruments, he was able to answer their needs using the skills he had developed as a broadcast engineer. Unlike some technical experts, who, in his words, regarded rock as "a fad – something people wouldn't need good tools for," he loved the

Below and right: Alembic California Special, 1998. This instrument retains the neck-through-body construction found on most Alembics, but its solid maple body and slightly Strat-like overall shape are, in the words of the company's publicity, "perfect for those situations where the 'hippie sandwich' look might not be appropriate." ("Hippie sandwich" is an affectionate and widely used nickname for "traditional" Alembic bodies like those illustrated in pages 380-383, which are built up from several layers of wood.) The California Special is fitted with two single-coil pickups in the neck and middle positions, and a humbucker at the bridge. Alembic staffer Eric Coleman created the custom finish on this example.
(Courtesy Alembic, Inc.)

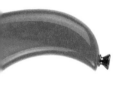

music, appreciated the problems posed by powerful amplification and high volume playing, and sought to give musicians the freedom to create the sound they wanted. "When you did provide a tool with more versatility, then more music came out, and people discovered the music that may have been trapped in their heads – [music that] they didn't even know they were having trouble getting out!"

Alembic's current instruments, like its earliest ones, aim to offer the widest possible range of tone-colors and to minimize noise and interference through the use of low impedance circuitry, active pre-amps, and specially designed pickups with ceramic magnets. Two fine recent models are illustrated here: the California Special, whose six-in-line headstock and distinctively shaped body are new departures for the company; and the six-string Orion bass – a set neck instrument also available as a four- or five-string.

Guitars by Ken Parker and Paul Reed Smith

Rock and jazz are radical forms of music, but the guitarists who play them often have strongly conservative views about instrument design. After more than 40 years, the classic Fender and Gibson solid-bodies are as popular as ever, and many musicians still believe them to be unsurpassed in terms of sound and feel. Significantly, a number of successful contemporary guitar makers share their customers' reverence for the past, and seek to develop, perfect, and even combine key aspects of the old "favorites" in their current models.

At first sight, there is absolutely nothing traditional or orthodox about the work of another leading American luthier, Ken Parker, whose Fly Deluxe is illustrated here. But beneath this instrument's carbon- and glass-fiber outer shell (or "exoskeleton") is a ▶

Left: Alembic Orion six-string bass, 1998. The Orion is based on Alembic's popular Europa model, but has a set neck of cross-grained maple instead of the Europa's neck-through-body design. Its body has a mahogany core, and is available with a wide range of top laminates; the fingerboard is ebony. It is fitted with two Alembic MXY56 pickups, and has controls for volume, pan (blend between the pickups), and treble and bass.
(Courtesy Alembic, Inc.)

Below: Parker Fly Deluxe, 1998. The Fly, which got its name because of its remarkably light weight, is fitted with two DiMarzio humbucking pickups as well as a piezo-electric transducer system designed by Larry Fishman. The piezo units, which are screwed into the body, provide a realistic "amplified acoustic" sound; this can be used on its own or mixed with the humbuckers. The Fly's many other unusual features include stainless steel frets set directly onto the fingerboard; they have no tangs (pointed undersides slotted into grooves at the fret positions) and withstand wear better than conventional fret wire. The guitar has a special non-locking vibrato system; its arm was removed for this photograph.
(Courtesy Room 335, Rose-Morris, London)

core of resonant wood, and Parker, who started out as an archtop maker, has likened his design to the construction of Renaissance lutes, whose sound was similarly enhanced by the use of softwoods covered in ebony veneers. The Fly is certainly an extremely responsive guitar, and its electronics – incorporating piezo-electric pickups as well as hum-buckers – offer the player a wide palette of "acoustic" and electric tones. It is also remarkably comfortable and well balanced, and weighs less than 5lb (2.3kg). Since its introduction in 1993, it has attracted a number of high-profile users, including David Bowie's guitarist Reeves Gabrels.

Maryland-based luthier Paul Reed Smith has brilliantly used "old favourites" concepts in his current designs. His guitars are elegant, versatile, and full of new ideas, while incorporating two familiar basic features: a Gibson Les Paul-style carved top and glued-in neck, and a Strat-like double cutaway and vibrato unit. Reed Smith's designs have evolved through years of experimentation and "field-testing" in live performance. As a struggling young craftsman in Annapolis, he would obtain backstage passes to concert venues and offer his instruments to star players on the understanding that "if [they] didn't love the guitars they didn't have to pay me even when I knew I couldn't make my rent the next day." His efforts eventually paid off, and today PRS guitars, which are favorites of Carlos Santana and many other famous names, are in demand all over the world.

Right: Paul Reed Smith McCarty Soapbar, 1998. This instrument pays homage to Ted McCarty, the former President of Gibson, who was responsible for the introduction of the Les Paul and many other classic designs. Its pickups are modern re-creations (built by Seymour Duncan) of Gibson's vintage single-coil P-90 "soapbar" unit. The guitar has a solid mahogany body and a rosewood fingerboard.
(Courtesy Room 335, Rose-Morris, London)

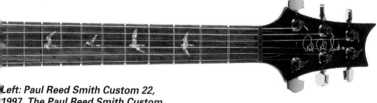

Left: Paul Reed Smith Custom 22, 1997. The Paul Reed Smith Custom range was launched in 1985; this 22-fret model (24-fret necks are also available) has a carved maple top, a mahogany back and neck, and a rosewood fingerboard. Its pickups are PRS Dragon I humbuckers. The instrument is fitted with three *control knobs: a conventional volume and tone, plus a rotary selector switch offering five different pickup configurations (including coil-taps and series/parallel switching).*
(Courtesy Chandler Guitars, Kew

Hugh Manson's Multi-necked Guitars

For many rock listeners, the use of double-neck guitars conjures up images of the progressive and jazz-rock scenes of the 1970s, with stars such as Jimmy Page and John McLaughlin reaching new heights of virtuosity on their Gibson double-necks – which combined standard six strings with twelve-string or bass necks and pickups. Multi-neck lap steels had been a familiar sight since the 1930s, but according to guitar expert George Gruhn, the first electric, double-neck Spanish-style instruments began to appear in the late 1950s, when Gibson produced a hollow-body six- and twelve-string (the EDS-1275) as well as a double-neck mandolin. These models were available only to special order, and in about 1962 they were joined by a bass- and six-string, SG-style guitar, the EBSF-1250.

Perhaps instruments like these were a little ahead of their time; it took the first stirrings of progressive rock to establish them fully. By the 1970s, with this musical movement in full swing (and the 1275 temporarily discontinued by Gibson), their popularity had grown considerably, and cheap double-neck copies had begun to emerge from the Far East. Meanwhile, at the other end of the price and quality scale, a number of famous players were commissioning individual luthiers to produce double- and multi-necked guitars to their own

Right: Hugh Manson custom double-neck, c.1996 This model is a combined six-string guitar and six-string bass. It has a maple body and an ebony fingerboard, and is fitted with EMG pickups. Both necks are headless; the standard guitar section incorporates a vibrato and a locking nut. The instrument's strings are tuned using the adjusters on each tailpiece.
(Courtesy Paul Evans)

Left: Hugh Manson custom triple-neck, c.1980. A one twelve-string/two six-string "neck-through-body" design incorporating illuminating LEDs. The body is mahogany and maple.
(Courtesy Paul Evans)

exacting specifications.

Hugh Manson, of Sandford, Devon, is undoubtedly the UK's leading maker of electric guitars of this type. His brother Andy, also a distinguished luthier, specializes in unusual acoustic instruments; their customers include John Paul Jones of Led Zeppelin, who, when asked about what he spent most of his money on during a recent survey, replied, "Buying guitars from Hugh and Andy Manson." Another of Hugh's regular clients, a leading rock guitarist, was so eager to see the blueprints for his new Manson guitar that the plans for it had to be redrawn to fit into the fax machine!

As Hugh explained earlier in this book (see page 440), he enjoys the challenge of designing and building wholly original instruments; and the three examples of his work shown here, all commissioned by musician Paul Evans, clearly demonstrate his ability to create guitars that are musically and aesthetically unique.

Emmett Chapman and The "Stick"®

The Stick® is an ingenious and versatile electric stringed instrument with a substantial, steadily widening base of players throughout the world. Its inventor, Emmett Chapman, started out as a jazz guitarist; in 1964, while stationed with the U.S. Air Force in Omaha, Nebraska, he built himself a nine-string electric, and used it to develop his own highly original fingering techniques. As he explains, "I was playing complex chords in the style of jazz pianists while trying to free my melody lines in the style of Jimi Hendrix. Under Hendrix's influence I had the urge to play standing up, sliding my left hand around on the fingerboard, and doing one handed hammer-ons and hammer-offs in his style." Hammering – making a string sound by pressing it firmly onto the ▶

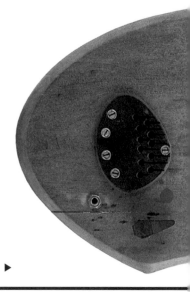

Below: Hugh Manson custom fifteen-string, 1992. This remarkable instrument is effectively a six-string bass and a standard six-string guitar with additional high A, D, and G strings. It has a maple body, staggered tailpieces to accommodate the varying string lengths, and a gradually widening neck reinforced with two truss-rods. *(Courtesy Paul Evans)*

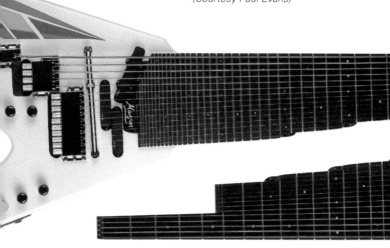

Below: Chapman prototype, 1964. Emmett Chapman's uniquely designed guitar, which led to the discovery of two-handed tapping, was built in the woodshop at the USAF base in Omaha, Nebraska, where he was stationed. Emmett's first attempt at instrument-making, it began with nine strings, but later underwent extensive modification to enable the "Stick" tapping method. It is a neck-through-body design, with a center section of maple; the pickup assembly has been removed, but the bridge, jack-socket, and one of the controls are still in place. *(Courtesy Emmett Chapman)*

fingerboard instead of picking it – is normally executed by the player's left (fretting) hand. However, during a practice session on August 16, 1969, Emmett repositioned his right hand perpendicular to the fingerboard (see photo), and began using both hands to hammer on and sometimes hammer off. This breakthrough revolutionized his playing style: "I threw out ten years of jazz guitar playing and started over".

Using Emmett Chapman's basic "two-handed tapping," players can, in his words, "do the common scalar fingering techniques with both hands equally, either independently or interdependently," combining chords and melodies in a rich, varied range of textures. Emmett modified his own guitar to take full advantage of these possibilities, changing its tuning,

lowering the action, raising the pickups, incorporating a string damper, and creating a double strap system to position the instrument more vertically. In 1970, he built a bodiless version of the newly evolved instrument out of an ebony board, naming it "The Electric Stick." This ten-string model went into commercial production four years later, and Emmett and his staff now produce about 50 instruments at a time over two and three month periods from their headquarters in Woodland Hills near Los Angeles. These include the original standard Stick and the twelve-string Grand Stick® introduced in 1990 (each encom-passing a range of over five octaves), as well as their newest model, an eight-string Stick Bass®.

Left: Emmett Chapman

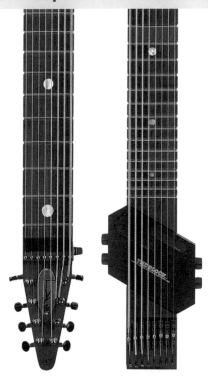

Right: Chapman Stick Bass, 1998. Unlike the Standard and Grand Sticks, the Stick Bass has a more conventional "top-to-bottom" tuning system; its eight strings are pitched in fourths, with the lowest (B) string corresponding to the note a fourth below the bottom string of a standard bass guitar. (The instrument can also be configured for other tunings.) Its neck and overall dimensions are the same as the standard ten-string Stick, but with wider spaced strings. It is fitted with active EMG pickups, switchable from stereo to mono.
(All photographs on these pages courtesy Emmett Chapman)

Left: "The Block"™ – the pickup housing is mounted on rubber-tipped set screws to isolate it from the body.

Below: Chapman Grand Stick, 1998. This model is made from laminated cherry wood; a variety of other timbers, including rosewood, teak, oak and some African hardwoods are also available. Unlike many electric guitars, whose fingerboards are designed to have a slight camber, the Stick's playing surface is absolutely flat. Its frets are stainless steel rods, slid into place from the side of the neck; these are far more durable than conventional fret wire, and are round and smooth to the fingers. The strings are divided into two groups – melody and bass – with the lowest pitched strings placed in the center. Each string's height, length, and position can be adjusted via the bridge and tailpiece assembly. The Block™ pickup module contains two active, humbucking transducers, and allows signals from the two string groups to be processed separately in stereo, or combined in mono.

The Old and The New

Acoustic "harp guitars", with up to twelve unfretted extra bass strings, were produced by a number of leading American companies, including Gibson, Martin, and the Larson Brothers (who marketed their harp guitars under the Dyer label) from the early 1900s onwards. The Dyer design, which had only five additional strings, proved to be the most manageable and successful of these instruments, and in the 1980s,

the brilliant young American guitarist/composer Michael Hedges (1953–1997) regularly played a 1920s Dyer model onstage and in the studio. A little later, Hedges switched to a new, electric harp guitar specially made for him by Californian luthier Steve Klein. This was fitted with two EMG pickups, and also had a Steinberger "TransTrem" bridge – a highly sophisticated transposing tremolo unit that allows the player to lock the

Right: National Reso-lectric, 1997. The Reso-lectric has a single, 9¹/₂-inch (24cm) resonator cone recessed into its solid alder body. The Seymour Duncan P90 "soapbar" pickup and the Highlander piezo device installed in its bridge are switched and

combined via two of the retro-style knobs on the upper bout; the third knob is a master volume control. The instrument's top is made of maple veneer, and it has a hardrock maple neck and rosewood fingerboard.
(Courtesy National Reso-Phonic)

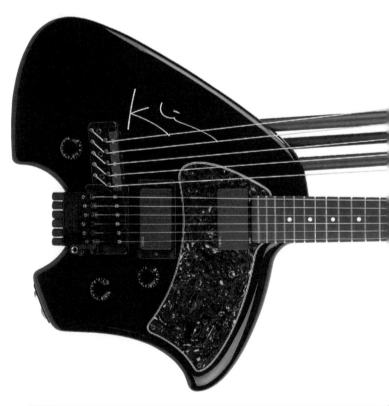

*eft: Steve Klein harp guitar, 1997.
The instrument's basic body
design is similar to Steve Klein's
six-string electrics, but with a
second headstock and supporting
bars for the five additional strings.*

*These have their own dedicated
pickup (controlled by the volume
knob beneath the five-string
bridge); the "regular" guitar is
fitted with two EMG humbuckers.
(Courtesy Klein Electric Guitars)*

six main strings into higher or lower tunings with its controlling arm. The Klein harp guitar shown below is almost identical to the one used by Hedges, but does not include the TransTrem.

National's Reso-lectric is another ingenious combination of old and new. It features a single resonator unit of the type first developed by John Dopyera (1893–1988), and subsequently used in a wide range of metal- and wooden-bodied instruments. The guitar has a Highlander piezo pickup mounted inside its "biscuit" bridge, providing a convincing electric version of the classic National resonator sound. Its output can be mixed with the signal from the magnetic "soapbar" pickup positioned near the neck. The Reso-lectric is also

effective when played acoustically.

The final guitar shown here is a more direct rendition of an earlier design. During the mid-1960s, Nathan Daniel (see pages 312-315) responded to the vogue for Indian music in American and European rock circles, largely inspired by George Harrison of The Beatles, who at one time took sitar lessons from Ravi Shankar, by creating a "sitar guitar" with thirteen extra "drone" strings. Jerry Jones, whose fine replicas of other Daniel models are featured on pages 434-437, has now revived this remarkable instrument as well. It is currently attracting a number of adven-turous players, many of whom are experimenting with custom drone tunings for special musical effects!

Above: Jerry Jones Electric Sitar, 1998. Like other Nathan Daniel designs, this guitar has "lipstick tube" single-coil pickups – two for the six main strings, and one for the thirteen drones, which are tuned chromatically in semitones. The extended, curved bridge is designed to enhance the "sitar-like" tone

quality by buzzing slightly! Daniel's original instrument appeared under the Coral brandname; it was endorsed by guitarist and mandolinist Vincent Bell, who worked with Bob Dylan and a number of other leading players.
(Courtesy Jerry Jones Guitars)